CAPTURING
THE HEART
OF LEADERSHIP

CAPTURING
THE HEART
OF LEADERSHIP

*Spirituality and Community
in the New American Workplace*

Gilbert W. Fairholm

Westport, Connecticut
London

Library of Congress Cataloging-in-Publication Data

Fairholm, Gilbert W.
    Capturing the heart of leadership : spirituality and community in
the new American workplace / Gilbert W. Fairholm.
      p.   cm.
    Includes bibliographical references and index.
    ISBN 0–275–95743–8 (alk. paper)—ISBN 0–275–97096–5 (pbk.: alk. paper)
    1. Leadership—Moral and ethical aspects. 2. Corporate culture—
United States. I. Title.
HD57.7F348   1997
658.4′092—dc20   96–26282

British Library Cataloguing in Publication Data is available.

Library of Congress Catalog Card Number: 96–26282
ISBN: 0–275–97096–5 (pbk.)

First published in 1997

Praeger Publishers, 88 Post Road West, Westport, CT 06881
An imprint of Greenwood Publishing Group, Inc.
www.praeger.com

Printed in the United States of America

The paper used in this book complies with the
Permanent Paper Standard issued by the National
Information Standards Organization (Z39.48–1984).

10 9 8 7 6 5 4 3 2 1

Contents

Illustrations

TABLES

FIGURES

Preface

Leadership is in flux. Our understanding of this most fundamental and pervasive of organizational relationships has undergone a series of transformations over the one hundred years of modern management. And, as with any universal idea, leadership has been defined variously by almost every writer contributing to this ferment. Analysis of this stream of ideas points up several common definitional categories around which academic and some practitioner authors have developed elaborate constructs to define and describe the leadership dynamic.

Thus, for much of this century, leadership has meant the technology of management. In this conception, leaders are those at the head of the firm who are responsible for accomplishing its work. Some reserve the idea of leadership to mean good management—the superlative qualities and actions of only the excellent organizational heads. A few writers couch leadership in personal power terms, suggesting that leaders use their personal power to get others to do what they want them to do. Leadership has also been defined in change terms, meaning the task of instituting meaningful change, managing the change process, and more recently, the job of transforming the nature and character of the organization and its workers.

In the last decades of the twentieth century leadership has come to allude to the task of setting and replacing the values guiding an organization and its people. Other current writers see leadership in terms of culture creation and maintenance. A few people are combining much of the discussion of the recent past and concluding that leadership is a function of the leader's concern for the whole soul, the inner sense of spirituality of self and group members. These writers counsel that leadership defines the leader's true self and determines what is good and true and beautiful for them and other organization stakeholders.

Leaders today are pressured to give their very best. They are asked to apply all of the secular knowledge available about work and leading others in doing work. They also are asked to bring to the task of leadership their whole selves, their knowledge of the spiritual dimension of life that, perhaps, more powerfully than any other force, guides daily action. Surely detailed knowledge about the theory and practice of leadership is important, but spiritual knowledge is essential. It is what we are, who we are, and why we think we are here in life that ultimately guides our individual lives and conditions our relationships with others.

The argument in this book is, therefore, a personal one. It defines my personal conception of leadership based on spirit as a result of my experience and review of the ferment of discussion and model building of the past few years. I have tried to buttress my position with the work of a host of contemporary authors, people who are in various stages of hypothesis formation and idea deliberation. But it seems to me that while the force of spirituality in our lives, including our work lives, is a fact, our understanding of its operational use and certainly of its control and guidance, is unclear. Spirituality is not easily susceptible to theory building using standard methods of search and research.

Theory building is accomplished in two ways. The first is to amass as much information as possible from the past, use it as a foundation, and extend common ideas into a model of what the world is or may be like. The second method is more creative, but perhaps equally valid, given the typical half-life of most leadership theories. This second approach is to immerse one's self in the lore of the field of leadership—its intellectual as well as practical manifestations—and then create a model that responds to essential elements of the operational surroundings.

The framework created in this personal, creative method is perhaps as valid as the more plodding accumulation of data to assemble a new paradigm from past ideas. This creative approach has, at least, the advantage of having the potential to add something new to our body of leadership understanding. It may even produce a better concept, one more sensitive to current needs, current values, and current operational reality, than a reassembled package of old and perhaps obsolete ideas. And, given the phenomenal changes in both work and worker's characteristics in today's workplace, something new is needed.

Building a theory of spiritual leadership, like getting in touch with one's own spiritual center, is an intensely personal, emotional, and passionate task. And, like getting in touch with our own spiritual center, building a leadership style on the basis of the spiritual sensitivity and power of groups asks the leader to create his or her own special version of leadership. This version of leadership centered on the spirituality of the leader and his or her followers is the author's personal take on this important, evolving, and potentially institution-changing phenomenon.

This book is my attempt to construct a coherent definition of spirituality in the workplace and to place it in the context of today's work cultures. To the degree that it makes sense, my personal goal will have been achieved. To the degree that it may aid others in coming to grips with this powerful tool to build organizations that meet the demands of today's customers and at the same time fulfill members' needs for wholeness, it will have served my other purpose: to expand our collective understanding of the ideal of leadership.

Leadership of the spirit is best seen in the life of leaders. For me, the best examples of leadership of the spirit is in the lives of Barbara, Ann, David, Paul, Corey, Dan, Laurie, Scott, Marcy, and Matthew, and in the potential of Jason, Craig, Michael, Kaitlyn, Sarah, Chad, Emily, Rachel, Jacob, Thomas, and Abigail. Thank you all.

Chapter 1

The Soul of Leadership

Spirituality is a new notion in leadership. For most of the one hundred–year lifetime of modern management and leadership, we have ignored this idea. It has not even been mentioned in our textbooks. Yet for that same period of time and, indeed, throughout all of social history, we have identified inner moral—spiritual—standards as the prime influence of human action. Our sense of spiritual wholeness defines humankind, determines our guiding values, and directs our most intimate decisions and actions. To leave spirituality out of our thinking about our leadership (or followership) is to diminish our theory, perhaps to make it irrelevant.

Our individual sense of who we are—our true, spiritual self—defines us. It creates our mind-set, defines our values, determines our actions, and predicts our future behavior. As such, spirit is a part of leadership and always has been, whether the individual leader knows it or consciously uses this fact in developing his or her leadership approach.

As our work world expands in importance and becomes, for many, the central activity of our lives, relating personal spiritual values with work values becomes the central task of leadership. Leaders must get in touch with their own spiritual nature. They must sense the spiritual essence of their followers and must deal directly with the task of creating an organization—defined as a group of people in voluntary relationship—where the essential spiritual needs of each member is considered and made a part of the group experience.

Growing numbers of people are beginning to talk about spirit and work in ways that are intended to enhance personal satisfaction, increase levels of personal commitment to organizational goals, and allow workers maximum freedom to function authentically to their spiritual values. To date little of this discussion has entered the formal academic and professional literature. However, there is growing pressure to include these ideas in revised definitions of leadership and discussions of a leader's tasks.

This book attempts to define spiritual leadership and assess its force as a new approach to leadership, one focusing and integrating current ideas such as values-based leadership, visioning, empowerment, and developing trust cultures. We will identify current pressures in the workplace that foster spiritual leadership. New scientific theories of chaos, new realities about the place of work in the lives of workers, and new demands upon work, the job, and career to fulfill needs formerly provided by home, church, and community combine to force our attention to the spiritual side of work and the leadership of workers.

NOW IS THE TIME TO ADD SPIRITUALITY TO WORK LIFE

The goals of corporate action have changed from profit alone to profit and individual worker development. This fact of contemporary U.S. (perhaps even world) life is in the process of instituting a sea change in the life and work of workers and their leaders. The full dimensions of this fundamental change are not always clear, but the fact of the change is attested to every day as workers are laid off, customers are asking for new and radically different products every day, and workers on the job demand more fulfillment from their work.

The preeminent goal sought by corporate leaders throughout the history of business has been profit. Concern for the bottom line drives business decision making. This has been the case throughout history and will continue into the future. Businesses are, after all, economic systems that use money as the primer of collective action as well as the goal of actions taken. Professional managers evolved over the years to focus corporate attention and corporate resources on the money flow and on maximizing return on money and other assets invested.

Perhaps the most significant change in the philosophy of business over the past several decades has been the introduction of another powerful drive, a drive that threatens to take an equal place with profit as the motivator of executive action. This drive comes not just from the core of managers at the head of the business hierarchy (or from their bosses, the board of directors), but from the rank and file workers. It is a drive to become all that they can become, a drive for self-development, within the confines of the corporate work unit.

This push for worker development and growth runs counter to the body of technique developed over the years by managers and solidified in past theory and technology. Indeed, there is evidence that managers cannot be fully responsive to this focus. Managerial tools, methods, and goals continually draw the manager into making decisions that intend to improve the financial performance of the organization even at the risk of hurting their employees through reduced work, layoffs, firings, and, perhaps most pervasive, reducing the nature of the work to its lowest and least costly but most mundane dimensions.

The rise of values-based transformational leadership ideas and their natural consequence, spiritual leadership, is a reflection of the rise in worker demand for the opportunity to use and hone more of their skills, knowledge, and abilities than those used on the assembly line or prescribed by confining standard operations policies and procedures. Spiritually attuned leaders accept as a prime goal the need to help workers become their best self as the corporation strives to maximize profit.

It simply is not possible to attain success today without considering the needs and desires of workers as well as the need to establish and maintain corporate health and vigor. The reasons for this reorientation of executive focus are many and have been thoroughly addressed in recent years. Among them the following seems particularly cogent:

- The rise of a labor pool made up of diverse workers entering the work force, each with different kinds of experiences and striving to honor different values systems contribute to this reorientation.

- Change in the nature of work done today also contributes to this new and equally important goal of worker self-development. This change in the nature of work asks most workers to be knowledge workers; people who use words and numbers as both the raw material and the results of their effort.

- The rise of knowledge work has brought better-educated and better-prepared people into the ranks of every organization, whether their tasks or their managers' styles have been changed to fully accept them. Indeed, knowledge work has changed the nature of the workplace into what Senge (1990) has called the learning organization. A learning organization is a workplace characterized by continuous worker growth, development—learning—to cope with ever-changing customer demand for unique products to meet their personal needs.

- And, workers today want more. Television and mass-selling techniques have educated workers to want the good life, a life style at home and at work that older workers were willing to wait and work for throughout their lifetime. Today's workers expect the firm to provide them with the kinds of work and the kinds of satisfactions that their bosses expected to receive only after promotion to supervisory ranks (Myers 1970).

WORK AND LEADING WORKERS IS LIFE

Work has entered a new dimension in our lives. Our work is fast becoming the locus where most of us find our sense of full meaning. As partial proof, for the first time in memory a book of poetry based on business themes is now available. *The Poetry of Business Life* is more than a title, it is a declaration and an invitation. It is tangible evidence that business is growing into this societal role of prominence. In his book, Windle (1994) calls our attention to the rich poetic language in the business world. His work evokes key aspects of modern human life and living. He rescues business from the narrowing constraints put on its meaning and application in society, liberating work and workers.

The word *business* is from the old English, *bisignis*, meaning *busy-ness*. Its core meaning was formerly related to task, work, occupation, profession, trade. Over time usage has limited the idea to concepts of commercial transactions such as buying and selling. Now business is becoming—has become—more than simply an economic reality. We all are, in some degree, in business whether we like it or not. Today business touches most lives. It consumes growing proportions of our time, energies, ambitions, and emotions whatever out profession is. Its ideas and language are part of everyone's thinking. Its motivations have become dominant in politics and social life.

Today the idea of business is recapturing its earlier meanings, which connote wholeness. For us business is our occupation, our intellectual orientation—our life. Chief executive officers are no longer the only ones in business. All members of our work organizations (industry, commerce, politics, government), no matter what their level of work, are also "in business." Because business has absorbed or replaced so many occupations that support a living, it would be a devastating blow if the poets found neither place nor inspiration in it.

The Western myth of managerial man (and woman) is one of the dominant myths of our age. Business is pervasive and powerful in society. It defines those human attributes thought appropriate to success in the formal corporation like competition, ambition, and financial astuteness. Managerial man has taken prominence over other, some argue more important, human attributes related to emotional needs, wider family relationships, and social and intellectual aspirations.

Nevertheless, to conduct business as usual is to conduct business into decline. The illusion of business as separate from humanity is similar to the idea of a head disconnected from its body. It just won't work any more—if it ever did—as a model for human interaction. If social transformation is to take place, it will probably take place at work because that is where we are most of the time. Yet, these obsolete ideas separating business from any other human activity continue. The commonly heard phrase, "the business of business is business" seems to mean that business is somehow disconnected from other aspects of life, somehow separate from us as sensitive, feeling individuals. It connotes business as a unique human endeavor, in which only a certain elite can participate.

This bifurcation of life from work is faulty. When we separate from our humanness—from our spiritual self—we give place to the other side of our character, our shadow self, our violent, animal nature. Evidence of this is in the jargon used in describing business and businesspeople: shark, dog-eat-dog, cut-throat, barracuda. We say he or she has a head for business. But we don't say he or she has a soul for business or a heart for business. The result of these absurdities is that business has taken on a largely negative meaning in human terms, one entirely without foundation in the routine practice of our jobs or in the nature of human beings.

Work Involves the Spirit

Rather than being a necessary distraction from life, business is business precisely because people bring their whole self, their spiritual self with them to work, not because they leave it at home. We need to reconnect to the fact that our hearts and minds, not just our bodies, are central in our business relationships. Our survival economically and as a species depends on it. For life is about spirit and we humans carry only one spirit that manifests itself in both life and livelihood. Our spirit is the vital, energizing force or principle in us, the core of self. It is the fertile, invisible realm that is the wellspring for our creativity, the core of our values, and the source of our morality.

We engage our spirit in all we do. Spirit lies at the heart of all life. Our spirit defines meaning for self and motivates our actions individually and in the groups we join. It expresses itself in beauty, aesthetics, and in our relationships with others (Jacobson 1995). In aggregate, spirit is what makes up our idea of who we are. In truth, it determines who we are. Spirit, along with mind and body, compose the soul—the whole person. Despite this intrinsic reality, our leadership theory for a hundred years has ignored the core self in developing its models and defining the leader's tasks and roles.

The result is that our formal theory and practice are defective. Unless both leadership theory and leadership practice develop ways to welcome the spiritual component into public conversation instead of demanding that leaders first deny their spiritual selves, the caricature of the leader offered by contemporary leadership theory will become more and more the operational truth. And leadership theory will continue its drift from a practical theory to a narrow elitist theory of productivity for the sake of productivity.

Spirituality and Work

There is now a quest to confront the universal spiritual frontiers of human consciousness (Nourse 1995). Leaders recognize the value of process as well as product. The higher leaders climb up the corporate ladder the greater their burden of responsibility and their need to reevaluate themselves and their whole self, their spiritual being. It is a kind of spiritual awakening. It starts with the realization that no matter who or where leaders are, there is always somebody more influential, more loving, and more knowledgeable than they are.

The root of spirituality is genuine concern for everything that is living. Integrity has to be the driving motive of any organization. In the twentieth century we have become so sophisticated, so modern, so enmeshed in the trappings of the secular world that we have overlooked that we have been enriched in many ways and impoverished in a lot of other, more important ways. We cannot afford that perspective in the twenty-first century.

Modern life has conditioned us to accept many immoral acts out of a societal sensitivity to others' emotions or their need for free expression. But there is something inside all of us that instinctively reacts against injustice. In fact, it is in the inner self—the visceral self—that the sense of morality is first born. There, almost instinctively, we realize that some matters are not subject to majority vote. Conscience tells us that some things are not even subject to the individual approval of our core values, that there are, plainly, some things you simply cannot do.

This inner moral standard comes out of our deepest traditions of right and wrong, out of our sense of spirituality. Spirituality transcends doctrinaire religion. It finds common cause with people of all religious persuasions, and even among those who profess no religion. There is a part of us that is not physical, a part that I am comfortable in calling my soul, that less-religiously inclined people may call personality or spirit. It is everything about me that is nonphysical: my identity, my values, my memories, my sense of humor, and so forth.

Spirituality is the essence of who we are. It is our inner self, separate from the body. It includes the way individuals think and the thoughts they perceive as well as their perceptions of the world. Spirituality has some religious versus secular overtones, but it has most to do with one's inner or private being. It is evident in emotional or intellectual activities or thoughts that transcend normal physical and biological wants or needs. Spirituality is the intangible, life-giving force in self and all people. It is a state of intimate relationship with the inner self of higher values and morality (Vaill 1989).

Spirituality is the goal. Religion is the path. Spirituality is not solely in the province of a particular religion, although the values of some religions are part of our spiritual focus. Our spirituality is the measure for personal values and meaning-making. It is a way of understanding the world, an inner awareness, a means of integration of the self and our world (Jacobson 1995). It is the acceptance of universal values that individuals believe guide their everyday actions and by which they judge those actions. In organizations, spirituality refers to the inner values of the leader and the followers.

The neglect of the spiritual in our natures helps explain at least in part, the whole range of problems we now face—the persistence of hopelessness, worker anomie, lowered productivity, teen pregnancy, substance abuse—which we have erroneously said stem from bad economics, politics, or racism (Raspberry 1995). Efforts aimed at improving people's lives that don't include a moral and spiritual dimension are literally a waste of time. A sense of spirituality is the anchor for most people's work ethics and social morality (Bennett, quoted in Range 1995). What is most needed today is not more intellect, but more soul (Boyce 1995).

There is a growing sense that America's failures are not political or economic, but moral. The cure for what ails America is in significant measure spiritual, or at the least moral. Show me a program that helps people to change their lives (as opposed to merely feeding their physical hungers) and I'll show you a program with a strong element of the spiritual. The most successful social programs are those that are driven—even if only tacitly—by moral values.

SPIRITUALITY AND LEADERSHIP

What we are is more important that what we know. What we are determines what we do with the things we know. Whether we go right or wrong at home or at work, depends on our souls. Matters of the heart transcend matters of the mind. More important than our knowledge, our skill, or our education, is simply our goodness—the quality of our hearts and our souls. People respond primarily to the way their leaders feel toward them. Leadership, as opposed to management, is a matter of touching people's souls, not controlling their actions. Leadership is connecting with other people at the feeling level.

A music metaphor may be useful in helping us understand spiritual leadership. Improvisation is a musical excursion into individual creativity. But the artist bases this innovation on an intimate knowledge and understanding of musical forms and principles. We cannot improvise until we know our craft. Improvisation is also a leadership skill. Leaders play a critical role in selecting the melody, setting the tempo, establishing the key, and inviting the players. But that is all they can do. The players must actually play (do the work of the organization). And they must be free to improvise on the leaders' general themes. Enthusiasm can't be taught, it must be caught.

Human beings have an inborn constitutional need to feel connected to others. The lack of human connection is driving some people out of organizations and away from leaders who don't provide for this need. Or it is driving them into unhealthy life styles should they decide to remain and endure the separations they find at work. This isolation at work is a prime cause for anomie, alienation, and dissatisfaction on the job.

We can relate follower spiritual well-being to the leaders' attitudes toward and the degree of comfort leaders enjoy in providing spiritual care (Cimino 1992). As leaders commit to the care of the whole person, they must include spiritual care into their practice. A positive correlation exists between a leader's spiritual well-being and his or her attitude and degree of comfort in providing spiritual care for co-workers. Leaders in the new century must consider and actively engage in making for themselves and then helping their followers make these connections.

This task asks for the best leaders can produce in communications skills and more. It asks them to intuit follower needs. Intuition is knowledge gained without rational thought (Rowan 1986; Fairholm 1991). The spiritual leader's influence comes out of a deep familiarity with the organization's culture, customs, values, and traditions. Such leaders develop an integrated framework based on core values—a vision—and operate out of this framework without stopping and thinking. It is this intuition that taps ingrained ideas and values also held by group members, which gives spiritual leaders their moral legitimacy.

Such a new philosophy of leadership will no doubt be controversial. Few will accept it easily. However, the time has come to engage in the production of new leader-follower structures that give place to the moral center in people. We need organizations and leaders who recognize the soul of the worker. We need people who can create a corporate soul within which workers can find harmony and satisfaction. Such leaders will seek out people who place more value on the spiritual side of life than on materialistic values (Walker 1989). A person who is sensitive to others has a high potential for success in the leading of others, while an insensitive or blunt person has to expend a greater effort in supervising or managing people.

The best leaders seem to have a unique ability to defend their ideas and a low self-consciousness, characteristics that conflict with the temperament of many contemporary managers. Tomorrow's leaders must be not only technically competent, but also wise, good, and honest. We can no longer afford to base leadership succession on appearances—size, attractiveness, and overall appearance—or even past performance. How our leaders look is not important. That doesn't tell us much about people. Unless we also look in their heart we are not qualified to judge our leaders. We need to know not only what people do but understand *why* they do it. To know another person we need to know their motives, their experiences, their level of spiritual or social maturity, their desires, their environment, their level of faith in themselves and others, their knowledge, their opportunity, and their intentions.

We need these qualities in our leaders: wisdom, goodness, and honesty. Without wisdom, leaders may make wrong (poorly thought through) decisions or honest mistakes. Without goodness, they will make immoral rules. Without honesty, they will show favoritism. Without all three, their leadership will be suspect. With all three characteristics, their preparation will be sufficient. The failure to find a place in our leadership for people with these core qualities is the cause of many of today's problems:

- politics without principle
- pleasure without conscience
- knowledge without effort
- wealth without work
- business without morality
- science without humanity
- worship without sacrifice
- peace without tranquility.

SPIRITUALITY AND ORGANIZATION

People establish organizations for the benefit of humanity. Too many contemporary CEOs have forgotton this core aspect of social living in the present stress to rightsize. Of course, organization structure and standard procedures help focus individual work effort. Properly designed they are simple, objective, rational, efficient. However, organization and system alone cannot guarantee protection of our innate liberties. The organizations we create should let members be actively involved in the affairs of their work communities.

Behaving rightly by itself is not enough. Given today's typical work environment, workers—leaders and followers—must raise their voices with others to seek leaders, not managers, to guide them. The loss of inner controls implicit in managerial action invariably brings an increase of external controls with a resultant diminution of individual liberty. We need to ensure that high moral standards underlay our laws. Successful leaders with high moral standards will not sacrifice those standards to achieve greater levels of power or more possessions.

The problems that organizations are facing today are not due to temporary downturns in the economy (Mitroff, Mason, and Pearson 1994). They are a vivid testimony to the fact that nineteenth- and twentieth-century organizations are obsolete. They cannot deal effectively with the new conflicts and challenges to the moral foundation of the communities in which we now live and that define our success. What we need are radically new kinds of organizations to meet the challenges of today's world and the work world of tomorrow.

To meet these challenges, we need organizations (and leaders to focus them) that provide not only training and direction in how to do work, but that engage workers in constant learning and personal development of their capacities. The future organization will have to be a learning center, a spiritual center, and a training center for multiple leaders. It will engage workers in work communities (teams) that recognize individual difference as they coordinate and focus individual talent and experience. Tomorrow's organization will provide opportunities for leaders to follow and followers to lead. It will be a school in every essential particular—all members learning and growing in their capacities to help the organization help its multiple stakeholders feed their souls along with their bodies.

Chapter 2

The Place of Spirit in Our Work Lives

The world advertises that the expanding scope of social organizations and institutions is good. That may be, but bigness often brings with it a loss of individuality. In many areas of life we subordinate the individual to the public weal. People are no longer directed by tradition or by the inner self. Rather, we are "outer-directed," made to conform to an external group standard.

For most of human history no one had to search for the sacred. At the core of every culture was a cult, with sacred times and places set aside for public rituals. Religion was the womb of civilizations (Woodword 1994). For most of our history religion was the core force that created our sense of morality, of right and wrong. Religious principles defined moral conduct. Religion defined good and evil and provided the context for human interactivity.

Today it is otherwise. Now we move in secular time and space. To the Pilgrim fathers America was sacred soil—a new promised land. Our for-bearers saw America as a land set aside by God as a place of refuge and hope for those believers who would conform their lives and their inter-course to known, religious principles of conduct. Thus, all social inter-action was conditioned on moral principles finding their source in religious principle and custom.

Now only the individual person (or, more typically today, the group) is seen as sacred. We have lost our religious moral roots. In a drive for so-called sophistication we have dropped our dedication to a specific religious orthodoxy. Instead, many of us are looking for the sacred from our work. Work is the place where we spend most of our time and to which we devote most of our true selves. It is logical that we should seek a secular substitute for our lost morality in our work, the place where we occupy ourselves most fully, and through which we define ourselves.

Unfortunately, many of us can no longer take satisfaction in our work. We don't make anything anymore; our contribution is often only a small part of the final product. How can meaning and satisfaction result in this kind of fractionated work atmosphere? How can we preserve a wholeness of personality if we are cut in two by spiritual aspiration on one hand and pressure for material aggrandizement on the other? We cannot. Our core values as individuals (and as a society) permeate our entire culture. The frustration and anxiety more and more people are feeling stem from a warring of these two competing value systems: spiritual versus material.

The idea of spirit at work is in reality a shift from a compartmentalized view of the universe, where each part of our life competes for its own self-interest in relationship to all other parts, to a view of the universe as a vast number of cooperative relationships with other independent units. This is nothing less than a total reinvention of the workplace, a redefinition of work as not merely an economic site, but a prime locus of life. Evidence of this transformation is rudimentary at best. The parameters of the change, however, are becoming clear. People in all kinds of occupations are voicing a cry for spiritual foundation in a chaotic world.

We have overcome nature and in large part are no longer dependent on it to satisfy material wants, but as a result we jeopardize the feeling of closeness (oneness) with our spiritual side. The central question for societies and for individuals is, Which value system will win? On the surface we must say that, at the level of the general society (and for many individuals) materialism is winning. Industrial work methods have dehumanized workers. Each person is dependent now on other people. Individual satisfactions are harder to come by.

Research by Jacobson (1995), which I confirmed, strongly suggests that experienced leaders and other members in our work organizations are seeking more than mere economic rewards on the job. Indeed, they are redefining work to include satisfaction of deep inner needs for spiritual identity and spiritual satisfaction. Jacobson's survey of national and regional leaders and my survey of mid-level managers using similar questions confirm a growing need for workplace cultures, leadership, and work processes that celebrate the whole individual with needs, desires, values, and a spirit self.* The results of these and a growing body of

*Jacobson, Stephen. *Spirituality and Transformational Leadership in Secular Settings: A Delphi Study.* (An abridgement of an unpublished dissertation completed in 1994 and available

similar research provide interesting insight about the presence today—and perhaps always—of powerful spiritual forces in the work culture and in our work relationships.

An implicit recognition of the need to recognize the spiritual side of our work lives should be at the heart of current talk about reinventing work, not merely efficiency and flexibility. Where current efforts to reinvent work ignore the human element, this kind of spiritual focus asks leaders to orchestrate a new personal context in and among organization members. Adding a spiritual element can produce meaningful change (Goss, Pascale, and Athos 1994). The challenge to leaders is to find a new language of the spirit, one that gives point and meaning to our lives, and then to use that language to shape the organization, because even reshaped the organization will remain the lynch-pin of our lives (Handy 1994).

Rather than seeking solutions for each "form over substance" problem, a shift of mind-set or a change of context can provide the spirit (or substance) behind the practice (the form). Albert Einstein said neither the world nor the individual can evolve past its current state of crisis by using the same thinking that created the situation. That is, a new belief can be entertained only when the previous one has been undermined, discredited, or demolished.

Part of the mind-set change is to view business not in a context of warlike competition but as mutually beneficial cooperation. There is great leverage in changing the context—the way we think—rather than attempting to revise each thought or behavior. It is a shift to inspirational leadership rather than dominating management. This shift of context could be from one fueled by doubt, fear, competition, and domination to one of cooperation, vision, and responsibility.

As society gets bigger and more complex, personal characteristics and personal attractiveness becomes harder to control. Strong personal ethics, a positive belief in others, and a compelling vision are characteristics of successful corporate leaders. When situations pull them back and forth between compromise and confrontation, leaders surveyed by Badaracco and Ellsworth felt they should have a clear predisposition toward confrontation. They say that leaders show by their own example that open confrontation is desirable so long as it is done in a spirit of mutual respect and goodwill (Badaracco and Ellsworth 1992). In effect, these leaders define leadership, in part, as one of spiritual community building.

through University Microfilm, Goleta, Georgia, 1995.) Fairholm's informal survey of nineteen graduate students, each with up to ten years of government service, used the same questions Jacobson used. Both sets of findings are compatible. Fairholm's survey is used as the basis for the data developed in this book.

People in organizations have three options: withdrawal, explanation, or fealty. To bond with any organization we need to be able to commit to a sense of mission, spirituality, and moral rightness (Flower 1991). Leadership is coming to mean the task of creating an arena in which competing interests come together and through negotiation strike a deal with workers, as long as that deal does not intrude on what the organization stands for implicity. An organization is a structure, a human resources problem, a political entity, and it is a culture with its own symbols, mythology, rites, and priesthood. Spiritual leaders emphasize all of these cultural features in attracting workers to full commitment.

THE NEED FOR SPIRITUAL LEADERSHIP

The growing incongruence between personal ideals and the traditional exploitation process is causing increasing numbers of concerned business leaders to question their leadership actions. The most effective way to achieve this global transformation is through the business community. Many business leaders and workers are making the quest for meaning and congruence with their innermost source of power a part of their work goals. Leaders in this quest are surfacing from all points in the organization.

Spiritual leaders value the human spirit and believe that modern society must make deep and fundamental changes in the way it thinks if we are to have a sustainable future. There are new business practices that are the result of new thinking, which requires a "change of mind" on the part of each individual—a breaking away from the underlying assumptions and deeply held traditional beliefs about how business should be done. New practices by some business leaders include honoring the human spirit, empowering employees, practicing social responsibility, and building stakeholder community.

This new leadership is understanding that people need to find the meaning of life through their work. These leaders know that that meaning is derived from creativity in the service of worthwhile purposes (Badaracco and Ellsworth 1992). Badaracco and Ellsworth's research with the chief executives of several large firms confirmed what many suspect, that leaders are motivated by self-interest and by a search for power and wealth in the face of self-interested behavior by others. However, they also confirmed that these forces fail to explain fully the motivation of the high-caliber individuals they sought for their organizations. The need is acute for people in leadership positions to move beyond being just models of management efficiency, to being examples of the highest principles as they lead business, social, and governmental organizations or activities. It is important that leaders not only have the right goals for their relationships with their followers, but that they employ spiritually based forces in those relationships.

Leadership consists of providing the right actions to produce right responses in followers. It is getting people to respond and sacrifice when they are under no obligation to do so. It is a persuasive task, developmental, growth-producing, other-directed. It is a teaching, not a directive role. It is a service role, one that involves commitment and sacrifice by both leader and follower.

Isaac Newton in the seventeenth century articulated the physical law of compensation: for every action there is an equal and opposite reaction. We can anticipate this reaction in our co-workers in much the same way. The law of compensation in human terms is nothing more than the Golden Rule ("with what measure ye mete, it shall be measured to you again"—Matt. 7:2). This law operates in all of our actions in relating with people—our families, our various social groups, our religious affiliation, our work companions, and all others.

The effect of the Golden Rule in leadership as expressed toward our followers is as certain as the physical laws of compensation under which we operate. Those who would practice corporate spiritual leadership must recognize, understand, and employ the leadership principles of stewardship, participative leadership, commitment, and dedication to the programs and purposes of individual freedom.

Success in leading on the basis of spirit is conditioned on the presence among both leader and follower of interactive trust, shared ideals, customs, and standards; in a word, it is based on a mutually accepted cultural morality. The task of the leader is to first create this culture, and then foster its values and customs among followers. Shared culture is the basis of leadership. Indeed, leadership is impossible outside a shared culture (Schein 1985; Fairholm 1994a).

Perhaps as never before has there been a more pressing need for spiritual leadership. The prevailing social culture is antagonistic toward many of the ideals that prompt the spiritual leader. Often attempts to analyze leadership fail because the observer misinterprets the issues. Too often we fail to deal with leadership, and instead focus on the leader's personal qualities of charisma, power, or wisdom. Some leaders possess these qualities but they are not the essence or spirit of leadership. Leadership is the accomplishment of program goals through others, but, more importantly, through the process leaders help followers become their best selves.

In accomplishing this purpose leaders may not necessarily exercise their charisma or power or wisdom. Rather, the leader's unique achievement is a human, spiritual one. It finds its basis in the leader's understanding of human nature, the aims and purposes of people, and the relationships that can or do exist among individual goals and the goals of the group. People want to work with a leader who believes in something and in whom they can believe—whose commitment they know is strong enough so they can "borrow" from it while their own commitment matures. We observe continually that the person with a sound value system, a moral orientation, and a stewardship concept of his role as a leader can be effective even if his or her technique or style is unsophisticated or unorthodox compared to traditional conventions.

A BRIEF HISTORY OF LEADERSHIP OF THE HEART AND OF THE MIND

Over the centuries leadership of the heart, spirit leadership, has lost favor because of its personal nature. Besides, it is hard to identify innate traits or characteristics of leadership before we hire (or accept) someone to be our leader. More importantly, charisma, personal magnetism, and the aura of invincibility stemming from having the "right" information, are hard to integrate into complex organizations. Leaders defined this way are hard to control and predict. We cannot tell beforehand what they will do or where they will take the group. Therefore, the world has moved away from leadership based on personal traits and toward management that is by definition concerned with control and predictability.

Large organizations need to control individual and group behavior to attain desired results. Management developed to supplant leadership and supply this need for control. Large-scale organizations need a measure of control of both human and material resources to ensure continuity. Leaders leading from the heart don't always provide this stability. Leaders are forever innovating, moving outside the constraints of structure. While this may be exciting, it is also sometimes disconcerting, and it is hard to predict and control. On the theory (not necessarily correct) that control is more useful (profitable) than innovation, secular society's institutions and organizations have moved to adopt control mechanisms that make it possible to constrain and predict behavior of work systems, resources, and people. That is, organizations tend to move to management forms and processes and away from leadership. The emphasis in management is to make the common work done countable, measurable, predictable, and, therefore, controllable. The purpose is to accomplish program goals according to preset standards. The values managers honor are those of hard work, efficiency, and conformity to those preset standards.

Leadership, on the other hand, partakes of different values. Leaders think differently, value people, programs, and policy differently, and relate to others differently. They have different expectations for followers and seek different results from individuals and from the group. We are moving away from seeing leadership as coordination of work in relationships bounded by structure and system. Rather, we now are coming to see leadership as a kind of contract in which the leader and follower cooperate voluntarily.

Leaders are more personal in their orientation to group members, more comprehensive in their thinking. They focus on worker and group values and expectations, not just task accomplishment. They set out to do the work by changing individual's lives, not just presiding over tasks or conducting meetings. They impact followers and constituent groups in a volitional way, not just through formal authority mechanisms.

The Rise of the Manager

Management is a modern creation. Given the range and scope of recorded time, it was only recently that management skills were developed and became necessary. There is no record of the counterpart to the modern-day manager among the social groups and chief people of our ancient and simpler past. The head people in the ancient world—the clan and tribal chiefs, priests, and generals—did not manage, they led their followers. They were in charge because they persuaded their otherwise independent followers to believe that they had qualities, information, or ideals followers needed for their own success. Something had to change if society was to ensure predictability and uniformity. The change we see in history has been from personal revelation to logic, from charisma to competence, from leadership to management.

The transition from headship, that is, being in charge, based on personal charm and attractiveness to one based on control is the history of the rise of management to preeminence in our social life. It is a movement from inspiration to ceremony, from prophetic pronouncement to managerial control of systems. Prophetic leadership made control over our religious institutions difficult, erratic, unpredictable, and unsuited in an increasingly complex society. Some other way to direct society's organizations was needed. It is seen in the change from the leader's personal concern with people, their needs, and support to imposition of management control.

Management arose as an alternative to this kind of charismatic prophetic leadership. It is a leadership that relies on internal logical consistency, repeatability, and subordination of the many to the few. In all of our social institutions—the military, industry, government, and the church—the movement has been away from the inconstant individual (prophetic) leader, to the stable, predictable, logically focused manager—from the minister of the gospel to the administrator of programs. The most absurd trait managers can have today is to act like they know what they are doing. The world is too complicated for that kind of arrogance.

The biggest problem with managers and leaders is that their egos get in the way of effective leadership. Consider a manager who consistently fails to inform her people of important developments so they are constantly in the dark. How carefully such a manager must orchestrate her every move, her every word, to marginalize her people so completely. It is not that she is not thinking carefully, it is that she is thinking about the wrong things. The difficulty is not with her mind, but with her soul.

Martin Buber called this kind of person I-it. He described the soul-oriented person is an I-you. An I-it manager, when interrupted by his or her workers, sees them as a problem, a distraction. The I-you leader sees them as in need of his or her help. The one is egocentric, the other is not. The I-you leader sees others in empathetic terms of their needs instead of just the needs of the leader.

Headship today is much more a matter of organization, management, and resource control than it is of prophetic vision. The prophet of religion has been replaced by the managerial bishop of today. The charismatic hero in the military has been supplanted by the logistics expert. In government, the shift has been from the appointed, hereditary, or revolutionary leaders to the calculating, power-preserving, authoritarian, master-bureaucratic managers of today. We have come to distrust spiritual powers in every aspect of society and have replaced them with pseudospiritual ceremonies that can be timed, organized, and controlled.

We have kept (albeit in adapted forms) the ceremonies, procedures, and sacred customs that have served to keep subordinates at a respectful psychological distance. Where the ancient leader once held symbols of power, managers now hold them. Today's managers have adopted the ceremonial robes and perquisites formerly taken by tribal chiefs and priests or by the Pope or General. These sacred leadership symbols are only changed to conform to the needs of the modern managers and contemporary civilization. Instead of fancy robes, head dresses, and mystic ceremonies, today we see these symbols in academic gowns, perquisites of office, $1,500 business suits, showy offices, and the fostered illusion that the manager has "the word" and is the centerpiece in the communication network.

What has taken place in modern social institutions over the past century is a fatal shift from leadership to management. This is the same shift that we have seen in the decline and fall of the ancient church, the Roman Imperial Army, and most older societies. The obvious intent is the same in both systems: to produce respect and obedience in subordinates. These perquisites of managerial power inspire awe for the professional manager (teacher, lawyer, doctor, etc.). They add an air of pseudosacred solemnity and mystery to replace our innate needs for inspiration.

The fall of leadership and the rise of management has brought mixed results. It has allowed us to attain remarkable material progress. Surely modern management has produced fantastically complex organizations able to cope with the pluralistic needs and desires of a growing and demanding population. But the costs are also significant. Without the bonding leadership produces we have produced a working population characterized by anomie, alienation, and despair. Our measures of productivity in our organizations and as a society are down, morale is low, creativity is off.

Management can produce tangible things extraordinarily well. It is less adept at producing motivated, inspired people. We cannot manage people into the commitment necessary to accept the risks of battle, for example, or any other significant social enterprise; we can only lead them in these life-changing social activities. And here is the crux of the matter: managers are not trained nor are their systems or theories geared toward inspiration or independent follower action. Rather, managers are successful if they can direct desired behavior, control deviation, and punish recalcitrance. This is in direct contrast to leadership, whose purpose is to inspire volunteer followers to common action whether or not the leader is present to oversee behavior.

The rise of management marks the rise of commitment to a stifling common cause. Uniformity is now the rule. Conformance to a common standard has replaced individuality, individual commitment, and innovation. Conformity, not innovation, is the mark of a good employee. The mark of good management today is a work force of people dedicated to the organizations' or the managers' goals and objectives.

This penchant for control through uniformity is seen in our organization structures, operating systems, reports, and management approaches. But as the authority of management spreads over the organization, quality deteriorates, if that is, indeed, possible. Management shuns excellence. It feeds on repeatable performance geared to the lowest skilled employee. It feeds on mediocrity.

The Leadership Role

As we practice leadership in the coming century and in different cultural settings some of the conventions of traditional management headship may not be helpful. Leadership describes an imprecise activity. Its manifestations are as diverse as the people who occupy leadership positions or who practice its systems and techniques. No one by virtue of position alone is automatically an expert in leadership. He or she must earn that title by study, hard work, discipline, sacrifice, and service.

A working definition of leadership must include ideas and the ideals of (1) teaching correct principles, (2) applying the techniques that encourage follower self-governance, (3) creating a situation where followers can function freely with the leader within their delegations subject to broad accountability, and (4) defining the leader in a servant-steward role.

Leaders share their leadership tasks with their core of counselors and other officers as they work together to provide the climate and conditions within which both leader and led can strive for perfection. This striving is personal, for the individual leader. It also asks leaders to inspire followers to want to strive for personal perfection themselves. Leadership is helping followers by empowering them to similar service. Leadership is also directed toward maintaining a climate that helps their clientele group of followers to accept freely the challenge to excellence. Conformity may bring unity, but it may also bring mediocrity.

Leaders escape mediocrity. The qualities of leaders in all fields are the same: leaders are the ones who set the highest examples. The great leaders in art, science, and literature lift their companions and their client groups to new levels of beauty, craftsmanship, appreciation, understanding, and skill. They open the way to greater light and knowledge. They break the mold. Leaders are inspiring because they are inspired; they are caught up in a higher purpose.

This is the role and function of the leader across the society. There is necessarily some leader and some manager in each of us. The problem is one of a proper balance of these skills in self and the organizations we serve. Unfortunately, in too many people and organizations, management predominates to the virtual exclusion of leadership. The cause can largely be traced to the simplicity and comfort of measurement and control, the central facets of management today. It is easier—not necessarily better—to manage than to lead.

Today we measure all that we consider important in terms of money. Indeed, our measurement systems are keyed to a money standard. Accounting, auditing, control, and success itself, all are defined, measured, compared in terms of that standard unit. We define values other than profit as ephemeral and irrelevant. Control over the money makes managers successful. By converting all activity to money (numbers), we can compare, control, and prescribe everything. Followers, then, can be processed, programmed, computerized, handled—in short, managed.

The manager knows the price of everything, but the value of nothing. Money cost becomes the prime value in management. By contrast, value-oriented leaders seem to always be pursuing small successes. If an organization seeks continuous improvement on the way to total quality excellence, it must travel along a parallel track—augmenting modern leadership practices with value-added behavior. While simple human decency is always a good idea, it is not to be confused with overly polite communication, which can often be nothing more than an agreement to take no action.

Leadership, in contrast to management, places a higher emphasis on values—on creativity, intelligence, integrity. Unfortunately, these are the same values and traits managers seek to screen out in interviews in favor of loyalty, conformity, and unit spirit. But it is precisely these qualities that are most needed today. Our organizations and their members cry out for interesting, exciting, challenging work and people who can make the work seem worth our personal time and identity.

Spiritual leaders add values to system and technology. Value-oriented spiritual leaders often work within existing situations and resources to leverage assets and outcomes beyond expectations (Myers 1993). They ratchet performance by displaying distinctive leadership in relationship with self and others. They open up avenues of awareness and choice. They focus the group they lead and integrate diverse perspectives and action patterns. They add innovation to performance. They are infectious self-starters who tend to influence others in the work environment with their spirit and enthusiasm. They keep the organization sharp by raising awareness of problems and opportunities.

Despite the silence of past leadership models on these topics, these philosophical values are present in the practice of leadership today and they probably were there in past leaders. We see them in most of our organizations. They are essential to understanding the work process relationships within which we work. And, in a real sense, these relationships constitute organization. Spiritual values are central to understanding and leading our social institutions. Understanding values is key to understanding leadership. And understanding leadership is central to our understanding of ourselves and our society and to making sense of our relationships in each of the societies in which we seek membership.

Chapter 3

Defining Spiritual Leadership

There is a crisis of meaning in America. People are searching for significance in what they do, the products they produce, and the services they offer. The community within which we work is becoming our most significant community. Work defines the "real world" for many people. The work organization, where we spend most of our waking hours, provides a focus for life, a measure of personal success. For some, it is replacing family, friendship circles, church, and other social groups.

We Americans have become obsessed with work. Yet in 1994 only 25 percent of workers were extremely satisfied with their work compared to 40 percent in 1973. According to John Renesch, more than forty million people in the United States are seeking a more "intrinsically valued" lifestyle, and the numbers are growing (Renesch May/June, 1994b). The vast majority of workers responding to his international survey claimed their values and the values of the organization were in conflict.

These numbers suggest that while our work has value in helping secure economic well-being, it is not meeting its human obligations. Now, as in the past, our work has rarely provided us with the opportunity to grow personally and fully express ourselves (Renesch 1992). Our jobs act to restrain us, perpetuating our insecurities and fears. The organization, the environment, fads and fashions, and the groups with which we affiliate, now provide the norms for most of our behavior. This kind of situation leaves us vulnerable to the propagandist, mass selling techniques, and mass manipulation of ideas, ideals, and mores. And, worse, the tendency is toward mediocrity.

The work we do can also act to enrich us. And more and more people are looking to their work to provide personal self-development and self-fulfillment. We have limited the basic purposes of people. Society leads us to believe that we can partition our lives, that we can separate our business (work, profession, trade) self from our social, family, or spiritual selves. Americans revere production, not people. Yet with the greatest economic system in the history of the world, the highest standard of living ever, one finds that one in ten people need psychological help. Fear, frustration, tension, and stress abound, as do anxiety and hostility. And, in the face of this stress, people are demanding change.

Whether we like it or not, work is becoming or has become a prime source of values in our society and our personal lives. Work has become the focus of our lives and our interactions with others. Its motivations are dominant in family concerns and in both politics and social life. Work, the work organization (community), and work ethics have become the fountainhead of values in our society, the site of our most useful social contributions. Indeed, our work is fast becoming the place where most of us seek our sense of full personal meaning.

American workers are uncomfortable, uncommitted, and adrift. They are searching for new organizational patterns and new paradigms (Lee and Zemke 1993). The typical organization is divided, compartmental-ized, and fragmented to the point that workers cannot or, more impor-tantly, don't want to attach themselves to their work any more. Workers are afraid that the current wave of downsizing will catch them next. They are alienated rather than bonded to their jobs, afraid to do anything but work hard, follow orders they often cannot see the rationale for, and swallow their complaints. They yearn for connection, attachment to the whole, but they cannot find it.

Some see the present clamor for organizational participation as a movement toward gaining this attachment and the individual freedom people desire. It is not. Participation may be a reaction against the tight controls many suffer under in the various formal organizations making up their economic as well as their social life; however, the participation many of these organizations fosters undermines the need to feed both the mind and the spirit. The organization persuades members that to cultivate one is to threaten the other. Hence the movement beyond mere surface participation to seek whole-soul spiritual satisfaction on the job.

Spirit is each person's vital, energizing force or principle, the core of self. It is inseparable from self. It is the fertile, invisible realm that is the wellspring for our species' creativity and morality. Our spirit is a part of all we do. Spirit lies at the heart of all things. Our spirit defines our meaning and motivates our actions. It expresses itself in beauty, aes-thetics, and in our relationships with others and ourselves (Jacobs 1994). Spirit, along with mind and body compose the soul—the whole person.

The spiritual in us describes the animating or life-giving principle within us; the part of us that we associate with the mind or feelings as distinguished from the physical body. We can define spiritual as the essential human values from around the world and across time that teach us how humanity belongs within the greater scheme of circumstance and how we can realize harmony in life and work (Heerman 1995). Secular and spiritual are not opposed because we need not limit the spiritual to only a religious context.

Our spirituality is a source guide for personal values and meaning-making, a way of understanding the world, an inner awareness. It is a means of integration of the self and our world (Jacobson 1995). Spirituality is another word for personal awareness. It is the acceptance of universal values that individuals believe guide their everyday actions and by which they judge their actions. Spirituality in organizations refers to the inner values of the leader and the followers—the mature principles, qualities, and influences that we implicitly exhibit in our behavior and interactions with other people.

Integrating the many components of one's work and personal life into a comprehensive system for managing the workplace defines the holistic or spiritual approach. It provides the platform for leadership that recognizes this spirit element in people and in all of their behavior. This new holistic approach will help companies realize a multitude of significant benefits. By using a comprehensive holistic approach, companies can focus their investments of people, money, time, and resources to get the maximum return possible (Kuritz 1992).

We've obviously reached a point where nonintuitive, leaner, rational management has made a mess of American companies. We sorely need true leaders. True leaders have a belief in the value of what they do—their vision and mission. But it goes beyond the spreadsheet analysis of vision and mission to their essence, to their spiritual core. Numerical surrogates for reality do not begin to take account of the rhythms of life or the rich dynamics of the human spirit. The true leader can see situations in different ways and then bring these alternatives to consciousness so other people can appreciate them.

What can those who prize spiritual values do to ensure the survival of these values? In part, at least, we can help others reject unlimited self-gratification as the goal of business and return to the ethics of responsibility. We can focus more on the "spiritual" dimension of America's social troubles (as many in government and other professions are now speaking publicly about). Spirituality is standing for something bigger than you that others can believe in also. That is also leadership.

An understanding of spiritual leadership must include understanding of some counterpoints to recognizing the spirit in self and others and the spiritual basis of interpersonal relationships. While the individual's inner spiritual self is and has always been a part of his or her interactions with others, it has only very recently entered into the arena of academic and practitioner conversation. Finding a legitimate place for spiritually focused leadership is fraught with challenges from traditional management and organization theory. It also challenges present practice and expectations held by today's leaders and workers. The following sections raise some key concerns and begin to build a bridge to what may be the new leadership paradigm for the twenty-first century.

FOUNDATIONS OF SPIRITUAL LEADERSHIP

The new spiritual leadership paradigm sees transformation of self, others, and the organization as important, even critical. This new leadership model is that of the servant leader. Servant leadership is not an oxymoron, it is a juxtaposition of apparent opposites to startle the seeker of wisdom. This model of leadership values the education, inspiration, and development of others. To function in this way, leaders need a change of heart (spirit), not just technique. This model asks leaders to put those they serve first and let everything else take care of itself.

Leaders are first servants of those they lead. They are teachers, a source of information and knowledge, and a standard setter more than a giver of directions or a disciplinarian. This leadership mind-set is radically different from the nonleadership, managerial mind or, even, common sense (Kostenbaum 1992). The difference is not one of quantity, but of quality. It represents a paradigm shift. Spirituality stretches the leader's mind toward vision, reality, courage, and ethics. The spirit leadership mind is touched by the unconscious. It lets us get in touch with eternal questions of the spirit.

The biggest mistake of current leadership texts is that they confuse dedication, mission, vision, and spirit with spirituality. People are looking for significance in their work and the opportunity to use their minds and feelings while appealing to the animating or life-giving principles within them. We spend more time at work than in any other part of our life. Popular culture celebrates the material and largely ignores the spirit. Competition and compassion need not be mutually exclusive. Indeed, the goal of work may ultimately be to become people of quality.

The ideas underlying the practice of leadership or management are elaborated in two parts. The first is about the *heart* of the leaders' task— the spiritual side of self. The second is about the *mind*—the intelligence, information, skills, and techniques leaders need to manage their programs effectively. Leaders need to understand and do both. Spiritual leadership asks us to do our best. Both our head and our heart must be engaged. Management is external—it gets its power and its sense of legitimacy from others. It is primarily a function of the head. Leadership is internal—it finds its definition and its power from the inner strength of its values, experiences, and assumptions developed by the leader. It finds its vitality in the heart.

Traditionally, leadership has been defined in terms of the institutional head; the person or small group who provide centralized direction to the larger group. For many the head of an organization is called the leader. Historically, leaders are those who are charged with ensuring that a program of activities is carried out, assignments made, and reports prepared and delivered on time. In reality, this conception more accurately defines the managerial role—only a part of the total task of leadership.

Management is a role that heads of organizations assume involving control over others' behaviors and actions. For most people a position of leadership centers around the management role, its tasks, techniques, and technology. It conjures up ideas like controlling interpersonal relations, making decisions, aligning individual member actions and perceptions with organizational goals, planning, budgeting, and directing the effort of the several followers engaged in the work with us. The leader's manager role involves ensuring that group activity is timed, controlled, and predictable.

Lumping these operational tasks under the name "leadership" has some merit. One part of leadership has to do with accomplishing organizational objectives and with development of the behavioral skills to get others to do the organization's work, to be productive. But we cannot think that being scrupulously accurate in computing profit or loss or ensuring that the letter of the procedure is adhered to is all that is needed. Management tasks are intellectual and skills based, requiring that the organization head learn how to manage others and know the laws, rules, procedures, tools, needs, and requirements for program success.

There is merit in understanding these control tools—the mind of leadership. Each of us develops over time a *mind map* that catalogs and interrelates the sum of our experience into patterns or theories of practice that help us make sense of our experience. The idea relates to the Lockean view that the mind of an individual at birth is a clean slate—written on (mapped) by subsequent experiences. The mind of leadership reflects life experiences and systematizes them into strategies that guide action. Applied to our business concerns, this mind map represents the intellectualized foundations of our experience, our expertise.

The managerial mind of leadership is critical to day-to-day success. Some routine behavior, some system is necessary in certain circumstances; some techniques work better than others in a given situation. Knowing these tools and becoming expert in their use is important. Knowing which rule to follow, which tool to use, can help us attain success in a given situation. They are important. But this is only part of the task of the leader. Just getting the work done, and reporting in a timely manner—difficult as this sometimes is—is not all that is required.

More important is the spiritual dimension—the heart of leadership. While critical, management is only part of the leadership role. Leaders who focus too much on the physical and technical aspects of leadership are in error. Limiting our leadership to management of system and procedure too narrowly defines leadership. The heart of leadership has to do with what individual leaders believe, value, dream; what they are focused on and committed to. It is about the leader's personal and institutional vision of life and what his or her place in it is. The leader's role in focusing group energy and commitment is equally if not even more critical than managerial control.

Leadership is a complex of spirit, intellect, and physical skill in action. A leader acts out of this complex of heart and mind and action. Our visions are keyed to our spirituality as leaders. Visions come from the central core of the leader and reflect (or come to reflect) the central core of the group.

The heart of leadership maps the leaders *interior spiritual world*. Our personal vision defines our heart-felt beliefs about what truth and reality actually are. Our vision, translated to the organization we head, defines its unique place in the larger communities of work and social life. The leader's vision defines his or her values-laden, spiritual focus. Leadership is trying to teach followers this spiritual nucleus and convince them of its truth (utility) for them and for other stakeholders.

The mind of leadership is shaped and focused by the heart. The heart drives what we do. When leaders respond to their heart-felt values, others will know truly what their leaders are about and can more freely choose to follow them. Then, and only then, can the rest of our collective needs be met, whether personal or in terms of our leadership assignment. That is, a leader's philosophy about life and leadership are given substance and meaning by the internal system of spiritual values focused on. These values become a vitalizing vision of the possible.

The heart is what the leader believes and values. This spiritual heart-vision, in turn, drives the mind and shapes the behavioral (managerial) tools we use in a given situation. Our behaviors, in turn, reflect and reshape the heart and the mind in an interactive, continuous, developmental dynamic. Truly, "as a man thinketh in his heart, so is he" (Proverbs 23:7).

Seeking focus (a vision) for the group is fundamentally a decision of the heart, a commitment. Actions to demonstrate that heart-thought follow acceptance of this mind-set. The mind is what is in our intellect that shapes and controls our particular worldview. We behave according to

Table 3.1
Most Frequently Defined Characteristics of Spirituality

Number of Responses	Definitional Characteristics
8	An inner conviction of a higher, more intelligent force
6	The essence of self that separates humans from creatures
5	The basis of human comfort, strength, happiness
4	The source of personal meaning, values, life purposes
3	A personal belief system
3	An emotional level, a feeling
1	The experience of the transcendent in life

that meaning. Together the heart and mind (our philosophical values and our intellectual skills) shape our behavior—our decisions, actions, and relationships.

DEFINING SPIRITUALITY: DEFINITIONAL ELEMENTS

One's spirituality is the essence of who he or she is. It defines the inner self, separate from the body, but including the physical and intellectual self. It includes the way people think and the thoughts they feel. It is a part of their overall perception of the world. Spirituality has some religious versus secular overtones, but it has to do primarily with our inner or private being, our "life-force" seen in religious (doctrinaire) terms. Our spirituality is the essence that separates humans from all other creatures, manifested in emotional or intellectual activities or thoughts that transcends normal physical and biological wants or needs.

Spirituality also is the quality of being spiritual, of recognizing the intangible, life-affirming force in self and all human beings. It is a state of intimate relationship with the inner self of higher values and morality. It is a recognition of the truth of the inner nature of people. Many perceive spirituality to include a much broader range of experience while they see religion and faith as limiting the discussion to experiences that arise in traditional institutions or ways of thinking (Vaill 1989).

Spirituality does not apply to particular religions, although the values of some religions may be a part of a person's spiritual focus. Said another way, spirituality is the song we all sing. Each religion has its own singer.

The respondents in my study define spirituality on several levels. Table 3.1 summarizes seven aspects of a definition of spirituality. It identifies relative frequency of use of each definitional aspect by surveyed managers in defining and describing their conceptions of spirituality.

An inner conviction of a higher, more intelligent force. For most people surveyed, spirituality is the inner conviction one has of a higher, more intelligent force. It is an awareness that certain principles or beliefs are intangible and may not rest on logical proof but are trustworthy and valuable. It is belief in the seemingly impossible. It is belief that people guide their actions through a higher power with whom they have a relationship. This conception of spirituality has strong religious overtones. It is a personal relationship with God.

While religion-based spirituality is a useful, valuable, and even critical dimension of the lives of many people, the idea of spirituality also describes a more secular definition of the essence of the person. Many people define spirituality as the acceptance of universal values that they believe guide their everyday actions and by which others should judge their actions. Spirituality is the essence of who the individual is, what he or she says, the being he or she is. It is the inner self, separate from the body.

The essence of self that separates humans from creatures. Spirituality is also defined as the essence that separates human beings from all other creatures. It refers to an inner awareness that makes integration of the self and world possible. Defined in this way, understanding spirituality is critical to understanding organizational life and leadership. Jacobson (1995) confirmed this perspective. He concluded that spirituality is important and meaningful to transformational leaders. The secular and spiritual do not have to be separate, and transformational leaders don't separate their inner self from the role they play. Instead they are integral to one another. This is a holistic view of leadership action, one more responsive to both our needs and our objective experience.

The basis of human comfort, strength, happiness. A large proportion of study respondents define spirituality in personal terms, but in less metaphysical ways. Human beings develop principles, certain qualities and influences, which they exhibit in their behavior and interactions with other human beings. For these respondents spirituality is the part of us that we use or rely upon for comfort, strength, and happiness. It is a source of contentment.

The source of personal meaning, values, life purposes. For some people spirituality is any doctrine or philosophy that lifts us and gives meaning to our lives. It is the side of us searching for meaning, values, ethics, life purposes. It is a guiding hand to our actions. It is the ethics we follow. It is the degree to which we seek to do things for the common good of all and to be better people. In this dimension, spirituality is a relationship with something beyond the self that is intangible, yet also provides a source of values, meaning, and broad understanding.

A personal belief system. Still others define spirituality as a personal belief system. It is being true to one's beliefs, internal values, and ethics. It is a goodness of mind and spirit.

An emotional level, a feeling. Spirituality is an emotional level, a feeling. It is how we feel emotionally in our soul and body.

The experiences of the transcendent in life. Spirituality for some also partakes of the transcendent. It is acting out in thought and deed the experiences of the transcendent in human life.

Spiritual leadership is new. And, like all new ideas, it challenges, by its very presence in the arena of ideas, all old ideas and practices. It is new in the sense that academic leadership theory has not considered the spiritual orientation in people as a factor in their theories of leadership, management, or organization. It is new in the sense that many people's professional paradigms have excluded any sense of the unique self from their preconceptions of work, workers, managers, and leaders, or of the interactions in which these organizational actors engage. As such, introduction of spirit to the workplace is new, even alien to many.

Spirituality, however, is also old. Individuals have always been responsive to their spiritual center. They have fostered its growth and often have let it dominate their lives both on and off the job. But they have not found a receptive community for developing individual and group spiritual values at work. As a result, many people compartmentalize their lives into work, family, religion, and social spheres. They fragment their self definitions into separate cells.

Nevertheless, people are the sum of their life experiences—physical, mental, spiritual. To try to compartmentalize our inner self and core values into a complex of disparate external relationships is to invite stress, tension, and dysfunction. Today where many people are spending most of their waking lives at work or in work-related situations and activities, such a bifurcated existence results in the social maladies that characterize contemporary American life. Some reintegration of the whole person is needed.

Spiritual leadership provides that holistic, integrated life. Through their personal efforts, leaders assure that the value system of the organization is integrated and holistic in nature so they do not have to sacrifice values (Cound 1987). A holistic approach includes services and programs that address both the professional and personal lives of stakeholders (Ruppert 1991; Autry 1992).

Holistic, spiritual leadership is no longer a choice. It is a need in today's world (Pinchot and Pinchot 1994). Workplaces are communities in which many of us live much of our productive lives. We need, therefore, to know what we can about how to make productive communities. Bureaucracies cannot do this. They so segment responsibilities that humanity becomes a departmental rather than a universal responsibility. We need new structural forms and new relationship patterns to accommodate this new leadership paradigm.

Chapter 4

Problems with the Current Leadership Situation

The idea of spirituality as a prime area of leadership concern makes sense intellectually. However, as leaders attempt to operationalize spiritual leadership they may encounter problems. Prime among these concerns is the fact that spiritual matters have never formed a major component of modern leadership or management theory. The result is that there is little concrete ideology supporting this perception of the leader's role. Consequently, young professionals are not exposed to spiritual ideas in their professional training. Indeed, they are taught to objectify, not personalize their profession.

Business success is, therefore, defined in much more objective terms. And spiritual satisfaction and professional success are seen as separate goals, not attainable by the same effort. Career and material acquisition, not spiritual peace are the measures in today's work world. These goals are held out as paramount in the face of individual longings for harmony, satisfaction, and peace; ideals held universally by all people, whether at home, in church, or in the office.

These pervasive human needs are ignored in leadership and management theory. In truth, the theory supporting leadership is based on obsolete philosophy and obsolete science. Based on three hundred–year-old science and an even more ancient philosophy, traditional leadership theory is insufficient to explain and predict contemporary corporate life. It is inadequate to deal with radical change and creativity typical of today's business world.

Spirit as the core idea in leadership theory is a radical idea. It is counter to accepted intellectual principles and ignores deeply held feel-ings. The classical model of the business firm is highly structured and focuses on control of tangible objects—products, services, people. The environment within which most people work is a bureaucratic one. While good at ensuring high productivity in yielding repeatable prod-ucts, it is not geared to meeting individual human needs. Hence, intro-ducing one's spiritual sense into the discussion of leadership is foreign to many.

Nevertheless, our spiritual self is our most accurate definition of our-self. It focuses who we are and what we do. It has to be a part of our work tasks and the goals we seek from our work. But acceptance of the spiritual side of both leader and led can be difficult given the history of separation of work and worker spirit.

Some of the problems spiritual leaders encounter in introducing spirit as a legitimate part of leadership thought and action are elaborated in this chapter. The intent is to introduce some of the limits on spiritual leadership in the workplace arising from present-day intellectual theory and practice. The sections here delineate the nature and scope of some of these forces in the present situation at work that mitigate against the full acceptance of the spiritual side of workers and leaders. Later dis-cussions will help provide a more positive rationale for this emerging theory of leadership in the workplace.

SPIRIT AND PROFESSIONALISM

Some may suppose that attention to the spiritual side of self discour-ages education and professionalism (see, for example, Peters 1994). They believe that it is the purpose of professional training to dispel the mists and shadows of religion and free the human mind from so much error and delusion. Like day and night, were either of them to gain the ascen-dancy the reign of the other must necessarily cease.

In fact, education is the expansion of the soul—the body and the spirit—to the fullness of its capacity. It is a bringing forth and perfecting of all the inherent powers of the individual. Education increases the qual-ity of our faculties. It imparts nothing but discipline and development. Like the work of creation, which is almost synonymous with education, it *forms* the human mind and spirit, it does not create them.

In a very real way, education does not happen in school. Life itself is the real school; all human experience is an educational process. Correctly understood, the entire human race is here in life as pupils. Education is the reward of experience and progress written upon all people. Human-kind is many-sided. Life involves the education of all sides. A perfect education is the full and uniform development of the mental, physical, moral, and spiritual faculties. Schools offer little toward this education of the mind and spirit, though if done well school is very important. Schools prepare and point the way to learning, but they cannot guarantee the student will reach the goal. Schools provide tools for us to educate ourselves.

If the above is true, education of the spirit; that is, experience with the spiritual side of self, must be a part of the daily work experiences of all people. If all we need is mental and physical discipline, prisons would not be crowded with educated convicts, the savings and loan fiasco would not have happened, banks would not break nearly so often, and war would be irrelevant. An educated man or woman who is devoid of moral principle, is just so much nearer a beast. Such a person is admirably adapted as an instrument of evil for the furtherance of base designs.

SPIRIT AND SUCCESS AMBITION

Americans work hard, but they don't often put work at the emotional and spiritual center of their lives. We may live well, but we no longer live nobly. Workaholism and its handmaidens, careerism and materialism, are not only social issues. They also are spiritual issues—dealing with the central core of the individual, often impoverishing all values but those of material success. In the quest for success, career professionals work an average of 52 hours per week. It is compulsive for some, nothing gets in the way of work.

Business people, however, have begun to question the deeper, underlying methods and motives of their leaders (Hickman 1989). Success has nothing to do with titles. It has everything to do with the faith, the vision, and the love we bring to our work. Sound moral principle is the only sure evidence of strength, the only firm foundation of greatness and perpetuity. Where this is lacking, no man's character is strong, no nation's life can be lasting. Spiritual leadership is more than a new leadership ideal, it is a paradigm shift. This shift impacts workers and leaders and redefines their standards of success.

How can people break the false gods of career and free the whole soul for growth? It is, perhaps, the ultimate statement that the world does not own us, that we are made for rest and holiness as surely as we are made for work and ambition. One road to dramatic change in tomorrow's leading organizations is the move from career dependence to career self-reliance. People need to take ownership of their careers (Waterman 1994).

Another thing people can do is to place work in the proper context. We don't have to sacrifice self on the altar of career. We can judge ourselves (and force others to also judge us) on a different measure: not by what we do, but by the way that we do our work. No matter what work we do, it can be done with heart and spirit. For example, a woman who died recently was eulogized as one who brought compassion and sensitivity to mastectomy patients whom she served as a clerk in a store. Similarly, but in a different context, is the position of a house mover, who recognizes that moving is hard for most people, a vulnerable time for them. Therefore he treats his customers with love and makes them feel that he cares about their possessions and their life. He said, "God wants me to help them, make the change smoothly. If I can be happy about it maybe they can be happy too."

The current leadership famine in America and the world stems from many people adopting other than suitable leadership styles. It has been deepened by an insufficient number of leaders striving to become orchestrators of their workers' environment so they (the workers) can realize more of their full self, not just acquire more material goods. To combat this tendency, people must take careful stock of their own lives and help their leaders be true to shared spiritual tendencies. They must monitor the soul of the leadership they receive, not just its outward form.

SPIRIT AND SELF-OVERCOMING

The greatest problems leaders face are not the surface challenges of work, worker, and product. Most leaders play to their workers' strengths. The leaders' greatest challenges lie deep inside their spirit and that of their followers. The spirit contains everything in our character we try to express (everything that makes us feel good) as well as everything we want to suppress (everything that is painful or makes us feel unworthy). Getting in touch with our inner self, our spirit self, lets us inventory and use our best qualities such as:

confidence	a sense of infallibility	quickness
sharp wit	alertness	dedication
courage	perseverance	charm
thriftiness	commitment	trust
faith	love	hope

We also can define our spirit by less than positive traits. There is a hidden part of our spirit, our hidden self, the aspects of our personality that we don't like to acknowledge or that society discourages us from showing. It too is part of what makes us human. We need to bring this less-attractive self to the fore of the mind for occasional scrutiny or it will turn toxic. Most healthy, well-adjusted people, for example, harbor traits such as:

a sharp wit	abrasiveness	narrow focus
workaholism	control	inflexibility
foolhardiness	resistance to change	manipulation
false economy	blind faith	sloth

Thinking about our negative inclinations and forming strategies to counter them is also part of sensitivity to the spirit. Applying spirit at work lets us consider the organization's spirit and to catalog its strengths and weaknesses. While assessing the group's strengths is a part of some organizations, assessment of its spiritual faults is less common. Symptoms we observe to analyze how the dark side of spirit operates in our organizations might include sensitivity to the following factors:

- We never discuss certain topics.
- We carefully guard information.
- Rituals serve to exclude rather than include.
- Politically correct propaganda dominates the culture.
- Language is characterized by deliberate obfuscation.
- Leaders openly or covertly scrape for power and turf.
- Those who dare to call things as they see them are shunted aside.
- Real dilemmas go unstated, unresolved, and unacknowledged.
- We don't promote and protect ethics and aesthetics as important.

Robert Bly said every part of our personality that we do not love will become hostile to us. The longer we persist in disowning the other side of our character, the darker it becomes and the more we fear to see what is there.

THE SPIRITUAL AND BUREAUCRATIC THEORY

Management science theory and practice in North America are in a state of intellectual disarray. Most management practitioners and theorists appear to believe in a mechanical, Newtonian world where we locate objects and events simply in time and space (Hurst 1989). While useful in our historical, simpler past, this sort of worldview breaks down when we have to deal with the radical change and creativity typical of today. And increasingly the present crop of professionally trained managers—MBAs—are unprepared for this task.

Masters of business administration (MBA) programs are faulty. We need to change these programs in the front-end, "pathfinding" area, where critical issues like leadership, vision, imagination, and values reside (Leavitt 1989). Among the subjects MBA programs teach quite well, and probably overteach, are analytic methods. While effective problem solving requires mental rigor and analysis of the environment, and while effective implementation requires competence in getting work done, effective pathfinding requires soul, imagination, personal commitment, and deep belief.

The three-world theory of Plato is more suited to today's environment. Plato's concept was of a physical world of nature, a spiritual world of the soul, and the world of ideas or eternal forms. This theory views the mind as a dynamic, evolving system that constructs a hierarchy of integrations by connecting the differences of the first world to make a series of transformations through information, data, knowledge, and meaning to achieve an identity.

The task of today's organizational/institutional managers is to continually weld imagination and experience. This task requires a philosophy of knowledge that does not mind talking about imagination and realizes that language cannot capture all of experience, some of which is mysterious, even mystical.

We often regard mysticism as something antiintellectual, obscure, and confused, or impractical and unconnected with experience. True mysticism is a vision of reality. It is like a form of perception that is absolute and so practical that we can live it every moment of life and express it in everyday duties. We need to be more fully "real." We need visions, goals, structures, and systems, and most importantly, leaders who will help us become all that we really are.

American (Western world) bureaucratic and managerial theory has remained largely unchanged for generations. A major shift in political thought has not taken place since the Enlightenment. For two hundred years the Enlightenment philosophers have discarded the time-honored belief that humans are subject to laws ordained by a source higher than their own understanding. The Enlightenment thinkers subverted the religious and traditional beliefs of older European philosophies in replacing the authority of custom and religion with the authority of "reason"—their term for the emancipated human mind.

They focused their intellectual energies on going beyond the search for the "good" in life. A noble aim, "good," but we must deal with the issue of what is good. Searching for the good has not produced a foundation for reform. So the Enlightenment philosophers tried to liberate human energies and reasoning power from the fruitless and contentious search for some transcendent "Good" or God and tried to redirect that energy toward the material improvement of the human condition.

The philosophers' argument was simple. While Socrates (469–399 B.C.) may have strolled about Athens questioning everyone's basic assumptions on matters like what is Justice and what is Good, he never assumed he knew enough to replace society's foundation of religion and custom with his own brand of legal and moral order. The philosophers of the past only interpreted the world, but the point, say modern philosophers, is to change it.

More modern intellectuals see the task as not so much a quest as a form of conquest. Jean-Jacques Rousseau (1712–1778) and Friedrich Nietzsche (1844–1900) argued that we can recover a sense of meaning through a further attack on traditions. But to do so we must obliterate the last limits on human freedom. This promised, they said, not merely physical comforts but limitless freedom, obtained by liberating humanity from even those limits (religion and custom) once thought to belong to reason itself.

Rousseau and Nietzsche sought deliverance from traditional authority for people by appealing to the law of nature. For them there is no standard but liberation itself. Jean-Paul Sartre (1905–1980) said human beings essentially create themselves. This idea suggests that self-actualization is defined as determining your point of view of right and wrong without interference from other authority. One example is today's public school curricula, which foster this self-actualization for teenagers without interference from parental authority.

The appeal to selfish reason is neither morally nor politically neutral but dependent upon a decisive reorientation of the mind toward secular or material ends. It is the intellectual equivalent of political correctness as used today. There are, of course, benefits flowing from this perspective. The project to construct a more rational and prosperous society worked. The problem is it worked too well. The risk inherent in reason—the Enlightenment philosophy—is that we are less and less satisfied by it.

We need to question the authority of self, the hallmark of the Enlightenment. What Enlightenment philosophers call tolerance for diversity is actually an attempt to shape a culture that recognizes the superiority of *their* ideas. What these so-called critical thinkers today say is that every individual should do his own critical thinking. What they mean, in fact, is that we should define individual freedom only as they—the intellectuals—define it. When we examine the assumptions of such nonconformists we reveal their bland acceptance of secular authority, not freedom at all.

We ordinarily seek the basis of human community in one of three ways: (1) in the rights of the individual and the partial delegation of them to political authorities, (2) in the mutual needs of people and the relations that spring from them, or (3) in the actual existence of the power of people over people—whether arising from natural relationship, from benefits granted, or from physical or intellectual domination. In this context, we maintain freedom in terms of an accepted agreement among free people to constrain their freedom for the common good.

The maintenance of society in theory is supposed to depend on a "social compact" between government and the citizens. True as an abstract idea, but it is untrue as an historical reality. Nonetheless the so-called social contract guides much of our contemporary political theory. The Mosaic Law, on the other hand, offers another theory of human relationships. It seeks the basis of its polity, first in the absolute sovereignty of God, next in the relationship of the individual to God, and then, through God to his countrymen. This theory of human relationships is more germane to spiritual leadership than old and obsolete political theory.

While it contradicts none of the common theories, the Mosaic Law lies beneath them all. It shows why other theories of social relations are only secondary deduction from an ultimate truth, which cannot be in itself sufficient; and, if only one of them claims to be the whole truth, it becomes an absurdity. The Mosaic conceptions of human relationship with matters of the spirit has permeated political theory, the sociology that supports it, and common human interaction.

The greatest problems facing our society are at bottom moral and spiritual rather than structural. It would, however, be a mistake to overlook the role of law and government policy in shaping our moral environment. All of criminal law is a moral code. It tells us how we can live with others in safety and security. Family law is morally based (love, caring, support). Business and commercial law is morally based (honesty, fairness). Most legislation has a moral foundation (AIDS, abortion, and gambling are current cases in point). We all need to commit to obey the laws we have as we work to improve them.

SPIRIT AND INTELLECTUALISM

When we talk about intellectuals we are talking about dissidents, about people who have some complaint against society as most people live it (Hancock 1994). Intellectuals equate critical thinking with the debunking of shared beliefs and established authorities. For them controversial means intellectual distinction. But it takes little intelligence to question authority without substituting something else.

It is fallacious to assume that intelligent means dissident. This undermines the need to feed both the mind and the spirit by persuading members that to cultivate one is to threaten the other. We can describe the essence of intellectualism in America and the world today as "liberationist"; we assume that a sign of intelligence and learning is to demand the liberty of the individual from all authority, liberation from all limitations, and an irreducible respect for human dignity and freedom.

Today's liberationists consider anyone who cannot accept their views as agents of intellectual abuse. Instead of bringing the lost sheep back into the fold, the shepherd must herd the flock to reconcile itself to the nonconformist member, wherever he or she may wander. Liberationists define themselves in the negative, as the enemy of all traditional and institutional limits and restraints. They see themselves as in an adversary culture making enemies of the general public. They criticize and seek to subvert any stable source of authority and meaning, acknowledging no responsibility for the consequences. Indeed, they see any adverse consequences as evidence of the need for further attack on tradition. The cure for the ills of a liberationist is always more liberation. Freedom requires no justification beyond itself.

Today the liberationists define themselves in terms of freedom and autonomy—my body is mine so I have the right to abort my fetus, exercise sexual deviance, or commit suicide. Over thirty years ago the literary critic Lionel Trilling observed the tendency of contemporary intellectuals to participate in an adversary culture that almost instinctively defines its identity by opposing the tastes and beliefs of ordinary people. No wonder the modern organization worker is alienated, isolated, and turned off. The spirit in each of us cannot move freely in such a constraining ideology.

SPIRIT AND ORGANIZATIONAL STRUCTURE

The environment within which we work is the firm, the corporation and the work groups with them. We model the modern large-scale (and the not-so-large-scale) organization after the classical bureaucracy—highly structured and geared to the production of tangible objects. In many respects, life in large-scale organizations sometimes resembles life in a totalitarian state. The worker is a labor bond servant of the managers who control his or her life in detailed fashion. And, in business organizations as in governments, totalitarianism is incompatible with high performance.

Too many corporations are run like miniempires, with no one caring about what anyone else is doing (Adair 1985). Few leaders do more than coordinate efforts in their small sphere. Management consists of more than mechanistic skills. This structure is no more sufficient to sophisticated workers today than serfdom was to the factory work of the early Industrial Revolution. Indeed, the corporation and other large employers may be among the last bastions of a stifling bureaucratic dictatorship.

We need to move beyond bureaucracy and rebuild the patterns of our formal relationships and the quality of our communications in the organization on the basis of freedom and rights (Pinchot and Pinchot 1994), not just objects. Bureaucracy is a structure defined by chains of dominance and submission. Initiative means asking for permission. Most workers get to use only a tiny fraction of their potential. The freedom of speech essential to adaptation to rapid change is at the sufferance of the boss. Bosses tell employees where they will work, what they will do, how to do it.

Some of the stress workers feel today in the modern organization may be due to this change of productive focus while maintaining obsolete structural forms. Bureaucracy produces simple and shortsighted answers in an era in which anticipating interconnections and dealing with long-term implications are requirements for survival. Merely changing bureaucratic structure does not mean only rearranging organization charts. It begins with liberating the self-organizing potential of working people so they can work in constantly changing units.

We need both management and leadership in any true definition of leadership. In today's competitive corporate market, managers must be more productive than their staff members *and* be able to lead (Rondeau 1988). Leadership calls for motivational and inspirational qualities, not just coordination (Adair 1985). In a word, work systems are moving to unit structures and group forms. A high-performance unit has at its heart a spirit—felt and shared by all members—that honors all people including workers and customers (Heerman 1995).

The spirit in teamwork is really about service and contribution—generous giving—and honoring those we serve with the finest we know how to provide (Heerman 1995). Worldwide, executives are realizing the need for better leadership to reach their company's and their workers' potential. To meet today's challenging markets and increased competition, many managers are getting more involved in the daily life of corporations. They are providing honest communication between management and staff. They recognize that happiness is the purpose of life—social and business life—that occupies the time and energies of all workers. It is something natural, desirable, and, when we recognize and foster it, it can be helpful in improving all aspects of corporate work life—at the bottom line and elsewhere throughout the organization.

Today's well-managed companies are guided by unit leaders. The core responsibility of the executive is to be an effective leader for the unit. Spirit supports and sustains each person in the group; therefore, the most effective leaders are those who create a unit spirit that makes the work exciting. For example, the mark of Lee Iacocca's success at Chrysler Corporation was that from the beginning he started building a team approach at every level. Indeed, unity was a key point in his outstanding leadership style.

Ideas of freedom and empowerment are competitive needs. The three guiding principles of wholeness and interrelationship, inner wisdom, and inner authority characterize this new paradigm. It is this paradigm that gives prominent place to many of the current ideas present in today's values-based transformational leadership. The new paradigm focuses on vision, empowerment, risk taking, creativity, harmony, trust, integrity, and compassion. It prioritizes culture creation and consideration of external forces. This new leadership paradigm is counter to the old one centering on short-term goals and a rigid culture, and is an orientation toward centralized direction and control, a procedural bias, analysis, and aggressive values.

The key issues and approaches that are part of this change include:

- Redefining profit to include providing society with services and goods, providing people with employment, and creating a surplus of wealth (profit)
- An attitude of cooperation, honoring diversity while establishing community
- Creating work characterized by a deeper sense of life-purpose, work that lets people feel they are making a difference, being fully alive, living with integrity, developing sacredness in their relationships, and turning the organization into a community where everyone can learn and grow
- Competition, cooperation, and co-creation
- Seeking inclusive communities that are open, frank, and accepting of mistakes
- Developing an inner wisdom that facilitates transformation.

Chapter 5

Pressures that Focus Our Spirit Self at Work

People are making the quest for meaning and congruence with their innermost self a part of their work goals. They are seeking more full personal (whole-person) development from their work, and in so doing are transforming the workplace and the larger society. People are voicing their craving to include inner spiritual needs as well as economic and production needs in the work experience now in ways not known even a few years ago. Leaders and workers alike expect more from their work than just a pay check. They are asking that their values and morals be not only considered, but openly reflected in work cultures. In so doing they are changing institutional structures and transforming their work lives.

My survey of mid-level professionals unanimously agreed that spirituality is a significant part of their work lives (see Table 5.1) and that their inner spirituality effects their values, ethics, and beliefs. Sixty-three percent said their spirituality was very important in shaping their overall ethics and values. The rest (37%) said it was important. None discounted their personal sense of spirituality in shaping their belief systems, including those at work.

The middle-level professionals surveyed identified several reasons why they felt that their spiritual selves were critical to work success. By far, the two most common reasons cited were that our spirituality is the motivating force for all life and it is the guide for life's actions. For them and, I dare say, for most other people, spirituality identifies and clarifies and places in context core values, ethics, and beliefs.

Table 5.1
Spirituality in the Workplace

Perceptions of the Importance of Spirituality in Shaping One's Values, Ethics, and Beliefs

     VERY IMPORTANT: 63%   IMPORTANT: 37%

     NOT VERY IMPORTANT: 0   NOT IMPORTANT: 0

Group Member Reliance on Spirituality in Doing Work

     A LOT: 100%   NOT MUCH: 0   NONE: 0

Connection Between Leadership Success and the Leader's Spirituality

     SIGNIFICANT: 84%   DEPENDS: 11%

     NONE: 0   NO RESPONSE: 5%

Significance of the Language and Values of Spirituality in Understanding Leadership

     YES: 74%   NO: 0

     DEPENDS: 5%   NO RESPONSE: 21%

Our spirituality is the underlying element in all major business decisions: hiring, firing, deciding with whom to do business, whom to trust, where to work, and how much of our life-force to invest in that work. It helps us think more clearly and more deeply. All managers surveyed rely on their spirituality in doing their work (Table 5.1).

Spirituality is a powerful force in shaping people's lives at work and in all other domains. We base our decisions and actions on our spiritual values. Our central values determine how we deal with people every day. Our spirituality is a shield in a sometimes corrupt and disappointing world. It is what guides our leadership and our followership actions. We draw on our inner beliefs for all significant actions we take.

Spirituality is at the heart of both self-esteem and self-actualization. It is the essence of our sense of morality. Our moral values determine our career path and all we do along that path. Spirituality gives us a value system beyond the boss or the organization and their policies and procedures. The Christian Bible says our work should glorify God, not just the boss. This and most other spiritual value systems suggest a similar priority ranking of an inner moral standard above materialistic rewards. The higher standard of moral conduct we adopt as our guide cannot help but shape our behaviors on the job.

There is a significant connection between a leader's spirituality and his or her ability to affect the organization (see Table 5.1). The leader's spirituality can be the basis for transforming the organization as it creates a culture based on values and ethics consonant with the leader's perception of spiritual self. Spirituality increases caring behaviors, changes the character of internal change and communications systems, is the source of our most powerful and personal values, increases effective group membership, and creates a dynamic, appealing, and creative culture.

The language and values of spirituality are significant in leader self-understanding, in understanding their activities as leaders (Table 5.1), and in giving meaning to follower behaviors. Their spirituality eases sharing of values as people think about doing what they know in their heart is right and true. People are motivated to action through shared trust that comes with shared belief in the utility of one value system. The leader's spirituality adds a vital source of strength and inspiration to interpersonal relationships. It lets us better understand others' values, beliefs, and motivations and, as a result, increases leader effectiveness.

Our sense of our spiritual self has always been a part of the dynamic of leader-follower relationships. That it is only now receiving popular—and some academic and practitioner—attention does not take anything away from its pervasive power and utility as an important tool in the leader's tool kit. Spirituality is, and always has been, a part of the life force of all people. It is in the workplace, whether our theory says it is or not. Surveyed managers are unanimous in identifying their spirituality as a significant, even vital part of their true self and a powerful force in shaping their actions at work and elsewhere.

The growing interest in spirituality and work gives promise of another "old-yet-new" idea to further refine and define leadership. It, like our current interest in leadership as distinct from management, trust culture maintenance, and the applied uses of power, represents still another new dimension of leadership that can increase the levels of satisfaction and productivity in our workplaces (Fairholm 1991, 1993, 1994a). Pressures are mounting to accept spirituality as another legitimate force in the cultural surround within which leadership takes place. We discuss some of these pressures below.

EXTENSION OF QUANTUM SCIENCE TO THE ORGANIZATION

Just when social scientists seem to have their science down and can connect the multiple strings of variables in social science to a coherent theory, the hard scientists have left us behind. They have forged ahead into the vast "porridge of being" that describes a new reality (Wheatley 1992). Present organizational and management theorists see organizations in the same images as our seventeenth-century hard science models imagined the universe to be. We manage by separating organizational structure and functions into subparts. We believe that influence occurs as a direct result of force exerted from one source (person) to another. We assume our organizations and our world are predictable and impartial.

This Newtonian model of the world is safe, clear, simple, logical, linear, and wrong. The early emphasis on established science as the route to ultimate truth has proven to be an unreliable and essentially unfulfilling road. In field after field we find that science does not provide the whole truth—even less so a satisfying life. Modern tools are neutral. Science produced the A-bomb and the computer, but doesn't guide us in their proper use. The world is coming to recognize that science has asked humans to give up feelings for sterile reason. But, reason is only positive when applied by highly moral people. And science doesn't guarantee morality. Indeed, it doesn't even include it in its formula.

Widespread disillusionment with science and technology is current. Science is characterized by materialism and reductionism. Its organizations are described in machine terms where tight control makes sense. If, as is more nearly true, organizations are seen as process structures (as the new science suggests), then seeking to impose control through permanent structure in the scientific mold is suicide.

However, the situation while bleak is not irreversible. People are turning from the old science to redefine and are re-establishing value systems that emphasize individuality, morality, and self-sacrifice. Church affiliation is rising. Humankind has rediscovered its inborn predisposition for spiritual fulfillment. The failure of abundance to assuage that need is observable in all age groups, especially the youth. Materialism doesn't attract so many adherents today. Many are disengaging from social systems that promise abundance without satisfaction.

Humanity is very much a part of this universe—it is not just immutable laws carried out neutrally. We are kin to all creatures past and present. There can be purpose without exact predetermined plan—the universe shows this, life shows this. Science is now defining a new science, the underlying currents of which are a movement toward holism. This new science defines every living thing as a spender of energy. Living entities will do anything needed to preserve themselves, including change (Wheatley 1992).

The Newtonian model of homeostases has been replaced with a model that says each living creature is constantly changing—it is a never-resting structure that constantly seeks its own self-renewal. We see change made in "quantum" leaps—abrupt and discontinuous changes where an electron jumps from one atomic orbit to another without passing through any intermediate stages. Surprise is the route to discovery.

We can see the principles of this new science played out in our organizations. Observers of the best organizations can tell what the organization's values and ways of doing business are by watching workers.

This is possible whether we are in a production shop, office, or behind the counter. It is not the formal structure that is the real organization as much as it is the relationships of the people making up the organization. Our relationships are key to our level of commitment and success whether they are formal or informal, planned or unplanned.

None of us exists independent of our relationships. Relationships exist even among ostensibly independent parts, even those existing between the person and the setting. Leaders need to be savvy about creating relationships and nurturing them as growing, evolving entities. Relationships have become the dominant theme in management today. Indeed, the movement toward participation is rooted, perhaps subconsciously, in our changing perceptions of the genuine organizing principles of the universe.

Reality changes shape and meaning because of our activity, not because of our abstract plans or theories. Because organization theories (all of the social sciences) have traditionally taken their models from the hard sciences, we are beginning to reconfigure our ideas about management in relational terms (Wheatley 1992). Leaders are at the center of a seamless web of mutual responsibility and collaboration. We need to stop teaching only facts—the tangible things or knowledge—and focus on our interpersonal relationships as the basis for all definition.

The participatory nature of reality has focused scientific attention on our interpersonal relationships. We are beginning to see autonomy, not as a small but necessary step away from control, but as a necessary part of life, more important than control and regimentation. We need to trust that something as simple as a clear core of values and vision, kept in motion through continuous dialogue, can lead to order and harmony.

An interesting idea coming from the new science of quantum physics is that of fields (Wheatley 1992). Fields are invisible forces that structure space or human behavior. They are unseen structures, occupying space and becoming known to us through their effects. Fields are the basic substance of the universe. Gravitation is a field. Magnetism and electrical forces are invisible fields.

We can also imagine organizational space as fields. Fields give form to our words. Space is never empty, even organizational space. If we don't fill it with coherent messages, if we say one thing and do another, then we create dissonance in the very space of the organization. In the same way we can envision our employees as waves of energy spreading out into all regions (fields) of the organization. They are minimally bounded. They are focused on interactions. They are centered on present energy exchanges (Wheatley 1992) and are a part of this invisible field of the organization.

Organizational vision is also a field—a force of unseen connections that influences peoples' behavior—rather than merely an evocative message. In human organizations, a clear sense of identity—of the values, traditions, aspirations, competencies, and culture that guide the operation—is the real source of independence from the environment. It is a self-organizing system. It may be volatile in a given circumstance, but it is stable over time. We build invisible, but powerful visionary fields through the collective behavior of a group's members.

Organizations are open systems (fields). They have the potential of continuously importing free energy from their environment and exporting entropy. They stay viable and maintain a state of nonequilibrium. They keep the system in balance so it can change and grow. Every organism in nature—including people—behave this way. They seek ultimate stability through creative local changes.

In the new quantum science of evolution and order in the universe, information is the dynamic element. It is the underlying structure. Information is the dynamic process that ensures life. Information organizes matter into a specific form. It both informs us and forms us (Wheatley 1992). Information is the key element in the continuous change characteristic of all human life—both individual life and organizational life.

The power of information is shifting to the individual. Indeed, we can say with Ray (1992) that we are in the age of individual creativity because power lies in the way individuals use information. The powers of the mind are everywhere ascendant over the brute force of circumstance. It is a move to spirit, to inner qualities such as intuition, will, joy, strength, spirit, and compassion.

NEW ORGANIZATIONAL STRUCTURES

Most current and past programs aimed at reinventing the organization have bottom-line productivity improvement goals. Recently, however, there is a growing interest in adding a human dimension to these programs. Downsizing and rightsizing efforts may reduce direct costs, but the impact on worker satisfaction and long-term survivability as a viable organizational asset is suspect. Hence the spate of research and discussion of spiritual dimensions on the job.

The exact dimensions of the human factor in downsizing is not clear. What is clear is that we affect people personally, emotionally, physically, and spiritually when we either lay them off or keep them on the job and ask them to accept increased work and responsibility. In one case the stress is obvious. In the other it is equally strong, but less considered, and its long-term impact on the individual and the corporation less clear.

We have long known of the powerful impact on the spirit of decisions effecting our work. It is unmistakable, if only tangentially, in more and more public discussion. We are all aware, for example, of the "high touch" reaction to the introduction of high technology that John Naisbitt discussed as far back as 1983. Part of the most recent pressures toward reinvention of the organization is clearly to invent organizational structures appropriate to this age of spirit at work.

Evidence is amassing suggesting there is a significant connection between a leader's or worker's ability to have a transformational effect on the organization and his or her disposition toward spirituality. Eighty-four percent of surveyed managers confirmed this link (see Table 5.1). The reasons are obvious. They can be identified under six headings:

Transformation. The organization is nothing more than a group of people in relationship. Given this obvious, but often overlooked fact, a leader or member with a defined sense of his or her own spirituality and that of his or her co-workers can have greater transformational effect on the organization, its forms, structures, and processes than some formal reorganization plans. The spiritually conscious person derives more passion and has stronger beliefs in his or her mission than the spiritually dormant member. Surveyed professionals see a correlation between reliance on spirituality and a person's ability to make tangible change in the organization. While this correlation is unquestionably not causal or exclusive, leaders can definitely transform an organization by sharing spiritual values with those they lead.

Subconsciously, and on very tangible levels, employees think about those with whom they labor for 8 to 16 hours a day. They decide whether their co-workers are worth the investment of their life-energy, a nonrenewable source. Spirituality is one factor that a skilled and intelligent person can use to change an organization.

Spirituality defines our effort. It makes us more passionate about our work and that passion is clear to followers. We can directly link inspiration to spirituality. Transformational leadership, though, allows followers to develop on their own terms. There are certain things about the way we feel (our spirituality) that positively (or negatively) effects our ability to create change in an organization.

Caring. We cannot separate a person's spirituality from his or her actions and disposition. Spiritual leaders exhibit positive traits like caring, honesty, and trust that can lift an organization and alter its basic culture. The leader is the pull for the organization. If a leader (or member) does not exhibit an inner spirituality that focuses on improving or helping the organization, co-workers will likely perceive any changes the person attempts as insincere. This increases the chances of having that suggested change fail because the changes suggested by the individual are not created in and valued on the basis of his or her spiritual self.

Communication. How we communicate our spirituality and how we use it to foster positive change is very important to the success of any effort to create positive change. Leadership and management technologies directed toward getting people to perform the organization's work can be great successes or dreadful failures. Which result we get depends on how we communicate our group's needs to others. As co-workers see our communications as laced with core, commonly held spiritual values, what we say will strike a responsive chord in these others and foster growth. Failure to do this will result in loss.

Values. Spirituality is the source of our most forceful and personal values. When leader and led can share spiritual values such as trust, faith, honesty, justice, freedom, and caring in the workplace, a true metamorphosis will occur and the organization can reach new creative heights. People have to believe in something bigger than self in order to love others. And we have to have meaning in a higher purpose than just material rewards to inspire others to greatness—whether at home, in church, or on the job.

Enabling. Leaders need followers to lead, but they need capable, energized followers who can and will do their share of the group's work including sometimes even taking over the leader's role. Enabled people flourish in an environment of interactive trust, shared vision, and common values. Moral leadership involves leaders in actions to enable followers to use many of their innate talents in pursuing group goals. Moral leaders train, educate, and coach followers, provide motivation, involve them in appropriate networks, and then free them from situational constraints that may hamper their growth or transformation toward full effectiveness. They endow followers with the capacity to lead themselves in accomplishing the organization's ends.

Endowing individual and organizational character with the desire and the capacity to be independent actors asks leaders to reconstitute themselves, their co-workers, and the organization. Reconstituting the individual worker, in effect, asks leaders to help their followers be *in* the system but not *be* the system. Effective workers detach their heart from the badness of the system and adhere only to the good parts. Spiritual enabling focuses on personal might, not organizational power; it is building capacity based on inner feelings of rightness, not rules and regulations.

Effectiveness. A leader who is comfortable with himself or herself is happy and strong and can convey these qualities to others. He or she can, in this way, be a part of another's spirituality. When this bonding is present, leaders or group members can be very effective. The leader is the primary and ideal role model for helping others in the development of unit efforts toward this process. It was the spirituality, as much as anything else (maybe more so), about them that made the great models of our past (John F. Kennedy, Martin Luther King, Jr., and Abraham Lincoln) effective in raising our standards and defining our best public self as a nation.

THE MOTIVATIONAL FORCE OF SPIRIT

Spirituality is what motivates an individual. Spirituality lies at the core of our values, ethics, and beliefs. It is at the epicenter of our self. It drives us and defines us. We and our core values are all one and the same. Our spiritual values act as a guideline for doing the right thing. It is *the* underlying element in decision making. In a word, spirit is the conscious motivating force in people.

Our spirituality plays a large part in shaping personal values, which, in turn, have a significant impact on our ethics and therefore our actions. Personal spirituality is at the root of a person's guiding beliefs. It is only our spirituality that can really motivate us. Our spiritual force is our primary guide in occupational choice and in day-to-day work in that career. It impacts daily decisions made. It guides all of our actions and all major business decisions.

WORKER ALIENATION

The current discussion of spirituality as an issue for serious debate by business professionals is not always propelled by the leader's concerns about personal faith or past religious traditions (Terry 1994). Rather, it often arises out of the present feelings of disconnection many workers feel. Spirituality provides the basis for a new connection between our own spirituality and the leaders who want to guide our professional lives. Spirituality in the workplace is moving workers and leaders away from ideas of us-against-them and, even, from the idea of taking ownership toward ideas of a unifying stewardship (McMillen 1994).

Spirituality may provide a bond that can respond to worker disconnection. Spiritual leaders make a concern for worker (and personal) spiritual needs a part of their vision for the group. In doing this, these leaders go beyond meaning and ethics into the question of hope. A focus on spiritual needs lets leaders and led unite on common ground—at the metaphysical, not the transactional level. As we make this connection, fleeting differences of policy or procedure lose essential meaning. Workers and leaders can accept these differences in the assurance that they share common core values and purposes.

A SHARED REJECTION OF CLASS WARFARE

The struggle many people face is to respond directly to the guidance of the inner voice in contrast with the demands placed on them for external compromise (Whyte 1994). Life is a challenge to overcome external pressures to conform and be authentic to the inner voice challenging us to excellence. This challenge is part of our work as it is part of other areas of our lives. Because we spend so much time at work, work has become the site where much of this struggle takes place. Our work experiences have to do with governing our conscious life according to core values. The soul finds its being because we voluntarily give up control to those powers greater than current human experience.

Workers are coming to recognize that many of the failings of our society are due to our past disregard for core values and a willingness to let a minority of the world lead us astray. The world has moved from the war against evil to reverence for three contending gods: race, gender, class. The conflict today is not against evil but black against white. There are good and evil black and white people. We waste our time when we let questions of race determine our decisions and control our actions. The conflict today is also of men against women. When men and women are in competition about such issues as feminism, abortion rights, and jobs, this conflict clouds our judgment. We cannot see the good or evil in these things or the qualities of the individual advocates. We see only the competition of the sexes that dissipates our energies and moves us away from realization of our powerful inner spiritual values.

And, finally, the conflict today is not against evil but is a struggle of the rich against the poor and the poor against the rich. There are good and bad poor and rich people. When we are conscious of economic class we cannot see the evils people do to each other in the push for pecuniary dominance of one class over the other. Our failure to recognize the powerful force that our collective spirituality represents and the tendency to waste our energies on unimportant ethical skirmishes has contributed to the contentious world in which we live.

THE VALUES FOCUS OF TODAY'S LEADERS

Spirituality in business means the organization really lives by values like living with integrity, treating every person with dignity, finding joy in what we do for a living, and experiencing the exhilaration of true collaboration. Spirituality enlarges our soul and gives it purpose. Covey (1992) says people are determinedly seeking spiritual and moral anchors in their lives and their work. They are feeling the need for values that don't change.

Spirituality is a leadership issue. It is the quintessence of leadership. Spiritual leaders see spirit as the basis for everything. They cannot imagine looking at the world in any other way (Magaziner 1994). They are people who feel safe outside what they know and who are passionate in what they have never tried. A focus on spiritual values gives us the ability to focus precisely. It is central to self-realization—the feeling that we are developing to our highest potential.

Spirituality is the process of living out a set of deeply held personal values, of honoring forces or a presence greater than the individual self. It expresses a collective desire to find meaning in, and to treat as an offering, what we do. It is developing a sense of community in organizations. Recognition of the spirit of work and of workers endows the organization with soul, or at least recognizes the soul of the organization that is there but which we previously ignored.

AN OLD/NEW DEFINITION OF SUCCESS

The present interest in spirituality emphasizes interconnectedness and wholeness. It is a growing awareness that although we may compete, we are also a part of a unity in which no one wins unless we all do. It is a shifting of our attitude toward the inner subjective experience— affirming inner wisdom, authority, and resources. The present-day focus on spirituality in the workplace has helped people become aware that they no longer have to adopt beliefs that they developed or accepted throughout most of their lives.

Society is increasingly viewing corporations as adaptable organizations, made up of many self-reliant, independent, and smaller organizations. Each suborganization exists and interacts with the larger whole. This idea runs counter to scientific materialism, a philosophy dominant in the earlier part of this century. It is a global mind-set change, a shift of an entire society's mind-set, the one scientific, the other spiritual (Harman 1992). It is a shifting of our core work paradigm.

We can characterize this change of mind as a repudiation of the competitive, exploitive materialism of modern society. It is an increased emphasis on values including improved quality of relationships, cooperation, nurturing, oneness of humanity, social justice, human and spiritual values, as well as respect and caring for the other creatures on the planet.

It is a kind of respiritualization. It is a third way (Mollner 1992); a shift from a worldview of the universe as a collection of separate parts, each of which competes for its own self-interests in relationship to all other things and toward a worldview that sees the universe as a vast number of connected parts, each of which benefits as it cooperates with all other parts.

Spirituality is a spirit of oneness and cooperation that must be the dominant spirit in all that we do. There are few activities that require more cooperation and concerted effort than service to others. Whether it is rallying to find employment for a displaced member, toiling on a production project, serving as a lead worker, or accepting foster children in the home, it is cooperation and mutual concern that determines overall success (Kimball 1982).

Spirituality brings a wholly different mind-set about business and a different way of organizing work. The measure of success is whether the organization and the followers grow. The focus is on genuineness. Love is used as a spiritual connection and an emotional bond within the organization. The focus is on oneness and valuing and preserving individual liberty within the collectivity of the group.

THE NEW LEADERSHIP AGENDA

Leading others today asks us to employ our head (the left brain, linear thinking), our heart (right brain, feelings), our body (physical muscle, health, wellness), and our spirit (the deep inner self, striving for inner peace, happiness, contentment, meaning, purpose) (Hawley 1993). Spirit refers to aliveness, the vitality dwelling in our body, the fountain of our energy. It involves constant spiritual awareness. Both the spiritual and the worldly coexist as a unified whole, overlapping. Spiritual and worldly values are two parts of the same thing, the same force.

Deep caring is the cornerstone of spiritual values. It is a kind of reverence for others and for our common activities. Reverence is treating all people with deference and respect. Reverence is a continuum of behaviors including politeness, caring, and respect. It is holding others in esteem. It is genuine kindness and politeness. Reverence consists of dedication, eagerness, and enthusiasm. There is deep admiration in reverence, a kind of devotedness. Reverence is an intensified state of commitment—a goal for leaders. In many powerful respects, leadership is nothing more than developing a reverence for mission, products, customers, employees, and all other stakeholders.

Leaders maintain power and influence in ways that enlarge the soul authentically. Leaders base their vision on spiritual beliefs. To be viable, our visions must contain a belief in the power of vision. These beliefs create our reality. Our affirmations lead to the reality of the affirmation. It is a kind of auto-programming, a self-fulfilling prophecy. The central drama of life is the fusing of one's personality with these manifestations of one's higher self (Hawley 1993). We need to be as constantly aware of our spiritual side as we are of our physical, worldly side.

Moving toward our higher spiritual self creates energy. Energy is the power that spirit activates. There is power in good thoughts. Leadership arouses and channels this human energy. Belief is the force that shapes all human affairs. Belief is power thinking—it focuses thoughts to produce actions. Belief is something we are as much as it is something we feel. It is the basis for doing anything, not the actual doing.

DESIRE FOR PERSONAL LIBERTY

Spirituality in the workplace enhances personal liberty. For many of us, if we don't make money we can't survive, and then, of course, we can't do anything. But, people want to associate with the firm for something more than just the bottom-line economic rewards possible through work. They need to be free to innovate, to alter their work processes, to do the organization's work in different ways, or, even, to do other work because in so doing they see personal spiritual growth and development. Spiritual values are the glue holding leader and led together. Leaders who cannot or will not see the power of spirit in what they do, who they think they are, and who their followers are and want to become, will fail to attract tomorrow's workers.

Chapter 6

A Shift to a Spiritual Focus for Leadership

Millions of Americans are embarking on a journey for the sacred in their lives. The movement is a shift from capital-centered to human-centered leadership. The baby-boom generation of Americans are at a point in their lives where they sense the need for spirituality, but they don't know where to get it. People are hungry for meaning in their lives. They feel they have lost something and they don't remember what it is they've lost. It has left a gaping hole in their lives. To fill this void, some are trying to blend their spiritual with their everyday work lives (Kantrowitz 1994).

Spirituality could be a strong force for personal maturation or another fad (Kantrowitz 1994). Whether it is a fad or a sea change, we can see a discernable shift in America from capital-centered to human-centered work systems. For a growing segment of the working population, leadership success is premised on gaining support from all stakeholders who make up the partisan political structure inherent in all institutions—employees, customers, business partners, government, the public, and investors.

Today, the notion of spirituality in business centers around the idea of service (Roddick 1993), not just productivity. Organizations must cease to look just at what it is and what it does. It also must look at how it does what it does. No society, no community, can function well unless most members behave most of the time because they voluntarily heed their moral commitments and social responsibilities (Etzioni 1993). People are now adding their work organizations to the list of social groups where this dictum applies.

Obviously, management in the traditional mold will no longer work today. We need a new type of CEO, a team leader, a coach, a builder instead of the dominant general of the past. Management will not work in this environment; leadership is needed. But the stumbling blocks to good leadership are part of the very structure of the contemporary organization and the training of its leaders. To overcome these obstacles, new leaders must learn to switch from traditional styles to those that focus on processes. To be effective today the leader shoulders an almost sacred responsibility to create conditions that enable people to have happy and productive lives (Senge 1990).

There are several causes for the recent shift to a spiritual focus for leadership in today's organizations and institutions. Some flow out of business practices and structures. Others come from changes in the nature and composition of the labor pools supplying today's business, government, and social institutions with workers. Each donates something to the dynamic mix resulting in both a disenfranchised workforce and a movement to make work more meaningful in our total—not just our economic—life. Understanding something of these causes for the present emphasis on a spiritual dimension of leadership in the workplace is a necessary prerequisite to understanding spiritual leadership.

BUSINESS REASONS FOR THE CHANGE

We can abstract several business reasons from the present situation that cause leaders and led to seek more than simple economic reward from their work. The present propensity to downsizing has produced a situation where corporation leaders pay half as many people twice as much for producing three times as much (Handy 1994). This may be a formula for productivity, but it is not very exciting for the portion of the work force dropped from payrolls. Their trauma is obvious. Equally significant, but less recognized, is the trauma of those workers and leaders who remain in the work force. This segment risks burnout from overwork and latent stress from worry about whether they will be next.

The upheaval in organizational structure caused by recurring reorganizations also adds to the present burdens workers face at work. Customer needs have shifted to demands for specific and exact requirements for the products they purchase, where they purchase them, and what color, size, or accessories they include. The magic of technology now allows organizations to produce at levels never before thought possible or to do more common work more rapidly, more efficiently, at higher quality levels, and with less human intervention.

The rise of baby-boomer employees in itself has produced change. These largely nonmanagers bring a new set of values to the workplace. Baby boomers want different things from their work than their predecessors or supervisors settled for. Many want a comfortable social environment. More want challenging work. Some want equality of treatment, not hierarchial advantage. They want to be first among equals, not a boss. And, many baby boomers don't want to be directed by managers any more. They want leaders—people who help, not control.

More and more employees are expressing a desire to involve themselves in managerial issues and decisions, whether they accept a supervisory job or not. They want to participate in the decisions that affect their lives, the work they do, the talents and skills they bring to bear on the work, and the approaches adopted to do the work. Workers are no longer willing to forego the use of most of their skills and capacities. They want to contribute to corporate goals to their level of competence, not just to the scope of a sterile position description. Official position descriptions are too narrow for today's new workers. They confine, rather than liberate people; today's workers want, not constraint, but freedom.

Management practice has for a hundred years been things-oriented not people-oriented. While effective in meeting production-of-things tasks, the large-scale organizations in which we work today do not engage so much in the production of tangible objects. Much of today's work is to produce information, facts, ideas. And the people—the knowledge workers—creating and using their facts need involvement. They want to manage their own work lives and contribute to their level of competence, whether they are in a leadership position or not.

The traditional organization doesn't lend itself to manipulation of ideas, the promulgation of ideals, or broad involvement in planning and decision making. Manipulation of knowledge requires flexibility, adaptability, and, sometimes even waste. Bureaucracies, on the other hand, fight waste by sponsoring programs of efficiency and tight supervisory control. Current management and structural models are incompatible with this new push for self-determination by workers and unique customer demands for products and services.

Clearly work is changing (Pinchot and Pinchot 1994). No longer do we need machine-like bureaucratic procedures. Rather, the movement is from unskilled work to knowledge work, from individual work to teamwork. We are replacing meaningless, repetitive tasks with innovative ones. We now ask our workers—and they are asking their leaders—to move from a system that once required of them single-skilled expertise to one requiring multiple skills. Power is moving away from supervisors and toward customers. We are replacing coordination from above with cooperation among peers.

The role of the middle manager—perhaps the most endangered species of worker in large-scale organizations today—has changed. It has moved from authoritarian straw boss through expert advisor and information conduit to coordinator of employee participation. The present circumstance has produced a situation where workers often do not need supervisors at all. The constant tension resulting from this condition of accelerating change places impossible pressures on traditional structures and on the people doing the work and on their leaders.

SOCIAL REASONS FOR THE CHANGE

The social organizations in which we live out our lives are likely to remain the linchpins of our lives (Handy 1994). Religion, family, and friendship groups remain critically important to life and its living. Unfortunately, they don't provide the closeness, harmony, and utility they once did. Part of this shift is to look to the work we do and the workplace in which we do it to replace some of this loss. Hence, the shift to new, more spirituality focused structures and processes at work.

Changes in family structure, work cultures, and social pressures to change all combine to move American society toward different goals and methods of interpersonal relations. We can list several reasons for the shift to a more spiritual focus at work, one that gives vent to the values we once found in the family, church, or friendship circle. For example, simple demographics is one cause. There are more young, highly educated people coming to work in our organizations and institutions today. Our educational systems and society generally expose them to ideas and styles of living that focus on self-fulfillment.

It is logical that these values be carried into the workplace when these young people enter the job market. They want to experience and use these values at work. They are no longer willing to accept the values and expectations of their parents or grandparents—or their supervisors. They see work as merely another extension of their lives, another venue to practice their own style of relationships, and an arena where they can receive the intellectual and spiritual stimulation they want.

And, too, today's is a widely heterogeneous work force. They come to the job with different values, work expectations, and interpersonal habits. Workers today are more wanting of involvement and self-determination on the job. They are demanding equal place for their personal development needs along with organizational needs. They are asking the company to weave personal, spiritual, social, and environmental dimensions into the fabric of corporate work. Business is, after all, simply another form of human activity. Workers are saying that we should not expect less from the workplace than we do other social institutions. Today's workers want work to be more human-oriented, more humane.

Managers are increasingly chasing excellence, trying to understand what it means and borrowing from the experiences of others (Wright 1987). However, we cannot introduce excellence ideas and values into an organization that is not ready for them. Most companies are not ready because they have not yet learned how to rise above the level of being mediocre. They have not moved beyond administrative efficiency to a concern for workers as human beings. We cannot attain excellence until we see the organization as more than a work site; we must see it as a culture where people come to satisfy deeply held needs, and to interact with others in mutually beneficial ways.

Excellence comes as people change to become more excellent. The majority of employees are motivated not by outward trappings, bonuses, or challenges to greatness as a company. Rather, people seek personal excellence through the opportunity of making meaningful contribution to others through their work and in the process growing themselves.

These and other individual and social issues represent our deeper motivations and are part of the spiritual side of work. The importance of learning to cope with stress, which is a natural human condition, is also a key reason for our focus on spirit at work. It is important to take time for stress reduction. Effective business communication is also critical to excellence, as well as networking and marketing skills. But, above all, the key to business success is not in management of objects, but in the leadership of people.

DIRECTIONS OF THE SPIRITUALITY SHIFT

We are in the midst of a kind of passage in our understanding of leadership and the leaders' relationships with followers. One of the distinguishing features of transitional periods like this one is a mixing and blending of cultures. We can characterize this present iteration of change as a plurality or parallelism of intellectual and spiritual worlds (Renesch 1994d). As we advance intellectually in our understanding of the nature of work and of the leadership of workers, it is necessary that we also advance in our understanding of the spiritual essence of our workers.

Our civilization has basically globalized only the surface of our lives. Our inner self continues to have a life of its own that is powerful and controlling of our individual and collective action. It is clearly necessary to invent organizational structures appropriate to the multicultural, global age. But, we doom such efforts to failure if they do not grow out of something deeper, out of widely held core values.

Many writers are adding to our understanding of spirit-based leadership. Following is a summary of some of their work. Each has proposed aspects of a definition of spiritual leadership. Some have suggested elements of a model for applying spiritual concepts on the job. Others have integrated spiritual leadership ideas into outline paradigm models that may serve as prototypes for more formal theory building.

We describe some of these archetypes briefly here. (More analysis of present theory building is presented in Chapter 8.)

Process Thinking. Process thinking is a way to address the complex issues and interrelationships facing organizations today. Thinking of the organization as a circular process of complex interactivity provides a new perspective from which to view organizations and their leadership. A circular organizational chart based on the organization's key process or processes is a way to graphically depict this interactive leadership model. Process-based leadership and the idea of the circular process is an extension of the continuous improvement concept.

The key points of a circular organization include the leader of the organization as the heart and center of the organization. Communications throughout the circular organization are open and unrestricted. The basis of the circular organization's structure is on the processes of the organization. Circular structure is more conducive toward the organization working as a team and is a visible symbol of the interconnectedness of the organization.

Circular organizational structures embody those practices proven effective in all types and sizes of organizations throughout the world. Indeed, more than fifty years combined experience in the design, application, observation, and measurement of human resource management effectiveness techniques supports this form of organization. We can visualize the model as a holistic approach, with the individuals making up the organization providing synergistic support for the whole.

Its environmental characteristics are a carefully designed corporate philosophy or culture, a balanced concern for people and organizational goals, and a commitment to teamwork. This model stresses simplicity and flexibility in organizational structure and systems. It includes internal stability and cooperation in system design and an environment that encourages openness, individuality, and creativity. Its leaders are committed to a management that provides leadership and support, and a process that emphasizes continuous evaluation of success.

Self-Esteem. The key to the success of any venture is strong leadership (Howe 1994). Courage, vision, and inspiration are key ingredients in the formula for success. Service to the community or communities also plays a critical role in the development of leadership potential. The importance of self-esteem in this model is fundamental. Every leader has some self-doubt, but using humor and spiritual authenticity to overcome self-doubt will lead to success and prosperity. And what we say for leaders we also can say for those who are led. The way to assure that we meet common needs is for leaders and followers to take some responsibility for attending to those needs. To do this continually, we need affirmation of each person's humanness, not just their skills. We need to know within ourselves that we can make the necessary difference.

The leader's job is to build self-esteem. The traditional way is through motivation. But, when seen from the perspective of the inner soul, the spirit in others, motivation takes on a different character. Two examples from sports may help illustrate the new motivational methods that build self-esteem. The first is used often and the second is used less often, but is more enduring. The first example involves the legendary football coach, Vince Lombardi, perhaps the most famous example of the orthodox sports motivator. Coach Lombardi motivated on the basis of control, fear, and insecurity. By contrast, and given today's breed of worker, Coach Bill Walsh's style is to inspire and encourage players to be their best selves. The foundation of Lombardi's style was on scientific management ideas of mechanistic linearity. Walsh's style is on innovation, intuition, and spontaneity. Walsh recognizes that the cement that holds organizations together is compassion—openness, receptivity to new ideas, honesty, caring, dignity, and respect for people.

Business—all work—is a spiritual discipline characterized by compassion. Compassion leads one to recognize his or her own inner strength and creativity and to see these qualities in others. It is the basis of the paradigm change in people who lead them to come to see their work in larger terms than economic exchange. It comes from inner consciousness or spirit. Compassion includes all the highest values—honesty, harmony, integrity. It fosters the growth of the new spiritual paradigm. Compassion makes empowerment possible. People today respond more to moral suasion than they ever did to coercion. Compassion carries no threat of punishment, rather it connotes caring, concern, and charity.

Pathfinding. Leavitt (1989) thinks professionals should emphasize critical issues like leadership, vision, imagination, and values, not just efficiency and control techniques. He calls these pathfinding issues and skills. More traditional managerial skills like effective problem solving require mental rigor and analysis of the environment. And effective implementation requires competence in getting work done. Alternatively, effective leadership pathfinding requires soul, imagination, personal commitment, and deep belief.

By contrast, business and public administration programs now teach "real" skills like analytic methods. To make spiritual leadership work we need to make changes in leader training curricula. We must alter them to accommodate the challenge leaders face to serve their followers' deeply held beliefs about what life is and what it holds for them.

The key to teaching these new leadership skills is experimentation. For example, we may need to modify selection criteria, consciously seeking candidates with pathfinding histories and consciously seeking to increase the diversity of professional school students. Core requirements in business and public administration schools could loosen core requirements to give students room to choose more of their own education. We need to broaden the vision of education to move beyond technique to philosophy, to redesigning the total MBA experience to include in-class and external personal experiences. And, importantly, we may want to recruit faculty from new, previously unimagined disciplines.

Principle-Centered Leadership. Covey's (1991) principle-centered leadership is a new standard that helps resolve several dilemmas encountered in applying spiritual leadership. One dilemma is to achieve and maintain a wise and renewing balance between work and family and between personal and professional areas of life in the middle of constant pressures and crises. Principle-centered leadership addresses this dilemma by asking leaders to develop a personal mission statement. This personal credo helps them to decide the high-priority items in their lives, and to learn to say no to the so-called urgent crises and problems that are, in fact, not vital.

Principle-centered leadership involves unleashing the creativity, talent, and energy of the vast majority of the work force whose jobs neither require nor reward use of such resources. Principle-centered leaders work from the inside out. They deal with issues of individual trustworthiness, interpersonal or group trust, empowerment, and with ways to attain organizational alignment. These are core values central to an understanding of our spiritual self.

Principle-centered leadership is a holistic ideal that can tap into these capabilities and resources. Covey (1991a) inventories seven habits of principle-centered leaders. He suggests these habits embody many of the key principles of human effectiveness. Thus principle-centered leaders are proactive, which involves taking responsibility for personal attitudes and actions. They begin with a clear understanding of the desired direction and destination they wish to take their organization and individual members. They organize and manage time and events around the personal priorities established, and they seek mutual benefit for all parties in their contacts with all others.

Principle-centered leadership asks leaders first to understand and then to be understood. They look for ways to take advantage of the synergy possible through creative cooperation and teamwork. And, they begin balanced, systematic programs for self-renewal of physical, mental, emotional, social, and spiritual aspects of self and all stakeholders with whom they interact. Principle-centered leadership focuses on the whole person of the leader. It is an approach that calls into play the soul of the leader and uses the leader's soul in defining himself or herself to the team.

Dharmic Leadership. Hawley (1993) developed a leadership pattern constructed of spirit, heart, and energy. Hawley notes that, while not all of us are consciously aware of it, we live in a state of constant spiritual awareness. This spiritual force moves us toward our source, beyond the senses and toward a perception of our spirituality. Spirituality is the goal of and the path to our social (including work) relationships. It is an individual, private journey. It contains elements common to all religions including love, belief, and the Golden Rule. Yet, for Hawley, it is not fundamentally religious in its focus.

Communitarianism. Free individuals require a community that backs them up against encroachment by the state or any monolithic force. America is becoming what someone has called a gorgeous mosaic of diverse ideas, values, and peoples. What any mosaic needs is some sort of glue to hold the pieces together. In this case the mosaic that America needs is a sense of community (Etzioni 1993).

We live in a state of increased moral disorder and social anarchy. We are bereft of clear leadership in most matters, especially moral. People are free to function fully under their so-called rights to do their own thing. But, to take and not to give is an amoral, self-centered predisposition that ultimately no society can tolerate. Those who advocate rights ought to be the first to accept responsibility.

For Etzioni the time has come to attend to our responsibilities to the conditions and elements we all share, to the community. We do this by responding to the human spirit in us all. The human spirit is a part of all we do. Business can be something more than making money. It can be something people feel good about. Business responsibly conducted ennobles the spirit by creating a sense of holism, of spiritual development, of feeling connected with the workplace, the environment, and relationships with one another. It is morally enhancing.

Organizational Chaos Theory. Most academics design organizations based on the Newtonian perspective of a mechanistic universe based on seventeenth-century science that value linearity and predictability to discover order. They come out of a science that sought order in nature and imposed it on human structures and institutions. Newtonian science has created a desire in us to create and have control over our own lives, regardless of the politics of the time or of the social patterns present.

Since the seventeenth century order and control have been very much a part of interpersonal relations. Recent advances in science, however, and the evidence of our experience challenge this traditional scientific logic. We do not live in a linear world. Yet, we often structure our work organizations on that basis. Instead, life is a dynamic circular place in which people base their actions on current conditions. These actions affect the underlying conditions and the changed conditions become the basis for future action. Rather than being like machines, organizations are more like intelligent social organisms.

Order, however, is inherent in all living systems. We base this order on conformance to our (and our culture's) core values and principles, not superficial or external rules and procedures. The spiritual leader's task is to create these heart-values and principles and use them to guide human systems. We can allow people enormous freedom with the understanding that common principles and values will order our collective behavior in ways that the organization desires (Wheatley 1992). Only when people agree on values can we safely empower them to work independently in self-directed teams with any assurance that they will do needed work.

Chaos is not randomness. It is order without easily seen predictability (Wheatley 1992). Uncertainty arises because the wholeness of the universe resists being studied in pieces. We call this kind of wholeness chaos. We see this mind-set in action as analysts try to separate and measure dynamic systems in terms of their individual parts (Wheatley 1992). As we take the new quantum science and apply it to the organization, we bring new insight into the inner workings of the people in interaction. It is people who collectively define the organization and do its work.

THE MAGNITUDE OF THE SHIFT TO SPIRITUALITY

Recent themes or approaches in leadership research have confirmed the need for a more holistic and interdisciplinary approach to leadership (Bargal and Schmid 1989). These themes consider the interaction of the leader's personality with followers' needs and personalities, the organizational culture, and the environment. The shift to more holistic forms of leadership that focus on spirituality is, in every sense of the word, a transformation (Renesch 1994). It transforms the people involved, the organization they collectively form, and the interrelationships through which they work.

While the essence of this transformation is on the inner needs and desires of people expressed in their personal work lives, the change is also significant in its geographic dispersion. That is, this shift is also discernable in other countries. Spirit in work is a part of changes taking place in the United States, but it is also seen in other industrialized nations. It appears to be worldwide in its incidence and in its impact on the lives of workers and their leaders.

The Western view of leadership focuses on the individual, to satisfy the leader's self-perceptions, and to rely on reasoning and a system of reward and punishment. By contrast, the Japanese form of leadership is more submerged (Noda 1980). We find it in group cohesiveness. It underlies operations of a simultaneous processing type. This emphasis on teamwork, uniform raises, and lifetime employment, gives Japan astounding productivity.

Decision making that considers the worker's soul or spirit is the responsibility of the people involved in the job. It does not even allow the corporate president decisional autonomy. In order to get input from all workers, the Japanese developed the *ringi* system, including the quality circle concept. When the circle leader and the foreman inform their superior of the circle's decision, the superior asks questions to be sure the circle received all necessary input and to assure unanimity. Then the supervisor formalizes the agreement. While this takes more time, it is much more error free and easily executed.

Profit consciousness is very high among Japanese workers, unlike American workers, many of whom often work only for their paychecks. Further, the lifetime employment policy, a part of many large-scale organizations in Japan, provides a stability that encourages research and development and marketing planning. It is this group spirit that sets Japanese industry apart from its American counterpart. It is to apply this group spirit in American corporations and incorporate its ideals in their leadership that motivates modern spiritual leaders.

Following the Japanese model of success in business enterprises is in part due to cultural and spiritual values. The Olga Company drew on principles from Judeo-Christian teachings to provide clear guidelines for a new style of corporate life they developed—a common venture enterprise model (Erteszek 1983). The guiding principles for this leadership approach revolve around the dignity of all people, the trusteeship of life and resources, leadership through service, development of a concerned community, and the right of the producer to a share of the production.

The common venture enterprise is a new corporate model that emphasizes and encourages consensus instead of promoting the traditional confrontation between labor and management. Components of the common venture include a highly intensive profit-sharing plan, ownership-sharing, and a commitment to permanent employment. Olga has enjoyed growth, annual new sales records and after-tax profits records, and only rare permanent layoffs.

Research out of China reports similar experience. Chenglieh (1987) reports that China has begun retraining large numbers of managerial personnel. In the Chinese way of thinking, management has two aspects. The first relates to productivity and the skills that are applicable to any firm or in any country. The second concerns the human side and differs according to the social, economical, political, cultural, and psychological backgrounds of participants.

Also, in China, the approach to motivation relies on unlocking each specific soul by a specific key. Although new management theory in the world has developed from the experiences of successful companies, for the Chinese theory and practice needs to conform to fundamental principles of Chinese philosophy. These considerations include shared benefits for the state and development of the spiritual character.

The economic reforms undertaken in the post-Maoist period in the Peoples' Republic of China have been shaped by the leadership's close adherence to three institutionalist concepts: holism, instrumentalism, and consentualism (Schlack 1989). The post-Maoist approach in China has been holistic in that the leadership has come to regard the economic system as part of the cultural process and human behavior as a constant readjustment to a world of ever-changing realities. Economic reforms have been instrumental in that they have emphasized technological behaviors and values at the expense of the ceremonial. Reform policies have been consensual in that there has been an absence of force in enlisting mass support for the new programs.

By contrast, the experience in Europe is less positive, although based on the same fundamentally spiritual values. In the Orient, they recognize and reflect spirit at work. In Europe, recent experience suggests that their problems may be due to ignoring spirit. The European Community is in the throes of a great failure because there are no leaders touched by greatness and there is not a major country whose people show confidence in their national leadership (Novak 1993). In 1992, Europe was a place of hope. In 1993, the continent turned sour because of the failure of a united Europe, in its first test, to show that it had learned the lessons of the Holocaust by intervening early and decisively against Serbia's aggression.

From an organizational and leadership perspective, perhaps the most important reason for Europe's sourness is the heavily regulated womb-to-tomb security promised by the welfare state. The Europeans call it democracy, but it is actually a new soft despotism administered by a motherly, smothering political class. Europe is not quite a community, for the unity of Europe lies in matters of the soul, a soul no longer much in evidence.

Similarly, evidence suggests that the institutions of the public service in the United Kingdom are weakening (Wolf 1987). Reasons for this change include the decline in the valuing of the bureaucracy by the country's political leadership and by society in general, and reductions and limitations on employees' support and rewards. The key, however, may be a loss of spirit, self-confidence, and efficacy, as many workers choose to psychologically disinvest from their work. Even the casual observer sees a shift away from core service values in changes focusing more effort toward the leadership's political bidding and less toward the responsibilities of administration.

Chapter 7

Understanding Spirit at Work

People are anxious for more spirit in their work lives. The recent wave of literature advocating a new age of spiritual awareness attests to this increasingly widespread need (see the bibliography). We've reached a point where traditional management has failed in many companies. What we can call the deregulation of employment—the abandonment of the traditional psychological contract connecting workers to a lifelong career with the company—has effectively destroyed the security and tranquility of the workplace. People need something to repair the damage. For a growing cadre of people—all of my survey respondents— spirituality is the answer.

THE POTENTIAL FOR SPIRITUAL POWER IN LEADERSHIP

The potential for the integration of spirituality into secular organizations is both positive and necessary. When asked about this extension of what many people feel to be a private and personal aspect of self into the workplace, 63 percent of my survey answered unreservedly in the affirmative. Another third answered yes with reservations (Table 7.1). Their responses come from widespread belief that spirituality is woven into all life's decisions and actions. We see it reflected in the example of people who won't compromise their values to gain power. It relates directly to individual and group success. It is part of caring for others, using the Golden Rule, trusting relationships, and other similar acts people engage in together.

Table 7.1
Should Spirituality Be in the Workplace?

YES: 63%	NO: 0%
DEPENDS: 31.5%	NO RESPONSE: 5%

The exact meaning of spirituality depends on our definition—whether we see it in religious terms or not. Most agree that as long as it doesn't surface as religion, but is more focused on spiritual values and ideals that are acceptable to all, it is a positive idea. In this form spirituality would be welcome. Our spirituality is an integrated part of our lives. We cannot easily separate it from our work. It is a personal issue for each person. In no way should others' beliefs of what spirituality is be forced on others.

The definition of spirituality affects the larger society as much as it does a specific business organization. Because some people consider spirituality to be unacceptable, it is often difficult to present the case for a more expanded application in routine work situations. We should not integrate spirituality into work practices from the top. Rather, we should integrate it through the creation of a receptive environment that leaders and workers can both create.

As leaders define spirituality in secular (practical) terms, it can influence the corporate culture, individual values, and routine operating practices. Leaders need to first educate the organization to accept this influence because people are not accustomed to spirituality on the job. Leaders need to adjust this approach and educate the organization to accept this influence. Over time, recognition and response to their spiritual side will help workers to improve their leadership. Leaders can do this through modeling and coaching, not preaching. Spirituality should come from the spiritual force present and recognized by individuals in the organization, not from outside.

Leaders also can make effective use of the power of spirit in the organizations in other less direct ways. They can use their own and their followers' sense of the spiritual by encouraging individual moral decisions at work. We can activate the power of spirit in others as we find out more about each employee and his or her individual needs and use this information to help them. Open communication aids in the leader's use of spirituality at work, as is a willingness to allow for the whole person to operate substantially independently in support of mutual values. Leaders can make spirituality awareness a part of training sessions. They can also foster corporate spirituality as they encourage ideas and suggestions that transcend the everyday business of the organization.

Workers who share in a common bond and have similar philosophies raise performance levels. They make more-informed choices, and they are typically more self-disciplined, honest in their evaluation of self and others, and are less competitive. When people become more aware of their spirituality and its meaning for all their life—including their work life—they are more focused and directed in their actions. In short, when we act against our spirit self, we act against ourselves.

Recognizing these cautions, there is still a need for a greater integration of spirituality in work life. People are hungry for meaning in their lives, and they want to seek it at work. In my informal survey, 95 percent of respondents wanted their leaders to give more attention to the spiritual side of people at work. Two of three of these survey respondents found a significant connection between their leader's disposition toward spirituality and his or her impact on their work (Table 7.1).

For these people, spirituality connotes the essence of who we are, our inner self, separate from the purely physical, but including the physical. Spirituality includes issues of ultimate values, transcendence, and subjectivity. It describes those essential human values that teach us how our basic humanity fits within the overall scheme of things and how we can attain harmony in life and in our work. Spirituality made manifest is the essence of leadership.

CAUTIONS IN APPLYING SPIRITUAL LEADERSHIP

Of course, thinking and acting in concert with one's inner spiritual self is new as a leadership technology in business settings. Almost one third of respondents, while also admitting to the power of spirit in their lives, expressed cautions about its unrestricted use. They caution leaders that their sense of spiritual identity and their use of spiritual power at work should not surface as religion. Rather, it should focus on shared moral values and ideals.

In a work context, spirituality is perceived to include a much broader range of experience while religion and faith are seen as limiting the discussion to experiences that arise in traditional religious institutions or ways of thinking (Vaill 1989). A sense of spirituality is the anchor for most people's ethics and morality (Bennett, quoted in Range 1995). Without taking anything away from doctrinaire religion, the new focus on workplace spirituality is one way to apply spiritual beliefs and satisfy the need to feel the spirit through work. In other words, we can nourish the spirit in diverse ways.

Leaders should not attempt to impose their version of spiritual values on others. Indeed, some suggest that spirituality has no place in the work force. Tom Peters (1994), for examples, says church and corporation do not mix with spirituality. He describes the United States as a nation that talks back to authority, that savors contention, and doesn't cower before petty political or corporate tyrants. Peters believes that imposing a spiritual authority on corporate decisions and actions may hamper individuality. He also claims that the right to be left alone is an important and cardinal human right. He believes that work situations are very intrusive on personal privacy as circumstances are now and that to add the power of our own inner sense of self and of a higher power would further erode individual freedom. Peters also argues that many people don't want to devote their whole being toward a higher purpose at work.

While his argument has intrinsic merit, it has little real meaning in day-to-day work. Even Peters' work credo (Peters 1994) implies at a minimum a deep, abiding dedication to the work, if not a whole-soul commitment. It includes ideas about doing fabulous work, being known for innovativeness, attracting exciting people, questioning the way we do work, attaining high ethical standards, working with people from whom we can learn and who we enjoy being around, and growing through quality service not just for growth's sake.

This credo shows obvious respect for stakeholders. While it does not use spiritual language, Peters wants his company to be a workplace where members feel encouraged to make something great and feel guilty if they fall short of that (Peters 1994). Corporate spirit is alive and well in Peters' corporate credo whether he says so or not. His credo is a call to the best within people—workers and leaders. Whether we call it spirituality or good management, the challenge to the leader is to help people come to realize that their work is a path to personal self-development as well as high productivity for the corporation.

UNDERSTANDING SPIRIT AT WORK

There is a clear difference between spirituality in religion, founded on sacred writ, and the spirit or soul of people, defined holistically as body *and* spirit, of the head and the heart. People are much more than a bundle of skills and knowledge, as many managers think. People also come to work armed with a spirit, a life-giving principle, that is concerned also with higher moral qualities. Defined this way, workers engage in work with their whole soul, whether management theory or managers (or management pundits) take note of it.

People want more from work than just excitement, a good job, and a chance to be promoted. The new work force is more intelligent and informed than those of a previous generation and, critically, they are more "wanting." Today's workers are typically better educated and aware of what is possible of the good life. Many come to work wanting to take responsibility, accept challenging work, and make a contribution to organizational success from the foundation of their whole self, not the few skills, knowledge, and abilities delineated in a sterile position description. Workers today want meaningful work, and they want to make a legitimate contribution to the betterment of themselves, others, and their community.

Success in today's global market demands innovation, creativity, commitment, and vision from all of us. These capacities cannot be measured using standard tools. Yet they are essential to the kind of employee every leader and every textbook advocate: people who work hard; who are innovative, exciting, curious, highly ethical, constantly learning, a joy to be with; and who seek growth and make money.

Of course church and corporate life differ, but committed religionists, like the committed corporate executives or subordinates, bring their passion with them twenty-four hours a day. Today's leaders recognize this and are creating corporate cultures that foster whole-soul (spiritual) commitment. Workers may, on occasion, talk back to authority, savor contention, refuse to cower before petty tyrants—political or corporate—but they want passionately to engage in work that makes a difference (Peters 1994). They do what they can—and, sometimes, even more than what their bosses will let them—to achieve it.

Leaders should build into any organizational culture a distinction between corporate rights and personal rights to the private enjoyment of religious convictions. But there should also be mechanisms present to allow workers to see the larger societal purposes and results of their work. There should be opportunity for workers to make personal, individual contributions in response to their highest order spiritual goals in addition to routine task accomplishment. We need to get past our confusion of doctrinaire religion and the personal spiritual needs we all have to become our best selves. Spiritually tuned workers want to do something great and they do indeed feel guilty if they fall short (Peters 1994).

Practical (Work) Spirituality

Spirituality provides a moral point of view that reflects the cognitive and affective foundations of a mature conscience. It is a disposition rooted in our true nature. It takes seriously *both* the partial imperatives on self-interest *and* the impartial imperatives of benevolence and justice. Leader and led alike must manage the tension between these two ideas (self-interest and objectivity) so they can remain whole on the journey of life. For Goodpaster (1994), spirituality is balancing the pursuit of purpose. It consists of cultivating virtues, policies, and practices that reflect a balanced mind-set in the Aristotelian sense. The call for spirituality in the workplace is a call for the moral point of view understood as harmonizing these two perspectives.

Spirit expresses itself in beauty, aesthetics and in our relationships with our customers, our employees, and ourselves (Jacobs 1994). Spiri-

Table 7.2
Degree of Reliance on Spirituality

A LOT: 100%	NOT MUCH: 0	NONE: 0

tuality is another word for personal awareness. Leaders need to be open to both hierarchial and community modes of functioning. Leaders who understand this will no doubt be servant leaders. This is not say that they will not relinquish their responsibility to guide those whom they serve. They will listen and empower, but they will not hide behind these ideals and shields against accountability.

Spirituality is an integration or balancing of person, organization, and social system. At the personal level, it means sacrificing part of our own deepest being so that devoting ourselves to our work experiences is not a loss but a fulfillment of self. Applied to our organizations, a business may be more healthy by being less competitive; by seeking a living balance, not just the maximization of profit. From a system perspective spirituality means shaping our cultural institutions and then letting them shape us.

Corporate leaders succeed who guide their leadership by a comprehensive picture of humankind, which respects all the dimensions of our being that subordinates our material and instinctive dimensions to our interior spiritual ones. Nevertheless, people cannot be everything to everyone. Human action is invariably action along several dimensions simultaneously. Spirituality is union of spirit and work through a reaffirmation of the moral point of view in business decision making. It is balancing the pursuit of purpose in the face of tendencies toward overfocus on overarching goals, lack of attention to shared values, a disregard of workers as equals, and a tendency to undervalue moral responsibility when it interferes with the achievement of goals.

There is some skepticism about the new emphasis on spirituality in the workplace, not about the accuracy of the observation, but about its desirability. Some see it as a dangerous intrusion on worker privacy, an invitation to inefficiency and unaccountability. Unquestionably, it challenges a safe secularity in the quest for ethical values. Nevertheless, the key questions for today's managers and leaders are no longer issues of task and structure but are questions of spirit (Hawley 1993).

The spiritual journey is a personal experience, an inner change. It is a change in the ways workers feel about the growing tension between their personal values and the values they need to conform to at the organizational level (The Compass Group 1994). Respondents to my survey report drawing on their spiritual half routinely in performing their duties and their leadership practices (see Table 7.2). Their reasons range from the practical to the philosophical.

Our soul is integrated with all aspects of our life. We respond to the force of moral and ethical values gained throughout our whole life as much, and perhaps more, than we guide our actions solely in terms of organization-set standards. Respondents to my survey say they base their decisions and actions on values and beliefs that are integral to their sense of spirituality. Choosing is, at its core, drawing on one's basic principles. Whether in a church, in the office, on the shop floor, or under the hood of a car, doing one's best work is a matter of determining what is really important to the individual and others and whether one's choices feel right. Seen this way spirituality is essential in the quality of the decisions we make. It moderates and contains the day-to-day life challenges that often cause us to question "right or wrong" choices. It is the basis for decision making, and it subliminally shapes the opinions that we see as viable.

All of our duties draw on individual spirituality. It is seen in individual effort and the way we work. It is not a program or policy or someone else's interpretation of quality, or effectiveness, or completeness (or whatever), that determines our success. We integrate our spirituality into the secular organization by our routine and special behavior. Spirituality is at the core of the person and if not expressed in all of life it is meaningless. Therefore, it has to have an effect on all behavior and choice including work behavior.

As people understand the difference between religion and spirituality, then spirituality will become an important part of all individual and group organizational action. Our spirit is what makes us human and individual. It determines who we are at work. It is inseparable from self. We draw on our central values in how we deal with people every day. Our values dictate whether we set a good example, take care of people, or try to live the Golden Rule as much as possible. Our spirituality helps us to think and act according to our values.

Spirit and Values-Based Transformational Leadership

Our beliefs and moral vision determine our career path and all that we do along that path. If secular organizations are to change and become more hospitable to today's workers, it will likely mean members inside the group will assault it. Present business practices that dehumanize the workplace, treat workers as economic objects, and prioritize organizational profit above humanness run counter to the intuitive forces within all of us. The white-collar angst many feel will take form in whispered and then spoken-aloud conversations as millions of people question the meaning of life and their life's work in this context. We cannot deny our individual and collective spirits.

Table 7.3
Most Frequently Defined Characteristics of Spirituality*

42%	An inner conviction of a higher, more intelligent force
31%	The essence of self that separates humans from creatures
26%	Values humans rely upon for comfort, strength, happiness
21%	The part of us searching for meaning, values, life purposes
16%	A personal belief system
16%	An emotional level, a feeling
5%	The acting out of the experience of the transcendent in life

*Percentages do not total to 100%. Respondents typically listed several characteristics.

Spirituality plays a large part in our ethics. Ethical behavior is, in essence, making decisions based on what we think is right and wrong. Following our ethical belief system is key to any type of behavior. We have to follow our gut. Ensuring a proper degree of fairness and respect is present in all dealings with others is a spiritual as much as a fairness issue.

From a leadership perspective, respondents to my survey define spiritually motivated leaders as those who work to make real their personal inner standards and not simply to please managers. Our spirituality is what guides our leadership actions. It inspires leader confidence and commitment in followers. Our inner beliefs define our level of self-esteem and focus our efforts toward self-actualization.

Some leaders may take the high ground and incorporate spiritual values into the workplace, probing employees for job satisfaction, asking them to take a more significant role in decisions. It must be a subtle process. It must be done very carefully; but it must be done. Those who have a mature value system, in effect, must leave a legacy for future generations by not compromising their values for power. We can demonstrate our spirituality through actions and values by casually rather than directly addressing the issue.

Spirituality goes beyond ideas of vision and mission and provides the necessary underpinning to make both work in our personal and professional lives. Defined operationally by survey respondents (Table 7.3), spirituality implies a relationship with something intangible, beyond the self. It is a source guide for personal values and meaning-making, a way of understanding self, the world, and as a means of personal and group integration.

It is in this latter context that spirituality has a place in our work lives. The increasing interest in the integration of spirituality into secular leadership and organizational development holds promise of further application of these seminal ideas in leadership (see Greenleaf 1977, Senge 1990, Vaill 1989, DePree 1989, Covey 1991, Lee and Zemke 1993, Fairholm 1994a). Spiritual leadership extends and broadens values-based transformational leadership ideas. It provides a substructure for the shared values that are at the heart of this new model of leadership action.

Based on the definitions in Table 7.3, we can define spiritual leaders as those who respond to central core values, the real sense of significance of someone or something, as do values leaders (Fairholm 1994a). Spiritual leaders live by a high moral standard of conduct in their relationships. This inner moral standard impacts all we do and become at economic (work) levels as well as at personal and social levels of existence. There is a part of us that is not just physical, a part that we are comfortable in calling spirit, which less spiritually inclined people may call nature. It is the essential, energizing force or principle in each person, the core of self. It effects our identity, our values, our memories, our sense of humor. It integrates guiding principles of wholeness, relationships, inner wisdom, and inner authority.

Jacobson's (1995) research reported that 59 percent of his cohort of national leaders felt there needed to be a greater integration of spirituality into the workplace. People spend a large portion of their time at work and should be able to relate their spirit sense of purpose and meaning in this part of their lives too. They reported that they practice this kind of values-based transforming spiritual leadership.

This kind of spiritual leadership is in demand today. Successful corporate operations are those that respect individual rights and dignity. Often without explicitly recognizing it, spirituality is at the heart of much of the values-based transformational leadership literature that is popular today. Transforming leadership based on core values counters the fragmentation of our spirit (Senge et al. 1994), which is the common description of our present and past work cultures. Far too many people live their corporate lives separate from each other, from nature, from the environment, from everything.

Surveyed professionals connect spirit at work to ideas about employee ownership, attitudes of cooperation, and honoring diversity while also confirming a sense of corporate community. Spirit also makes use of the idea of creative work, work with a deeper sense of life-purpose. It defines work that lets people feel they are making a difference, creating meaning, being fully alive, living with integrity, and developing sacredness in their relationships. It involves turning the organization into a community where everyone can learn and grow. Spiritual leaders integrate values like competition, cooperation, and co-creation. Workers need to interact in concert with all three.

The Values Foundation of Spiritual Leadership

Spiritual leadership asks us to reject past models of human leadership, which focused on values of self-interest. The energy driving these earlier models were implicit values focusing on power, wealth, and prestige. Power, wealth, and prestige are not definitive of spiritual leaders (The Hartwick Humanities in Management Institute 1993). Rather, the transcendent values of spiritual leaders include a rejection of self-interest and a focus on servanthood. Surveyed professionals say that they focus on core ethical values including integrity, independence, freedom, justice, family, and caring. In responding to these values, spiritual leaders engage in activities that include the following:

- Doing good for their people
- Helping and expecting nothing in return
- Promoting those who show the same values foundation
- Refusing to impose their will on others who contest it
- Basing standards for followers on personal example
- Caring without bias
- Trusting in the belief that their mission will succeed even if they cannot always be there as it happens

These corporate values draw heavily on Judeo-Christian teachings (Erteszek 1983). They reflect core American values (Fairholm 1991), and they reinforce our traditional beliefs in the dignity of all people. They define corporate leaders as the trustees or stewards of life and resources, and they reflect ideas of what is good for individuals and groups—convictions about what will promote the faith, protect the country, build companies, and transform our schools. Spiritual leaders clarify followers' moral identities and strengthen and deepen their commitments. Spiritual leaders make connections between others' interior worlds of moral reflection and the outer worlds of work and social relationships.

Chapter 8

Spiritual Leadership at Work

Like anything else, spiritual leadership is susceptible to structure and system, to form and format. Many people are conscious of their spiritual side and respond to it in most circumstances. Unfortunately, there is little to guide us in its application in the more or less prescribed confines of the organization or in terms of the strictures of process and procedures peculiar to corporate life. Nevertheless, we are also responsive to the force of our spiritual standards at work. The work we do, the people we interact with, and the skills we use all challenge or reinforce our sense of self; they have a spiritual dimension.

Work can be a drain on our spiritual capacity. It can also be a source of renewal and growth. Our work situations are a powerful part of our sense of self. Work defines in large part who we are socially and, perhaps, who we are at our core self. When that work is sensitive to our spiritual needs we grow and mature. Spiritually attuned colleagues can provide role models, sustain values and principles we learned in the family or in church, and otherwise reinforce our spiritual nexus. When our work ignores, or is actively antagonistic to our spiritual sensibilities, we encounter stress, sometimes so severe that we experience physical or emotional trauma.

Leaders who accept the challenge to relate to followers in terms of a shared reverence for things spiritual can add another tool to their professional tool kit. Spirituality helps leaders understand self and others better. It helps the leader motivate and inspire others. In understanding another's values and beliefs, leaders learn to know their co-workers better and understand their motives. Spirit-centered interaction helps leaders and led work more effectively together.

The work of a growing number of contemporary researchers is beginning to shape a coherent model of spiritual leadership, one that the leader can use to hone his or her particular leadership style. This model integrates a variety of ideas implicit (and recently made explicit) in leadership. These ideas include issues of optimism, balance, capacity, and continuous improvement. Spiritual leadership is also an amalgam of culture, mood, moral tone, and awareness of the inner core self. Leaders set the standard of excellence for the group. These researchers see the organization as both an economic and a human enterprise. Leaders are moral architects. They seek to liberate the best in others. Spiritual leaders expand work-life concerns to relate inner spirit to the "soft" ideas of meaning, fidelity, and caring. Leaders bring unity to organizations.

Leaders reflect their own inner strength and create bonds that fulfill people's needs. They help followers find the sacred everywhere. As stewards, leaders hold work resources in trust. In this way they help unite the group and focus collective attention on mutual results. These researchers, whose work is reflected in this book, see leaders as stewards of virtue and the role of leadership as covenant making. Leaders create oneness within the group.

Based on this research and personal experience with the sacred in self, we can define some key elements of spiritual leadership. These elements are in dynamic relationship to each other and manifest themselves in leader-follower interactivity. Spiritual leadership is a dynamic process of building special skills—visioning, servanthood, and work competence. Spiritual leaders engage in special processes of community building, building personal wholeness, maintaining stewardship, and creating a higher moral standard. Leaders seek one primary goal among all the others challenging their time and attention: continuous improvement of the whole self (both leader and follower) and the group.

THE PRACTICE OF SPIRITUAL LEADERSHIP

A legitimate question may be asked: How might we apply spirit in our work lives? Comments by respondents to my survey (incorporated in the following material) suggest some ideas and issues spiritual leaders need to consider. For example, nourishing the spirit at work asks leaders to consider and respond to yet another dimension of human life beyond those commonly identified with leader-follower relationships. No longer is structure, system, and procedure sufficient (if they ever were). Nor is it enough to consider only the recent challenges placed on leaders to create and articulate compatible and shareable values.

Table 8.1
Most Important Activities that Inspire, Encourage, and Renew People

Percent of Responses*	Activity
73%	Group interaction
31	Private contemplation
26	Achieving difficult goals
26	Reading that I can personally relate to
21	Experiences in nature
21	Implementation of my thoughts
21	Helping others
21	Time with my child/family
21	Church or other inspiring experiences
10.5	Stories from real life or the workplace
10.5	Traditions review
10.5	Wishing for the right things
10.5	Volunteering

*Respondents typically identified several activities.

A working definition of spiritual leadership today must include ideas like teaching our followers correct principles and the application of techniques that enable self-governance. It means creating circumstances— cultures—where followers can function freely with the leader and within their work group subject to only broad accountability. It means redefining the leader's role in servant and steward terms. Leading on the basis of spirit asks leaders to recognize not only the deep inner needs and values of co-workers, but to define leadership in terms of the spirit self. It asks leaders to provide environments that both recognize and feed the spirit in us all while we are directing work activity.

REINFORCING SPIRIT AT WORK

Inspiring, encouraging, and renewing the spirit in followers becomes the central task of spiritual leadership. There is a strong probability that to create and maintain beneficial values of any kind we need to be conversant in areas of spirituality. The data in Table 8.1, taken from my survey, identifies a wide range of experiences—some present in current work situations now and others that could be added to the work experience—abstracted from available current research about spirit at work. The activities noted in this table describe leader actions to accept and foster personal spirituality in their own lives and those of their followers. These spirit renewing activities effect their values, ethics, and beliefs and, thus, the spiritual force of their leadership. Spirituality in the sense implied by these leader activities is a highly significant factor in the development and practice of values-based transformational leadership.

Some group interaction that is typically a part of normal work life can inspire and "in-spirit" us. Spiritually grounded group activity is by far the most significant endeavor we can engage in on the job to recharge our spiritual batteries. This kind of group socializing, which includes discussing the meaning of major life (or corporate) events and actions with others, bonds people and excites them. So does participation in such simple events as conversation with other, like-minded (and like-valued) people. Relating stories from real life or from the workplace where someone takes risks based on his or her beliefs and receives a reward also nurtures the spirit.

Anything we do that helps us learn and grow as humans and as a society can help us spiritually. Indeed, any activity that challenges us to listen, share, and review our value system with others builds our spirits. Even routine activities like group brainstorming, staff meetings, and other seemingly mundane interactions with others provide a venue where individuals can share in planning and decision making. We also feed the spirit sometimes just by observing how others deal with defeat or hardships.

Activities done individually are also "re-spiriting." Quiet contemplation, reflection, challenging study, and time to reflect on our circumstances in a beautiful, natural setting all renew the spirit. Private contemplation is a spiritually reinforcing and spirit-strengthening activity that we human beings can engage in almost any place, at any time. Leaders who recognize this fact of life and incorporate opportunities for personal reflection in the corporate philosophy and vision may help make work a spiritually meaningful, as well as an economically emotionally rewarding, experience for themselves and their co-workers.

Achieving difficult goals, or sometimes merely meeting preset goals, and overcoming hardships and other challenges—whether failing or winning—inspire people. When our leaders or colleagues with whom we associate act against a deteriorating and immoral world, it rejuvenates and uplifts us. Winning victories for people who desperately need these victories is spiritually strengthening. Reading that relates personally to our needs at a given point in time also can be renewing.

Table 8.2
First Choices of Spiritually Renewing Activities

Percent of Responses	Activity
37%	Contemplation
21	Group interaction
11	Achieving difficult goals

*Respondents typically identified several activities.

Other individual activities also recharge us spiritually. Thus, being close to nature—a hike, a swim in a lake, watching the stars, a stroll on the beach—can inspire us. Helping others, spending time with a child or the family, church or other inspirational experiences, review of traditions, even wishing for the right things are potentially inspiring activities that leaders need to engage in and promote for their followers.

Implementation of our thoughts through activities that provide a sense of mastery where an impartial evaluation reveals that we have completed needed work competently and of high quality also builds spirit. If people cannot get this feeling at work they will seek it away from work. Survey respondents cite fixing a car, completing a research paper, setting goals and objectives for the future as examples of activities engaged in off the job that inspire and stirs them. An opportunity to feel this sense of accomplishment on the job will increase loyalty and productivity and will help link workers and leaders at deeper, spiritual levels.

When looked at in terms of the most significant activities that renew and inspire people, a slightly different picture emerges. Table 8.2 shows the ranking of the activities mentioned first by a group of working professionals. Individual contemplation is most significant with group activities coming in second. Other rankings appear to be similar to the composite rankings of respondents reported on in Table 8.1. Nevertheless, leaders are cautioned that attention to the individual, private thoughts and needs of their followers is a critical component of spiritual leadership.

SOURCES OF SPIRITUAL SUPPORT

We may ask the question, Where do leaders get the strength to lead in a spiritual way? What are the sources of strength that allow leaders to emerge and to endure over time and in the face of problems, competition, and recalcitrance of followers? Perhaps the best answer is: from their own spiritual foundations. Leaders gather strength from their inner conviction that their vision values are correct, right for their followers, and true for them and the group.

Added strength for leaders comes from the support of their followers as they come to share the leader's vision values, accept the constraints defined by those values, and participate actively in accomplishing the joint vision. The vision becomes a kind of defining moment in the life of the leader and the organization members he or she leads. A defining moment is when we receive insight that illuminates an aspect of self, an idea, or a concept and makes it a part of our self-image and self-definition.

Leading others from a foundation of the spirit self places heavy burdens on leaders. Leaders have the arduous task of learning the corporate business, whatever it is. They also must stay current with contemporary managerial technique. And, as the foundation for their leadership, they must get in touch with their core values and communicate them to followers through vision statements and personal actions that vitalize follower actions. Spiritual leaders also need to renew constantly their spirit self and encourage self-renewal in their stakeholders.

Professionals responding to questions about how they renew themselves spiritually listed a variety of communities of support. Some spiritually renewing sources were other people. Others were renewed spiritually by the activities in which they engaged. And still other sources were community and social institutional groups. These sources of personal spiritual renewal confirm and revitalize the individual's values, ethics, and beliefs. They provide a source for restoring their spirit self. Table 8.3 summarizes the most significant of these sources of spiritual support.

For most people, family is the most sure place to find the personal spiritual renewal necessary to continue in life and work. Professionals who participated in my survey chose family most often (84%). Family was the first listed source of spiritual support for 68 percent of respondent professionals (Table 8.4). The security and familiarity of family and the counsel of parents provide an environment where we can regain our most sacred, inner self. Family, especially parents, are important in forming our values both early in life and throughout life. Fathers, initially, and more recently all working parents, instill in us their beliefs about work that carry over into the rest of our lives.

Church, deeply held religious values, and the support for and example of living according to the values we see there in the lives of coreligionists and in the shared doctrines of life, revitalize our spirits. Some people can find examples of religious principle anywhere, even where we work. For many, it is in church, through religious programs on radio and tele-

Table 8.3
Sources of Spiritual Support

Number of Responses*	Sources of Support
84%	Family (73.4%)
	Parents (10.5%)
53.5	Church/religion/prayer
47	Friends
36.8	School (26.3%)
	Teachers (10.5%)
15.7	Professional colleagues/peers

Note: Also mentioned were the following sources of spiritual support: Local culture; literature; the media and TV; expectations from community role models; life experiences; the power of the human spirit; groups that value freedom/justice/peace.

*Respondents typically identified several sources.

Table 8.4
First Choices of Support Sources

Number of Responses*	Communities of Support
68.4%	Family
5	Religion
5	Parents
5	Friends
5	School
5	The power of the human spirit
5	Groups that value democracy, freedom, justice, peace

*Respondents typically identified several sources.

vision, and in the lives of others who believe in the power of the human spirit that spiritual renewal is most often fostered.

Like-minded friends and family members also can renew our spirits. The example of their lives, the counsel they give, and the nonjudgmental friendship they offer confirm our self-worth. Friendships help bond (rebond) us to our core values and ideals. Similarly, school relationships in our early life and in adult educational contacts set and reconfirm periodically our core values and goals. Teachers and fellow students provide role models for our life and define, often, the targets for personal professional behavior at work.

Both student and work situation role models can provide a clear focus and exemplify professional expectations. Our work organizations also can offer high standards by which to compare our actions. While it is, perhaps, true that organizations from the past may offer higher standards of professional conduct than do some today, those that espouse values of democracy, freedom, justice, and peace—all nonreligious political values—can also reinvigorate our spirit.

Of course, different communities are important at different stages in life. Early on, parents, teachers, and peers provide much of the basis for our personal values and beliefs. Later, individuals, professional colleagues, and religious principles may be paramount. And, for some, literature, life experiences, and (for good or bad) the media and television shape our spiritual essences.

In a work context, it is often our colleagues and corporate values that shape our spiritual self. If, as often is the case today, these values denigrate the spirit rather than renew it, individuals must seek spiritual support elsewhere. Hence the movement today to change work cultures to be more accommodating to the spiritual lives of members.

In his study, Jacobson (1995) surveyed the communities of support of values-based transformational leaders to identify those most helpful to them. His list (in order of frequency of response) included the work environment, community service groups, family, spiritual support groups and communities, personal support groups, worshipping religious communities, ethnic origin groups, and friends. While there is much similarity in this listing of spiritual support groups and individuals, respondents to Jacobson's study find a high degree of identification with the importance of spirituality but find communities of support in environments that are not overtly spiritual.

While Jacobson's listing prioritizes secular and professional support institutions, his list matches in many respects the list in Table 8.5. Spirituality is a means of integrating self and world. And the boundaries between what is spiritual and what is secular are vague and in some cases absent. There may be a discrepancy if one tries to separate the spiritual from the secular, but it creates no discrepancy if one does not

Table 8.5
Most Frequently Mentioned Values

Number of Responses	Values
11	Integrity, honesty
6	Freedom, independence
5	Fairness, equality, justice
4	Family
4	Love, caring, charity, respect for others
3	Commitment, perseverance, persistence
3	Ethics
3	Faith (in God and people)
3	Sanctity of human life
3	Treat others as you want to be treated
2	Belief in one's own ability
2	Choice, autonomy
2	Friendships
2	Happiness, enjoyment of life
2	Honor
2	Kindness, goodness
2	Service
2	Working

Note: The following values were also noted at least once: contribution; dream power; health and well-being; trust; courage; experiencing the meaning of life; learning; truth; discipline; growth; relationships.

anticipate such a separation. Spirituality is available in ordinary places as well as at church.

THE VALUES SUPPORTING PERSONAL PROFESSIONAL SPIRITUALITY

Each religious community is bound together by common values, a body of doctrine, and a set of ethical standards that serve to guide mem-

Table 8.6
Frequency of First-Mentioned Values

Number of Responses	Values
7	Integrity, honesty
2	Fairness, equality
2	The sanctity of human life

Note: The following values were also noted at least once: discipline; love; security for family; faith (in God and people); personal independence; service; freedom; respect; equality.

bers and shape their belief systems. In this respect, spirituality at work is like a religious community. Work spirituality is a kind of mind-set. It relies on common values held in concert with others in the group culture that set them apart from all other similar groups.

Tables 8.5 and 8.6 summarize values based on the kind of spirituality defined by professionals. These tables rank values in order of frequency of mention. They seem, however, to fall into several clusters of values centered around ideas of:

• Integrity
• Freedom and fairness
• Family values
• Service to others
• Personal growth and development

Integrity—bone honesty in one's dealings with others—is a prime value guiding spiritual leaders. It was the single most often mentioned value and it was the first named value for over a third of those surveyed, further adding to its perceived importance in defining our spiritual self in work terms. Integrity involves ideas such as honor, courage, and pursuing truth and continuous learning. It is a combination of discipline and freedom. Almost 58 percent of surveyed professionals described integrity in these terms. It is a primary value in their definition of workplace spirituality. Indeed, it defines their ethics.

Following closely behind honesty are freedom and justice. Working professionals see honesty in our dealings with others, respect for their freedom and independence, and treating others with fairness and justice as key. While seventh overall in frequency of mention, respect for the sanctity of life was a first choice value for 10 percent of those responding and is implicit in all of the above-mentioned values. Integrity, fairness, justice, and independence have special utility in work situations and help prepare the culture for spiritual leadership.

Family values of closeness, love, caring, and charity follow as prime spiritual values. Faith in God and people, looking out for the other person, working for what you believe in, nonviolent respect for the sanctify of human life both for self and others, happiness, enjoyment of life, and respect for others all comprise the core family values for many working professionals. Apparently workers want to be free to practice these values in their family associations, but also to have them recognized in the work setting. The Golden Rule of treating others as we want to be treated and caring for others are at the core of family values. The Golden Rule honors this value cluster on the job. Leaders who incorporate security for family, health and well-being, happiness, and fellowship in their organization's work values are responding to the spiritual needs of their followers.

Several values noted in Tables 8.5 and 8.6 deal with the value of service to others. Service—helping people realize their own power and using that newly realized strength to win improvements in their situations—is an important part of the idea of spirit at work. Commitment, perseverance, and persistence in rendering service through work ranks as significant operating values guiding worker activity. Professionals see work as a place and a way to demonstrate kindness and goodness. Belief in our own ability and that of our co-workers and feeling that work is where we can live up to our potential for service define this values cluster.

The opportunity for personal maturation and self-development is also a part of the values mix of those surveyed. Working professionals see a need for opportunity to experience the meaning of life in their workplace relationships. They want to find opportunity there to continue their pursuit of truth and learning at work. They appear to use work as well as leisure time to find ways of making a positive contribution to society. Personal growth is a combination of discipline and freedom. Those leaders are organizations that foster these values and provide this regimen may add to their fund of enabling tools.

THE INTEGRATION OF SPIRITUALITY INTO SECULAR WORK ORGANIZATIONS

Spirituality is a part of all life's decisions and actions. It is in the example of people who won't compromise their values to gain power. It is part of caring for others and using the Golden Rule. Spirituality relates directly to individual or group success as work values take on spiritual meaning and context.

Table 8.7
Reasons Spirituality Is Significant in Leadership

Number of Responses	
7	The leader's spirituality helps workers understand self and others.
6	The leader's spirituality facilitates sharing of values as people think about doing what they know in their heart is right, true.
3	Leaders motivate others to action through shared faith (trust).
1	The leader's spirituality adds a vital source of strength and inspiration.
1	The leader's spirituality lets workers understand others' values, beliefs, and motivations better and increases effectiveness.

There are obvious risks in trying to act authentically in terms of values formerly relegated to religion. Few will argue that the typical workplace resembles the average church, or typical workers the average believer. But these religious believers are on the job eight or ten hours a day. And many are coming to see their work as the prime activity of life. They want to relate the best of themselves to the activity in which they spend the bulk of their time. Hence, leaders must give attention to the spiritual center in people, even as they rigorously avoid imposing a particularized view of spirituality in their work actions and decisions.

The leaders' efforts to connect at the spirit level should not surface as religion. Rather, they should focus on values and ideals, like those noted above, that are normally accepted by all. Leaders should not impose their idea of spirituality on others. It is only as leaders encourage the use of individual moral decisions—not by providing any religious content—that spiritual values can be effectively and morally useful on the job.

There is a significant connection between a leader's ability to introduce change in the organization and his or her disposition toward spirituality. The language and values of spirituality are significant in helping leaders understand self and in understanding their activities as leaders. Seventy-four percent of professionals queried suggest that the spiritual sense is a significant factor in their leadership success (see Table 8.1). The reasons they give are powerful in documenting the power of the spirit (soul) in shaping mundane as well as sacred human life activity. Table 8.7 summarizes five critical ways that a leader's spirituality can impact his or her capacity to be successful in leadership.

Spirituality Helps Leaders Understand Self and Others Better. A spiritual perspective on our leadership actions and the actions of others helps us understand our self better. Spiritual values form the basis of self-understanding. They guide our activities. They can provide each of us with a sense of mission in life. A focused self-understanding based on spiritual values rather than a mere chronicling of skills and attributes makes leaders more likely to succeed. A greater familiarity with genuine values-driven language and action will promote greater self-awareness that gets to deeper levels of spirituality in meaningful ways.

Spirituality helps people to define their motives and to understand what is actually important to them. Shared values surface as we think about doing what is right, what we know in our hearts is true. Our inner beliefs are significant in this role. They define self for each person. Our values are the core of who we are. They frame the options a leader sees as viable.

Spirituality Helps the Leader Motivate Others. One's trust in someone or something motivates them to action. Leaders can use this awareness to communicate to others and to link organizational goals to motives that everyone in the organization should understand and support. Ideally, followers will recognize those motives as their own and devote their best efforts to realizing stated goals.

Spirituality Is Another Source of Strength for the Leader. It is a part of all we do. When we ignore spirituality in group activity then we lose a major source of strength and inspiration.

Spirituality Helps Leaders Know Their Co-workers Better. In understanding others' values and beliefs, leaders and members know their co-workers better, understand their motives and can work more effectively together.

Chapter 9

The Search for a New Leadership

It is hard today to generate even a reasonably long list of recognized American (or world) leaders. There is a leadership famine in our social, business, and civic communities. One cause may stem from the fact that many would-be leaders opt to focus their leadership on special groups, not the larger community encompassing all groups. And, the leadership gap has been deepened because too few leaders have been willing to give up tight control of their group members to become orchestrators of their independent actions. The root cause of both situations may be that, unlike their more numerous predecessors, today's business and civic leaders do not offer a high moral standard around which potential followers can cluster.

We need to look at ourselves more deeply and honestly and create a greater capacity for ethical, moral, and meaningful leadership and followership. For surely the moral standards of our civic and corporate institutional leaders affect us. The familiar biblical proverb has as much application now as it always has: "When the righteous are in authority, the people rejoice and when the wicked beareth rule, the people mourn" (Proverbs 29:2).

As Hickman (1989) suggests, business people have begun to question the deeper values, methods, and motives of their leaders as well as their own actions and values in the various organizations and communities to which they belong. To combat the tendency to fragmentation of our leadership relations and our standards of social conduct, we must take careful stock of our own preferred leadership style. We must monitor not just the form, but the soul of our leadership.

The ideal leader for today's business climate knows the true power of an organization lies in people. Leadership success lies in the people who are led. This kind of leader continually seeks to bring out the best in people. They are sensitive to the needs of others to grow, change, and mature. They vary their responses according to the person and the situation. They understand that their behavior has a major impact on their followers. People resist being told what to do; they really commit when given the chance to make their own ideas work. The new breed of spirit leader understands that as people feel cared about they will go to extremes to help those who help them.

This harking back to the soul—the heart, the essential being, the spiritual essence—in leader and led alike is the heart of this emerging spiritual iteration of leadership theory and practice. Because of the power of the organizations we live and work in, the leader's actions and policies affect member performance, and the standards of ethical conduct set by the leader and exemplified in the leader's words and deeds define the essence of the organization. Leaders have a duty to lead with the best interests of their workers and other stakeholders in mind. Given the demanding nature of today's work force, this focus on follower moral, even spiritual, development and transformation is the hallmark of holistic, whole-soul leadership models some current writers are sketching out today.

ELEMENTS OF THE EMERGING SPIRITUAL LEADERSHIP

There is a myth that excellent leaders are always alone in coping with stress and change. Actually there are a wealth of mentors, teachers, and support people who are willing to act as guides. But the reality is that today's whole-soul oriented leaders do listen to their inner feelings. The more a person knows about his or her inner self, the easier it will be to lead and stay healthy. Another myth is that it is necessary to think harder and work harder to achieve organizational change. Perhaps the truth here is that spiritual leaders think and work deeper, not just harder.

Leadership in essence is from the soul. The nature of leadership stems from the leader's personality and soul rather than just from his or her behavior (Keifer 1992). Management will not suffice for the future. Modern organization members need leadership. Organizational leadership ultimately must depend on the leader's inner capacity, from a source very close to if not from within the soul of a person.

Such a leadership style will consider both the worker's capacity and his or her needs. John Renesch (1994b) identified that the workers' greatest dissatisfaction level concerns their desire for openness throughout their organization. Fifty-five percent of the respondents in a study by the International Workplace Values Survey had experienced what they called a "personal transformation" in recent years. And 69 percent of the respondents expressed a desire to become part of a formal organization to further "new thinking" and humanistic values in the workplace (Renesch 1994b).

Past leader models have lost sight of the need to energize, inspire, and enthuse workers, not just control them. Leadership should seek to create a climate in which the leader and members of the group bring forth the best they have to offer. Sometimes, however, the best that individuals have to offer is not of a high quality, but we must assure them about the acceptability of their proffer. Of course, our task is avoiding unnecessary mediocrity. However, too often our tolerance of poor performance by ourselves and others is not tolerance at all, but simply lazy leadership.

True leadership is setting standards and values and persuading others to accept them as personal and group guides. By setting clear standards and helping ourselves and others to grow within these standards in mind-stretching and ability-stretching ways we will experience an infinite variety of results. For the individual, this can mean closing the gap between what he is and what he might become (Maxwell 1973).

Foundations of the New Leadership

Several writers have begun the process of defining a new leadership grounded in spirit. Their contributions range from openness to community, from individualism to team strategies to stewardship, from standards to values, from economic materialism to human systems, from personal growth to service to others, from growth to competence, from caring to love. These foundations provide the base upon which we can begin theory building.

Several recent books and articles share a common interest in leadership focused on a deep sense of purpose and meaning. They reflect a growing need to find comfort and meaning in the stressed-out insecure workplace of the 1990s. This movement builds on the work of many people. These spiritual leadership pioneers—whether they define themselves in these terms—include (alphabetically):

V. Anantaraman. Anantaraman (1993) suggests that current leadership models shift their emphasis from one person, whether bureaucratic or charismatic, to a top management team to meet the challenges of environmental turbulence. This model includes a holistic conception of the organization both as an economic enterprise and as a human system.

James Autry. Spiritual and religious values and those of a free democratic society go hand in hand. Religions have evolved as structures or forms designed to support and perpetuate specific beliefs or dogmas about spiritual matters. Religious dogmas are expanding to include work concerns and relate spirit in business. We need to consider the "soft" topics of meaning, spirit, and caring. Holistic leadership addresses both the professional and personal lives of stakeholders (Autry 1992).

David Bargal. Bargal (Bargal and Schmid 1989) sees the leader as a servant and a steward. Both are similar in nature and action. Leaders are servants of stakeholders. Leadership is giving, whatever the situation needs, and management is getting.

Peter Block. Block (1993) concludes that leadership is a spiritual endeavor. It requires leaders willing to know themselves first and act out of their true self in relationships with others. Spirituality for Block is a process of living out of deeply held personal values, of honoring forces or a presence greater than ourselves. It is treating as an offering what we do. It is choosing service over self. Block says leaders are stewards. Leadership without stewardship relegates the leader to the role of parent and is demeaning to the follower. It is operating in service to, rather than in control of, those around us.

Tom Chappell. Spirituality recognizes our connection with all other things including a higher power. Spirituality brings mind and spirit back together in commerce (Chappell 1993). It is about how mind and spirit can work together to compete for profit and market share. It is a middle way—managing to grow while navigating a course between profits and the common good.

Stephen Covey. Covey (1992) suggests that one problem with contemporary American business deals with unleashing the creativity, talent, and energy of the majority of the work force whose jobs neither require nor reward such resources. His is a holistic paradigm intended to tap into those capabilities and resources. To resolve this dilemma, he says leaders must work from the inside out. Covey believes leadership involves developing relationships based on individual trustworthiness, interpersonal trust, empowerment, and organizational alignment.

Max DePree. DePree (1989) says leaders create conventional relationships or bonds that fulfill deep needs and give work meaning for employees. For him, the purpose of the organization is redemption, not profit. The measure of leadership is not structural, but attitudinal. It is not of the head, but the tone of the soul that makes leaders outstanding. Leaders are servants characterized by ideas like integrity, awareness of the human spirit, and breadth.

Peter Drucker. Drucker (1988) suggests that management's job is to find out what it is doing that keeps people from doing a good job, and stop doing it. Leadership does the opposite.

Amatai Etzioni. Many people have a deep desire for more fulfilling work, and more than that, a commitment to manifest our dreams in our community life. Most organizations take away our individual power.

The quest for spirituality allows us to win back active control over our life. We need to relate work and leadership to the elemental matters of the spirit that lie at the heart of all activity. In leading, complexity, a synthesizing and global vision, extending to ultimate and spiritual significance, counts for more than analytical powers (Etzioni 1993).

Gilbert Fairholm. Trust is reliance on the integrity, justice, or fairness of a person or similar quality or attribute of an event or thing. We base lasting trust—real trust—on truth. We do not continue to trust unless the aspect of the person we trust eventually proves to be authentic. Leaders who make a difference to others cause people to feel that they, too, can make a difference (Fairholm 1994a).

Matthew Fox. Fox (1994) says spirituality is about life. It is about responding deeply to life, to accepting life as a mystery and as something sacred. He says it is about finding the sacred everywhere, including in self. We are spiritual beings in a human experience, a major part of which is work.

Kenneth Goodpaster. Doing business requires interaction with our fellow human beings and within those interactions are enormous possibilities for spiritual growth and connection (Goodpaster 1994). Spirituality is a response to a growing tendency in organizations toward teleopathy. Goodpaster sees organizational life and leadership characterized too much by a situation—a syndrome of focus on superordinate goals, lack of explicit attention to shared values, less than full regard toward workers as equals, and a tendency to pass the buck when moral responsibility interferes with the achievement of urgent and risk-laden goals. He calls this "teleopathy."

Goodpaster defines teleopathy as an unbalanced pursuit of purpose. This is the single most significant stimulus to which business ethics is and must be a practical response. The principle symptoms of teleopathy are fixation on narrow goals, rationalization of people and situations, and detachment—a separation of the head from the heart. Compartmentalization of our selves and our leadership into prescribed and traditional roles limits and constrains our leadership. It places our responses to internal and external stakeholders and communities in known and predictable boxes from which we cannot easily extract ourselves when market or other forces dictate change.

Teleopathy is the most significant stimulus to which business ethics in this century has been the response. It is a principle hazard of business leadership. It is a kind of goal sickness (Goodpaster 1994). Unchecked, teleopathy results in alienation, stress, unreasonable demands on work time, loss of creativity, and, most notably, loss of community.

Robert Greenleaf. The secret of leadership, especially leadership founded on spirit, is that the leader is a servant first and then a boss. Many of the problems we have as leaders, or in working with other leaders, result because we often reverse this order of things (Greenleaf 1977). A major part of spiritual expression on the job and elsewhere is in the idea of service to others. It is looking beyond the immediate—job, industry, nation—and connecting the human being with the cosmos. Servant leadership appeals to the spiritual side of people. It appeals to the intrinsic common sense of people.

William Gross. Business in America faces two challenges at this juncture in history: the challenge to do good and do well simultaneously. Spiritual leaders recognize, understand, and encourage the concept that employees must have a working environment in which they can grow personally and spiritually. We need to reconnect the practice of business with those inner values most easily defined as spiritual. This connection refers to the need for the human spirit to express itself in a way that generates personal meaning and fulfillment in work-related activities. Wholly integrated people are at the heart of empowerment and true team work. The important part in leading others is really this delicate, almost imperceptible fabric of feelings, thoughts, and behaviors that forms the sum total of one's life (Gross 1995).

Jack Hawley. All leadership is spiritual (Hawley 1993). We need expanded, spiritual leadership today more than ever. Leaders work in the abstract realm of people's energy, heart, and spirit. Leadership is coming to mean re-inspiring, which literally means to take in a new breath. Leaders seek to liberate the best in people. Management is action, growth, advantage for someone else, competition. This often ignores the spirit in self and others. Leadership is finding peace of mind as we work. Hawley calls this "dharmic management."

Dharmic management is infusing spirit, character, human values, and decency in the workplace and in life (Hawley 1993). Dharmic means deep integrity, living by your inner truth. It is about re-empowering spirit in the individual. For Hawley, dharmic leadership involves constant spiritual awareness, working with energy and spirit, love and reverence in work and life, realigning beliefs, thoughts and being, and strengthening personal and organizational integrity. Leaders define reality for the group. They set the vision goals and give people and systems a sense of purpose.

Frederick Herzberg. Herzberg (1968) confirmed that Douglas McGregor's theory was correct. Employees treated as McGregor specified in his theory Y—with a basic respect and confidence in their ability and desire to work to high standards of effectiveness and responsibility—were more productive and hard working.

Craig Hickman. Hickman (1989) focuses our attention on the leader's role in questioning their own core values and motives and those of the group. Development of a common core of values is the central task in building corporate community.

Susan Howe. True leaders live in an organizationally healthy manner, and the key to daily rejuvenation lies in actively making choices about the care of one's body, mind, heart, and spirit (Howe 1994). The basis of real health and leadership is on a holistic vision about how to work and live. Spiritual leadership is holistic precisely because it considers equally the physical, mental, social-emotional, and spiritual in us all.

Charles Keifer. The nature of leadership stems from the leader's soul rather than from his or her behavior (Keifer 1992). Keifer suggests that management will not suffice for the future, but, rather, our organization members need leadership. Ultimately, organizational leadership must depend on inner capacity, from a source very close to if not from within the soul of a person.

Herb Kelleher and Colleen Barrett. Kelleher and Barrett (1994) say corporate spirit is a spiritual force that honors excellence in the leadership of job performance. It is manifest in compassion, concern, and understanding of others, individual contributions, and individual personalities. It combines good humor, a warrior's courage when attacked, and ideas that operationalize group goals and methods such as customer service. Our spirit needs to connect to the natural world and to each other. Leaders need to respect both the human spirit and the environment.

James Kouzes and Berry Posner. Kouzes and Posner (1993) focus on the dilemma of achieving and maintaining a wise and renewing balance between work and family. Life is a balancing of the personal and professional in the middle of constant pressures and crises. This is also a holistic approach including services that address the personal and professional lives of workers. It is illustrated in practical programs like flexible benefits, career development services, telecommuting, wellness programs, and employee assistance programs.

Leadership is of the heart; management is of the head. When we ask people to do things with their heads rather than their hearts, they rebel at the implied control and demand to control themselves (Kouzes and Posner 1993). We express spiritual leadership by letting people do work with their minds not just their hands, setting an example for others about the rightness or wrongness of particular actions, and addressing the personal as well as the professional lives of workers.

Chris Lee and Ron Zemke. There is a connection among love, trust, and energy. Felt love inspires trust. Trust makes it possible to commit to something with energy. Love is the source of a leader's courage to do what the group needs. There is an interest in making sense out of the present management chaos by proposing a leadership filled with heart and soul (Lee and Zemke 1993). Leadership training has a sacred dimension—we talk about being committed, a better person, and treating others as we would want to be treated. Lee and Zemke advocate turning the organizational pyramid over and serving all the people.

Abraham Maslow. Maslow (1971) theorized that work was a major part of human life and was necessary to fulfill fundamental human needs. Some work only fulfills the lower-order needs, not the higher ones. He said the goal was not survival alone, but self-actualization—to be all you can be. Maslow's work presaged McGregor (1960), who said that people want to work, take responsibility, be innovative, and be energetic.

St. Matthew. Matthew 23:23–24—"Woe unto you, scribes and Pharisees [leaders of that day], hypocrites! for ye pay tithe of mint and anise and cummin, and have omitted the weightier [matters] of the law, judgment, mercy, and faith: these ought ye to have done, and not to leave the other undone. [Ye] blind guides, which strain at a gnat, and swallow a camel."

Matthew 20:27—"And whosoever will be chief among you, let him be your servant."

Neal Maxwell. Spirituality in business is a passionate dimension of work life. While energy and spirit come from within, we must share it with others to fully experience it. The spiritual values we traditionally express in church are present in the business environment as well. We must somehow express them there too. Business is becoming more entrepreneurial and less bureaucratic. What we see of the corruption of business, governments, and other social institutions is partially portrayed in the covering of sins, the gratifying of pride, the role of ambition, and the passion to exercise control or dominion (Maxwell 1976). Most of us tend to do these things if we are not careful. But Jesus' model of leadership is not only loving, but also long-suffering. Under this approach, when we can we should enlarge our soul without hypocrisy or guile.

Douglas McGregor. McGregor (1960) advocated Theory Y views that workers are responsible, ambitious, energetic, ingenious, and creative.

Terry Mollner. For Mollner (1992) leadership is the process of initiating the young into a mature understanding of who they are. This process, which he calls "eldering," requires credibility in the leader. Credibility is the foundation of leadership, and yet there has been a large-scale erosion of employee confidence in management during the 1980s and 1990s.

Keshavan Nair. Mahatma Gandhi's life is and has been inspirational to millions of people around the globe. According to Nair's (1994) analysis, Gandhi's was a nontraditional, postmodern leadership style. His influence was worldwide and rooted in a devout individual spirituality. Gandhi's impact on his followers was a kind of personal vow and each follower had to decide whether he or she possessed the inner strength to keep it. His style of leadership was challenging, inspiring, enabling, and encouraging. Much of current spiritual leadership theory-building stems from ideas and actions Ghandi and a few others reflected in their lives and leadership.

Nair's analysis of Ghandi's leadership embraces a concept of leadership that is heroic in its commitment to moral principles and service rather than one driven by acquisition of power and mastering the forces of violence. People have an inner self that defines who they are and dictates what they do. Gandhi exemplified this. There was a majesty to Gandhi's life that came from his inner strength.

Gandhi's religion drove his leadership: truth and nonviolence (physical and violence to the spirit) and a life of service to others. He symbolized service rather than power. He founded his leadership in integrity based on a single standard of conduct, a spirit of service, decisions, and actions bounded by moral principles.

Nair makes a convincing case for the application of these principles in modern leadership of our institutions, businesses, and public life. Continuous improvement is the path to the higher standard of leadership (Nair 1994). Improvement is helped by colleagues who share our values. Following Gandhi's example, we must rate our every action on the measure of absolute values. The discipline of evaluation will help us rise to the highest level of our performance as leaders—as it does for athletes. He also said that attachments to possessions limit our ability to improve.

The principles of governance Nair found in Gandhi's life include moral criteria in rating decisions and actions as we do economic factors, acknowledging the fusion of ends and means, and respect for the intrinsic good in every individual. The moral direction set by our decisions and actions determine the nature of the society in which we live.

For Gandhi, it was essential that leadership have a moral or spiritual dimension. Change is not enough; the change should lead to a spirit of community. To do this, everyone involved must trust the decision process. Openness allows all affected by the decision to evaluate the process as well as the outcome. Gandhi's higher leadership asks us to follow a single standard of conduct in personal and professional life, to act within a moral framework. Leadership asks of its leaders moral courage—doing what is right and accepting the consequences.

Leadership is a life of service. People followed Gandhi because they came to know he devoted his life to serving them. Power has only one legitimate use—service. Nair's analysis of Gandhi's leadership found a pattern of five steps to help make service the centerpiece of leadership (Nair 1994): (1) focusing by example on responsibilities, (2) emphasizing values-based service because it is right, (3) making a commitment to personal service, (4) understanding the needs of the people you serve, and (5) reconciling power with service and acting as a trustee toward others.

Robert T. Pascale and Anthony Athos. In the West we have devolved a culture that separates each person's spirituality from his or her institutional life (Pascale and Athos 1981). What we need in the West is a nondeified, nonreligious spiritualism that enables a firm's superordinate goals to respond authentically to the inner meanings that many people seek in their work, or, alternatively, seek in their lives and could find at work if only that were culturally acceptable.

Bruce Payne. Leadership is about sharing intentions (Payne 1994). Effective leadership, a pattern of actions deliberately and successfully influencing change in groups, is more likely to occur, and more likely to be beneficent, when it comes from people of strong character. Leadership means leaders must attend to choices they make in their relationships with others. Leadership aims to affect people's values, encouraging them to discover contradictions in their views. It is about persuasion, about arguments of better or worse, right or wrong.

Acts of leadership at every level typically reflect ideas of what is good for individuals and for groups—convictions about what will promote faiths, protect countries, build companies, or transform schools. Leaders cannot avoid the ethical ingredients of group cohesion—a subject Payne calls the moral aspects of morale. Leaders want to clarify their moral identities and to strengthen and deepen their commitments. They make connections between others' interior worlds of moral reflection and the outer worlds of social relationships.

Insight is knowledge about the world that surprises the self, or knowledge about one's own mind, passions, and interests, that can illuminate a portion of the world. Good acts come from reactions and reflections in response to several kinds of forces. If we are not talking a lot about ethics, we may not be talking about leadership at all.

M. Scott Peck. Peck (1993) writes that we need a more civilized world based on values. Leadership for Peck is a spiritual endeavor reached most easily in the corporate world. Individuals and small groups institute community. Community works only in the largest organizations and institutions. There is evidence today that government and other social institutions are not taking the lead in this community-building activity. It may be that only the business world is willing to pay the price of building community.

We base corporate community on a values basis. It is a necessary step to rebuilding a unified society. It needs visionary leaders to show the way. Visionary leadership is based on wholeness, spiritual values, and concern for the human side of life, rather than materialistic models of the past. This kind of leadership includes vision, credibility, courage, and adaptability. Visionary leaders demonstrate a sustained ability to build consensus and lead democratically. These are also the qualities of a true spiritual leader.

Robert Rabbin. We experience truth—also called Tao, Self, Spirit, God— as a state in which the mind is open and silent and the heart is suffused with encompassing love. Only when individual behavior affects adversely the organization's performance should leaders step in. Until then they should refrain from regulating the private affairs of their people. The spiritual message is simple, clear, and universal. It is important to know who we are by directly perceiving our true nature. Everything in this world is alive and conscious and deserving of our respect and care. Love and compassion arise naturally in the experience of our oneness with life (Rabbin 1994). Applied to the workplace the application of truth calls up the innermost secrets of the soul.

John Renesch. Renesch (1994b) documents worker dissatisfaction levels and identifies personal transformation and a desire to become connected with the organization to further humanistic values in the workplace.

Tom Robins. Our purpose is to consciously, deliberately evolve toward a wiser, more liberated and luminous state of being. Some kind of mystical evolution is our true task (Robins, as quoted in *The New Leaders* 1994). The new breed of business leader is not a religious guru, but an individual who assumes responsibility for an outcome, who is self-empowered, and who can work in harmony with his or her environment.

Frank Sonnenberg. Trust is critical to spiritual leadership. Trust makes you free to put your deepest fears in the palms of your colleagues' hands knowing that they will treat you with care (Sonnenberg 1993).

Peter Vaill. Based on an analogy of the performing arts, Vaill (1989) suggests the formulation of the organization's mission and strategy in terms of values. He suggests that in a work context, we perceive spirituality to include a much broader range of experience while we see religion and faith as limiting the discussion to experiences that arise in traditional religious institutions or ways of thinking. Spirituality is, for Vaill, a core basis for our values, beliefs, and ethics. This source of individual ethics is also recognized in the recent leadership literature dealing with values-based transformational leadership.

SUMMARY

When people work with leaders they admire and respect, they feel better about themselves. Admired leaders do not place themselves at the center; they place others there. When people perceive their managers to have high credibility, they are significantly more likely to tell others of their affiliation with the organization, feel a strong sense of team spirit, and see their personal values as consistent with the organization's.

We don't have to mix religion with business. Neither do we have to shy away from the spiritual side of our work and the deeper meanings of our mission. Building a bridge between the secular and sacred worlds may be a natural outgrowth of the search for meaning and identity. We need to treat people out of their wholeness, not just that part needed by the corporation today.

Spiritual leadership involves many ideas, some common in today's values-based transformational leadership, some more commonly seen in metaphysical, religious, or philosophical literature. But, based on the work of the authors listed in this chapter, leadership deals with (alphabetically):

Affirmation. Leaders acknowledge a basic optimism.

Balance. Leaders strive for balance between work, family, and professional areas of life.

Capacity. Leaders tap into worker capabilities and resources.

Ceremony. Leaders define new ceremonies and rituals that bring people together.

Community. Leaders relate to the organization as a community.

Continuous improvement. Leaders help others express their highest potential in ways that generate fulfillment in work-related activities.

Corporate spirit. Leaders create a spiritual force that honors high performance, compassion, empathy for others, and individual contributions.

Credibility. Leaders are more likely to feel a strong sense of team spirit, and see their personal values as consistent with the group's and thus be seen as creditable by members.

Culture. Leaders build a sense of community, of oneness, by creating cultures consonant with the shared values of the group.

Emotions. The leader is a mood setter. Leaders deal with contentment, capacity, equanimity, detachments, and connectedness.

Ethics. Leaders set the moral tone of the group.

Heart. Leaders are a guide to spiritual awareness, through a sense of their inner core self.

Higher standard. Leaders set the standards for excellence for the group. The standards are the basis of their ethics.

Holistic. Leaders see the organization both as an economic enterprise and as a human system. Both are equally important and equally controlling of individual and group action.

Integrity. Leaders are moral architects, truth clarifiers. They model moral truth in their actions.

Liberation. Leaders seek to liberate the best in people. The best is linked to one's higher self.

Love. Leaders love their followers, the common work, and the people served. They care for, respect, and honor followers.

Meaning. Leadership is about sharing of intentions.

Morals. Leadership raises the levels of human conduct.

Nonsectarian spirit. Leaders expand work-life concerns and relate inner spirit in business to the "soft" topics of meaning, fidelity, and caring.

Oneness. Leaders bring unity to organizations.

Organizational health. Leaders strive to help stakeholders make choices about the care of their body, mind, heart, and spirit.

Power. Leaders are models of inner power, they maintain an attitude of unbending intent.

Presence. Leaders reflect inner strength.

Relationships. Leaders create bonds that fulfill deep needs of employees and the purposes of the organization.

Sacred. Leaders help followers find the sacred everywhere, including in the self.

Servant. The leader is first a servant, then a boss.

Spirituality. Leaders recognize the process of living out deeply held personal values, of honoring forces or a presence greater than self.

State of mind. Leaders seek inner peace for self and others.

Stewardship. Leaders hold work resources in trust for a temporary period. Stewardship is a collective idea, it is by sharing equally all power that we become one, united.

Team. Leaders use their power to help accomplish the group's ends, not only the leader's ends.

Trust. Leaders rely on the integrity, truth, justice, and fairness of others in trusting them.

Trusteeship. Leaders hold work resources in trust for a temporary period.

Truth. Leaders apply the truth. The application of truth calls up the innermost secrets of the soul.

Values. The leader is a values steward, a steward of virtues.

Visioning. Leadership is sense-making, covenant-making.

Wholeness. The leader is a whole-maker, a creator of oneness within the group.

Chapter 10

The Spiritual Leadership Process

There is peculiar power in this new leadership process defining a *holistic* approach to dealing with people and centered on a community conception of the organization both as an economic enterprise and as a spiritually human system. This holistic approach includes services that address the personal as well as the professional lives of workers (Kouzes and Posner 1993). The dilemma is to achieve and maintain a renewing balance between work and family and between personal and professional areas of life in the midst of constant pressures and crises. To resolve this dilemma, we must work from the inside out at all levels— individual credibility, interpersonal trust, empowerment, and personal and other development.

The new breed of leaders fulfill their role as moral and spiritual anchors in these turbulent times (Rasmussen 1993). It is a risky responsibility. Today, leadership means putting your life and your money where your values are. Spiritual leaders work primarily to enable their team. Personal gain is not often motivating to them. This new leadership springs from a regenerated school of thought that focuses on leader service to followers (Greenleaf 1977).

Successful leadership depend on a carefully designed corporate philosophy or vision imbedded in a corporate culture. We can summarize the idea of leadership in the idea of commitment to serving others. It incorporates values honoring self and other development or growth to become one's best self. It is a stewardship orientation to the leader's tasks. Bradley (1993) suggests that is the only way to lead in the new world toward which we are headed.

Leadership today incorporates a sense of interactive, mutual trust. We can characterize trust in the workplace as an authentic concern for people *and* organization goals. Leaders need to create work environments that encourage openness, fairness, individuality, and creativity as the pillars of trust. The leadership of trust is commitment to group unity, teamwork, and sharing and to integrity in all interpersonal relationships. It employs simple and flexible structure and systems and a process emphasizing continuous evaluation of progress (Fairholm 1994a).

OUTLINES OF SPIRITUAL LEADERSHIP

We can abstract a skeleton outline of spiritual leadership (Goodpaster 1994) from the growing research defining spirit in the workplace described in Chapter 9. This model is as much a creative result as an abstraction of available data. It addresses what is essentially a new environment, a new culture of leadership, one that demands new solutions. This model tries to embody those values, traits, and practices proven effective in various kinds of organizations and with some individual leaders over time.

Spiritual leadership also incorporates new ideas about what leadership is and the important role played by the leader's and follower's inner spiritual experiences, values, and expectations. However, it integrates these ideas in new ways and adds others not previously considered in older leadership theories. The new spiritual model defines by this integration a new conception of leadership and the role of the leader in modern organizations.

This approach is holistic and dynamic, with the individual parts providing synergistic support for the total. This new leadership is keyed to enduring principles (Covey 1992), is people-oriented, and focuses on service to all stakeholders. It concentrates on a few principles of human interpersonal conduct that elevate and ennoble the individual within the group. It, like any assumption, is a best guess about what leadership is really like and what are the key elements and dynamics activating leaders.

This particular image of leadership is my hypothesis about what leadership is and, more importantly, what it should be. Some of it is grounded in a repeatable reality. Other parts are extrapolations from other dimension of human life, not easily measured, defined, and rated. Still others come from an ethic that prioritizes service, other-development, and personal professional maturation. Together they attempt to define an integrated pattern of reality.

This leadership pattern recognizes the whole person for the first time in modern leadership theory. It accepts the fact that people come to work owning all of their human qualities, not just the few skills, knowledge, and abilities needed at a given time by the employing corporation. Workers today—and perhaps always—come to work armed with and ready to use their total life experience. They have and want to use all of their skills. They want to apply all of their pertinent experience, and exercise all of their capacities to think, act, be creative, and take responsibility (McGregor 1960).

Spiritual leadership is a holistic approach that considers the full capacities, needs, and interests of both leader and led, and the goals of the organization. Spiritual leaders see leadership as a contextual relationship in which all participants want to grow and help others in their self-development activities. While the parameters of this model are unclear—indeed, we are still uncovering them—we can adduce some elements of the process. Table 10.1 lists the key principles and some of their definitional characteristics.

These eight spiritual leadership elements comprise the core of a new leadership pattern (Figure 10.1). It focuses on the whole person and not just on the few talents of the worker that managers want to integrate into a monolithic structure geared to repeatability, predictability, and uniformity. Such a bureaucratic conception of organization for the production of goods or services cannot be effective today. We must develop other than traditional management methods to fill this gap.

Two reasons—among many that commentators redundantly argue—may suffice to prove this point. First, today's worker is a knowledge worker: better educated, more aware of alternative ways of doing work, and more aware of alternative consequences of that work. They come to the workplace differently (better) prepared, and differently motivated. They are more intelligent, better prepared, and want more than their counterparts did in previous generations. They can do more, and a greater variety of, tasks and want more opportunity to guide their own work lives than did their counterparts of a generation or two ago.

Second, the tasks, products, and services we ask our organizations to produce to meet present-day demands are no longer stable and predictable. Assembly line processes and assembly line mentality will no longer suffice to realize success. Customers want tailor-built products and services, not off-the-shelf versions. Technology is changing so fast that manufacturing methods to produce even stable products make traditional assembly line processes inappropriate. And today's organizations are serving global markets, not just local ones. We cannot conduct business as usual and survive and prosper.

While we can list many other causes—increased size, complexity, globalization, ambiguity, adaptability, technology—for the current situation,

Table 10.1
Elements and Characteristics of Spiritual Leadership

Community: Leaders relate to the organization as a community.

    Ceremony   Culture

    Holistic   Oneness

    Wholeness

Competence: Leaders demonstrate spiritual competence.

    Balance   Credibility

    Trust   Power

Continuous Improvement: Leaders help others express their highest potential.

    Capacity   Organizational health

A Higher Moral Standard: Leaders set the standards for excellence for the group.

    Positive affirmation   Ethics

    Heart   Integrity

    Love   Presence

    Meaning   Morals

Servant: The leader is first a servant, then a boss.

    Liberation

Spirituality: Leadership is the process of living out deeply held personal values, of honoring forces or a presence greater than self.

    Corporate spirit   Emotions

    Nonsectarian spirit   Relationships

    Sacred   Truth

Stewardship: Leadership is a collective idea; it is by sharing equally all power that followers become one, united around the leader's vision.

    Team   Trustee

Visioning: Sense-making, covenant-making.

    Values   State of mind

---

these two suffice to focus on the need for new paradigms focusing on leadership, not traditional management, not even traditional leadership theory. Spiritual leadership meets the needs of today's workers and organizations for comprehensive approaches to work activity and flexibility in responding to environmental pressures. It does so by appealing to

Figure 10.1
Model of the Spiritual Leadership Process

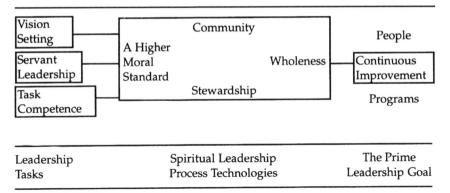

Leadership	Spiritual Leadership	The Prime
Tasks	Process Technologies	Leadership Goal

and energizing the inner senses of the leader and connects these inner forces to similar drives in followers.

Leaders cannot conduct spiritual leadership or any other kind of leadership in a vacuum. It is a dynamic process engaging in unique ways the model elements. Figure 10.1 pictures the dynamics and interrelationship patterns of this new leadership approach.

A more complete description of each of the core elements of the spiritual leadership model appear in the following chapters. The brief descriptions and elaborations of the eight core ideas of spiritual leadership summarized below help us circumscribe this version of leadership for the twenty-first century. Later chapters provide a more comprehensive examination of the eight dynamic elements of spiritual leadership.

THE THREE SPIRITUAL LEADERSHIP TASKS

Competence in three tasks define the preparation phase of spiritual leadership: task competence, vision setting, and servanthood (or servant leadership). Spiritual leaders accept primary responsibility to know intimately the tasks their team is in business to perform. They integrate these tasks into a vitalizing values-laden vision. As they do these things they relate to their co-workers in a servant relationship. Functioning out of this role they are prepared to oversee the day-to-day process of a spiritual relationship with their stakeholders.

Task Competence

Spiritual leadership asks leaders to be competent in four kinds of tasks: credibility, teaching, trust, and inspiration as well as to be knowledgeable about the actual work of the group. Group members are likely to perceive the spiritual leader as having a strong sense of team spirit, see his or her personal values as consistent with the group's, and thus to see the leader as creditable when they perceive the leader is competent. The process of attaining this sense of credibility is keyed proficiency in several areas. One is communication skills. Leaders tap into worker capacities, capabilities, and resources primarily through persuasion. Leadership is, at its heart, a teaching task and the leader a teacher. Leaders teach—that is, transfer meaning to—followers in ways that help followers do needed work. The unique feature of spiritual leadership is done in ways that maximize the potential that followers will commit to the tasks required of them and to the purposes these tasks serve.

Another factor in gaining follower acceptance is trust. Leaders rely on their integrity, justice, and fairness and in their willingness to trust others, and in so doing leaders gain the trust of their fellows. Trust is a key ingredient in leadership (Fairholm 1994a). Spiritual leaders inspire trust in followers. Our level of trust is a function of many particulars. It refers us to our theistic or atheistic values. Trust was not unidimensional because both orthodox and unorthodox views affect our willingness to trust.

Trusted people make known their confidence in the others' ability, expertise, and skills by sharing information and ideas with them. They trust in the other's ability to work with people. They value the other person's overall sense of the task and in their capacity for common sense. And they advertise their confidence in their followers.

Such leaders are inspiring. Inspiration is the leader's use of words, ideas, and deeds to convey a sense of connection, excitement, and shared commitment to group goals or methods. Development and use of this spiritual leadership technology is a critical part of spirit-based transformational leadership. Inspirational leaders who have high self-confidence and a conviction of their moral rightness transfer these qualities to followers (see Burns 1978, Peters and Waterman 1982, Bass 1987, Maccoby 1976, and Fairholm 1991).

Vision Setting

In a genuine sense, vision setting is sense-making, covenant-making. Leadership is about creating and then sharing meaning and intentions. Leaders are mood setters. They deal with contentment, capacity, equanimity, detachment, and connectedness. Through their vision, leaders affirm and acknowledge a basic optimism. Their visions have a universal concern and respect for every individual. They reflect love for their followers, the common work, and the customers they serve. The leader's vision reveals a commitment to fairness and justice. Visions optimize follower independence and freedom of choice.

Spiritual leaders develop visions and mission statements that foster development of a spirit of cooperation, mutual caring, and dedication to work. The source of the leader's vision is his or her individual sense of spirituality. Employees need to feel related to the organization's mission statement to feel connected on a personal, intimate level. The source of this motivation is the values held by the leader that followers see as uplifting to them. They must see them as inspiration not control.

Spirit leadership requires people who are unafraid to offend, who bravely stand apart from the rest, and who willingly give voice to ideas that may run counter to the status quo (Graham 1994). Leadership is the major responsibility of a chief executive officer, and visioning is a tool used to facilitate the exercise of leadership (Stata 1988).

Servanthood

The leader is first a servant, then a master. Spiritual leaders realize that they cannot do all of the work of the organization. They must assign all or most of the work of the group to others, and in so doing they give up their so-called authority to their followers. And, as soon as they devolve responsibility for group success to followers, leaders go to work for them. The leader becomes their servant, providing resources needed for success.

In a very real sense, leaders lead because they choose to serve others. They serve by making available to followers both their needs for information, time, material, and other resources and the higher organizational purposes that give meaning to what workers do. They are simultaneously leaders and followers of others in the team. Leaders have to be the best follower of the organization's goals or others will not trust and follow them. The leadership of service asks leaders to create and facilitate a culture of self-leadership.

The idea of the leader as servant of their followers comes out of the work of Robert K. Greenleaf (1977). Greenleaf wrote in the late 1960s and 1970s, partly, perhaps, in reaction to the ferment of that era that questioned authority and legitimacy. He postulated service as the prime definitional characteristic of true leaders. Since then, the idea of the leader-as-servant has become a persistent theme in the current research on leadership.

THE FOUR SPIRITUAL LEADERSHIP PROCESSES

Spiritual leadership process technologies include building community within the group and a sense of personal spiritual wholeness in both leader and led. Spiritual leaders set and live by a higher moral standard and ask others to share that standard in measuring their collective work. In their relationship with stakeholders they act in a stewardship role, forming a cohesive, shared responsibility team (Bradford and Cohen 1984).

Building Community and Personal Wholeness

The new spirit-based leadership denotes the creation of harmony from often diverse, sometimes opposing, organizational—human, system, and program—factions. It is an exercise of community building, of making one out of many. It is a task of generalizing deeply held values, beliefs, and principles of action in ways that all stakeholders will find acceptable and energizing.

Spirit-based leadership also preserves and honors personal individuality. Human beings strive for community. Belonging is a fundamental human need, but human beings strive for independence too. These two basic needs are and have always been in conflict in our organized group relationships. Spiritual leadership recognizes the simultaneous need we all have to be free to act in terms of our own reality *and* to be part of a similarly focused group.

Setting a High Moral Standard

Spiritual leadership raises the level of human conduct. Spiritual leaders set high standards for excellence for the group; they set the ethical moral tone for the group. In real ways, leaders are moral architects and truth clarifiers. They set the individual and corporate mood. Indeed, the character of the corporation is a direct function of the level of morality present among the members. Leadership is about sharing of intentions that raise the level of human conduct. They maintain an attitude of unbending intent, and they are models of this inner moral power.

Spiritual leadership is, in part, a task of connecting business decisions and actions to their natural and logical consequences. Rather than narrowly viewing business decisions within the context of the immediate situation, spiritual leaders take pains to understand—and see that stakeholders understand also—the natural and logical consequences that flow from their actions, the impact of these consequences on lives and careers as well as on profits, and the nature of the world created by the sum of the corporate decisions made. They consider these consequences before making decisions, and they form their choices in light of the longer-term impacts on both the corporation and the individuals making up the corporation.

Spiritual leaders have presence; they reflect inner power along with their technical capacities. They seek and help others find the truth and apply it in the collective work. And the application of truth calls up the innermost secrets of the soul. Spiritual leaders are a guide to the spiritual heart of their business—to spiritual awareness, the process of living out deeply held personal values, of honoring spiritual forces or a presence greater than themselves in the confines of the corporation. They expand work-life concerns and connect nonsectarian spirit to the "soft" topics of meaning, spirit, and caring. Leaders seek and teach inner peace for self and others.

Stewardship

Leaders understand that their leadership is temporary, held in trust for a limited period. Stewardship is a collective idea. It is only by sharing all their power with followers that leaders help the group succeed. The leader as steward idea is one of whole-group leadership. Leaders may propose plans, choices, and programs, but followers have an opportunity to consent so the actions taken are universally accepted.

Leaders use their power to help accomplish the group's ends, not just their ends. In this way individuals become bonded as a team. Leaders are values stewards, custodians of virtues. They set the values foundation for the group and model these values in their actions. They may set the values foundation, but until followers give their consent to let others govern them based on these communal values, a true leader-follower relationship is not possible. Only when the core values serve the best interests of team members is stewardship possible or spiritual leadership present.

THE SINGLE GOAL OF LEADERSHIP: CONTINUOUS IMPROVEMENT

Leaders help others express their highest growth potential in ways that also generate fulfillment in work-related activities. Leaders tap into as many worker capabilities and resources as they can, not just the few required for the immediate task at hand. They strive for balance among work, family, and professional areas of life. Leadership is by nature developmental (Fairholm 1991). It can only take place in a situation (culture) where members trust each other enough in working together to risk going beyond the safe and sure to the unknown in both institutional and individual behavior.

Leaders seek to liberate the best in people, and we link the best to our higher self. It is a follower development task. Leaders strive to help followers, all stakeholders, make choices about the care of their body, mind, heart, and spirit. They focus on creating and maintaining organizationally healthy people. Leaders seek a state of mind of inner peace for self and others.

Leaders of organizations in all sectors of our society are coming to see enhanced service to stakeholders as a new challenge and a central feature of work cultures. The movement toward increased quality throughout the organization is a cultural challange more than a technological one. While both are important, the prime need is to develop a culture that supports continuous progress and improvement in customer service through the accomplishment of cultural shifts. This task is one of education of the heart more than training of the head or hand. It is a task of leadership and not merely managerial resource control. It is a values-change task that sets up different, challenging expectations for all workers.

Expectations are a kind of self-fulfilling prophesy or Pygmalion Effect. Leaders make full use of (often imprecise) assumptions and expectations as a means to inspire and stretch followers. People usually rise to meet others' expectations of them. By raising his or her expectations of workers, leaders can increase follower efforts to succeed. People who feel their leaders have concern for their personal, individual development and maturation as human beings tend to be more committed to their leader. They will follow a leader whom they feel shows concern for them quite apart from what they can do for the organization.

THE DYNAMICS OF SPIRITUAL LEADERSHIP

This new spiritual approach to leadership asks leaders to behave differently and to seek different goals than former leadership types. It engages leaders in new tasks, new processes, and seeks a unique goal. Spiritual leaders have the task of becoming expert in vision setting and servanthood and, in addition, teaching their followers to be competent in traditional work tasks unique to a given corporation. Spiritual leader task competence involves leaders in helping followers grow, develop, and continually learn. Indeed, the key task in spiritual leadership is building and operating a continuous learning organization.

Spiritual leaders also focus their attention on the process of building a sense of community among their stakeholders. They build wholeness, integrity, and completeness into their relationships with followers. They seek to follow a higher moral standard in what they do. They build team stewardships. The goal sought by these tasks and these process technologies is continuous improvement for the leaders, their followers, and other stakeholders.

The following chapters interpret each of the elements of this twenty-first century leadership approach. The reader is cautioned, however, to remember that spiritual leadership, like all leadership, is a dynamic, interactive process, not a series of separate events. Success in this kind of leadership is dependent on the leader recognizing that leadership is a relationship, not a skill or a personal attribute. A leader's leadership is successful only as he or she develops relationships with their followers that are or become important to the followers and valuable in helping achieve their personal needs and desires.

Chapter 11

Spiritual Leadership Task Competence

As noted in Chapter 10, the organizational environment within which most people live and work today is changing. The transformation we see is from bureaucracy based on control of physical objects to one centered on organizational intelligence. No longer is the focus of organizational activity on the control and management of materials, parts, and product units. Now the focus is on information. Our organizations are becoming learning organizations guided by and using information (intelligence) as the raw materials of production. And our people are becoming knowledge workers.

The era of the knowledge worker places new demands on leaders. It asks of them new kinds of expertise; new skills, knowledge, and abilities that we normally associate with teaching and learning. To be creditable with today's workers, leaders must be in a continual mode of teaching. Leadership is helping followers be successful in their (the followers') terms. It is directing follower attention to the future. Leaders must gain follower trust and, in turn, trust their followers. They need to appeal to their followers' highest motives. Skill in these capacities may have always been a part of leadership. That it is only now being advocated as past of leadership preparation and theory marks a milestone in our progress.

THE LEADER AS TEACHER

Learning, not physical capital, is the ultimate source of all profit and growth. Knowledge has become more important for organizations than financial resources, market position, technology, or any other company asset. Assets key in leadership and, therefore, organizational success are no longer tangible. They are the skills involved in linking solutions to particular needs, the reputation that comes from past success, experience, expertise, and individual and collective capacity. Knowledge (information) is now both the means of production and its raw material. And knowledge (capacity, expertise) moves with individual workers as they move from organization to organization.

Today's leaders need to become designers creating the governing ideas and animating community values to guide individual and group action. Today's leaders are teachers. They help everyone in the team to gain insight through coaching, guiding, encouraging, and giving attention to individuals' mental and spiritual paradigms. Leaders are stewards, in service to their stakeholders, but the service they provide is mental and spiritual, not material and physical as former leadership theory defined it.

The Learning Organization

The learning organization is the wave of the future (Senge 1990). The new way is to integrate thinking and acting at all levels. The learning organization is an adaptive enterprise. The impulse to learn is an impulse to be generative—to expand our capability. It appeals to the spirit and the heart more than to the mind. Leaders respond to their followers' innate need to expand their understanding.

Learning organizations make the company work horizontally. It is a decentralizing trend. Learning organization leaders delegate parts of responsibility to suppliers, customers, and their co-workers. They outsource many of their traditional leadership work tasks. Learning organizations are free; they remove barriers to the free flow of information.

Eliminating constraints on the flow of intelligence is only the beginning. More difficult is creating public motivation and attitudes that inspire people to rise above personal, parochial interests and be responsible for the common good. Learning organizations create the self-restraint and inner spiritual essence that allow freedom to prosper and give it its vitality and dynamism.

Leaders are preeminent spiritual communicators. They are symbol users, whether it is words, songs, speech, or something else. Leaders communicate meaning. They create a community of learning (Bennis 1986). Persuasion implies an interaction between leader and follower, engaging the hearts (spirit) of both. Persuasion, as a form of communication, is different from informing or ordering. It implies equality, caring, and respect for the ideas, logic, and of the central self of the other person.

Fred Koffman and Peter Senge (1993) base the learning organization on three pillars: culture, cooperation, and capacity. The following brief discussion of each may help elaborate the parameters of the learning organization.

Culture

The culture leaders create is intangible, intellectual, spiritual. It is not physical—as in brick and mortar, formal structures, or standard practices. It is spiritual in the same sense a neighborhood is connected to the soul of the people. The basis of culture is human values like love for other people and wonder at the world of opportunity available to us all. Our work cultures—at least those that work for all stakeholders—include values of acceptance of the idea of growth and compassion for all co-workers. These cultural communities are defined in terms of justice, individual freedom within the team, and happiness.

These values replace the traditional will to homogeneity, a characteristic of most prevalent management theories. While cultures unite people and make them whole, they do not have to force everyone into the same mold to promote control. Articulating a shared vision can unite people more forcefully than can company policies, standard operating procedures, and rigid organization charts. Spiritual leaders create cooperative, action-oriented communities that, in turn, provide the environment, the culture, within which leaders can operate out of a sense of spirituality. They engage in teaching and immerse their followers in learning defined as understanding meaning.

Culture defines the communities in which we live and work. It bears on leadership in specific and direct ways. Unless the culture is supportive of the community, leadership based on common values is not possible. Culture determines a large part of what leaders do and how they do it. Culture determines organizational practice and confirms that set of practices. In actuality leadership is an effect of organizational culture and culture a result of leadership (Wildavsky 1984).

The organization is a learning community when both leader and led sense the ever-surprising possibilities that any group of people sharing a collective task generate. Learning organizations are those where members see opportunities to grow in daily work tasks and problems, not frustrating breakdowns to blame someone for. Leaders of learning organizations are humble. They can see the pattern of organizational life as a process always ready for improvement.

The core purpose of organizational culture is to create community. A community is made up of the climate and conditions of mutual trust within which all persons can decide to grow and develop to their full potential as leaders and followers. It is only in a shared learning culture that leadership can evolve, develop, and flourish. In overemphasizing the personal characteristics of the leader, we have ignored the community context that makes a spirit-based learning community possible.

Leaders of learning organizations also show compassion in their relationships with co-workers. Leaders appreciate actions, even those they cannot condone, if they come from people whose viewpoints are legitimate to them. And leaders understand that even those actions which are currently unacceptable may eventually become valid. Through giving their acceptance, leaders may be capable of influencing positively their own behaviors and that of the organization.

Leaders need skills for building shared vision and encouraging personal vision. They must prepare to let go of perfected skills and strategies long enough to develop and cultivate new ones. For example, they need to be expert at communicating and asking for support. They need to lead from their ongoing vision, build extrinsic and intrinsic visions, and distinguish positive from negative visions. Spiritual leaders surface and test mental models. They are systems thinkers.

From an organizational perspective the problem of creation of community is one of leadership. Creating the kind of physical, psychological, and spiritual environment necessary to get others to *want* to follow them taxes leaders' abilities on all levels. The task of creating an organizational community that engages both the intellect and the emotions to attain the best efforts of members and organize them into a unity is daunting. Leadership means fostering and then training workers to accept a system of mutually acceptable assumptions and expectations. As such it is fully within the context of the idea of the learning community (culture). It is a central leadership task. And it is, at its center, a problem of developing oneness, wholeness (i.e., community), out of many individuals.

Cooperation

Learning organizations are founded also on a set of practices for generative conversion and coordinated action. They honor information (intelligence) as the source of corporate life, progress, and internal harmony. Information both informs the individual and forms them. Learning organization leaders understand that information is the building blocks of the modern organization peopled with knowledge workers. They use information they get from any source to inform and shape their organization in ways that build community, foster cooperation, and improve performance.

Information of use to leaders of knowledge workers ranges from history to forecasting the future. It runs the gamut from system and process ideas to detained procedures. Each business unit should look to its roots to rediscover the elements that made it unique. It should reinterpret founding values such as those for individual achievement, competitive spirit, tenacity, and resourcefulness (Blanchard 1993). American institutions, including the business community, can regain their worldclass status if they can build on these deeply rooted values and work toward the goals they foster.

Learning organizations link employees' self-development to the progress of the organization as a whole and to its history and experience. The assignment is developing a relationship-oriented worldview (Mollner 1992). The universe is made up of a vast number of connected parts, each of which cooperates with all other parts. Learning organizations attempt the process of discovering these linkages and connecting past with present and future.

The spiritual leader's task is also to undo much of past leadership theory that focused on the management of objects, not the leadership of people in relationships. These models see the universe as a collection of separate parts, each of which competes for its own self-interests in relationship to all other parts. The modern science of quantum physics, on the other hand, says nature is always cooperative. Competition is anti-nature. Helping today's workers and managers come to see this new physical universal truth and apply it to work relationships is the task of the spiritual leader as head of the learning organization.

Leadership is a process of introducing group members into mature understanding of who they are. It requires credibility in the leader. Spiritual leaders gain this credibility as they relate to their followers honestly, act justly in their interactions with others, and foster cooperation in fulfilling nonwork related needs of the work force (Mollner 1992). Spiritual leaders honor their co-workers. They create ways to let all group members participate in planning, decision making, and management. They let their co-workers feel the joy of participation in the spirit of ownership of the collective enterprise.

Capacity

The leaders' role is as a teacher and a persuader, not a dictator, of follower action. Leadership calls on our ability as communicators. They persuade stakeholders to change their values and the behavior to conform to the vision potential. To be effective, leaders must develop the skills and technologies of collaboration. Leaders must communicate a level of commitment to stakeholders. They must communicate with, inform, and persuade followers to cooperative action; that is, they must teach them.

Without the leader's vision there is no creative tension. Increasing flexibility, not lockstep thinking and acting, is the key to modern success (Senge 1992). Spiritual leaders can see and work with the flow of life as a system as they pursue their collective ends. They develop strategies to increase power in areas of perceived weakness. They struggle to improve continuously (Marquardt and Reynolds 1994). They see work as a continuous process of learning how to create the future rather than react to the past. They relish the unknown. They plan and use reflective time regularly.

The principle of creative tension teaches that an accurate picture of current reality is as important as a compelling picture of a desired future. Time after time we see that solutions to problems emerge not from some systemic approach to a problem but from a sudden leap of intuition and the courage to act on it. The real breakthroughs in technology come not from the human intellect but from the human spirit (Berson 1994). In one survey, for example, only 6 percent of survey respondents from eighteen countries say they never use intuition at work; 45 percent say they use it frequently, and 49 percent say they use it sometimes (The Compass Group 1994).

The role of the leader is to attract and motivate workers: They reward, recognize, and keep them; they train, educate, and improve them. That is, spiritual leaders use learning methods to serve and satisfy workers. Learning organizations are organizations where workers are continually expanding their capacities to create the results they truly desire, where new and expansive patterns of thinking are nurtured. As workers mature, leaders let them govern themselves.

We can define spiritual leadership as a process by which people gain new knowledge and insights to change their behavior and actions. It includes both cognitive (intellectual), affective (emotional), and psychomotor (physical) domains (Marquardt and Reynolds 1994). Leaders become designers, teachers, and stewards. They build shared vision. They design the governing ideas of purpose, vision, and core values, and they design organizations that embody purpose. They bring to the surface and challenge conventional mental models, and they foster more systemic patterns of thinking. They act as coaches, guides, and facilitators.

Leadership is almost solely a matter of attitude. Analysis alone will not generate a vision. A specific leader creates a vision with specific values, in a specific situation, with specific people. It comes from the creative tension resulting from the task of adapting the organization's efforts to integrate new ideas and forms into work processes because of changing external and internal forces.

Continuous learning, creativity, and sustainability are the hallmarks of learning organizations, and the spiritual leaders who head them will lead the corporation into the next generation (Miller 1993). It is a new paradigm, a new mind-set similar to the mind-set change—the quantum leap—of modern physics. Miller (1993) says spiritual values like well-being, truth, inner peace, right conduct, and love directly support established business values like service, communications, creativity, responsibility, and excellence.

Given this reemphasis on dimensions of interpersonal relationships beyond mere productivity, interaction with colleagues at work based on managerial control skills will not suffice for the future. Peter Senge (1990) says the popular system of management is destroying people: rewards are for the ones at the top; punishment is for those at the bottom. Organizational survival today is a function of the organization's ability to run experiments at the margin. The old model where those at the top think and those at the bottom act cannot work anymore. Our work relationships must depend on everyone's inner capacity, from a source very close to the soul (Horton 1979).

We need leadership of the spirit in addition to leadership of the task. Spiritual leadership even goes beyond leadership of the vision of the group. The spirit is that mysterious inner life, the fertile invisible realm that is the wellspring for our species' creativity and morality. It is the core of our personality. We should not give up, neglect, or forget our inner life for a moment, but we must learn to use it, to work with it so that the unity of the soul may break out into our activities (Meister 1994). It is essential that we become aware of the light, power, and strength within each of us and that we learn to use those inner resources in service to our own and others' growth (Kübler-Ross 1994).

To summarize this point, we can only achieve true excellence in leadership by encouraging the self-leadership system that operates within each person. This new kind of leadership is spiritual leadership. It is that leadership that recognizes the inherent spirit in us all and responds to it. Spiritual leadership offers the most practical approach for enabling independent followers. Spiritual leadership is servant leadership. It begins with a natural feeling that one wants to serve (Greenleaf 1977).

The best test of leadership of the spirit is to ask if those who are served grow as persons. Do they become healthier, wiser, freer, more self-sufficient. Do they become more likely to become leaders sensitive to the spiritual needs of others.

This kind of leadership is a holistic approach to work and decision making. It promotes a sense of community and a sharing of power in the critical dimensions of the work interrelationship. It creates a positive impact on a work community instead of using profits as the only motive. Spiritual leadership allows people to turn to the collective wisdom of the total stakeholder group to glean knowledge. Ken Blanchard (1992) says leaders need to admit to their vulnerability, acknowledge there is a higher power, and get their lives in line with it. This kind of leadership sees the whole person and responds to that total follower self.

THE SPIRITUAL DYNAMIC OF TRUST

The thrust of spiritual leadership is toward seeing the leader as a developer, not a controller, of followers. This task is developmental and integrative. The challenge is to mold a follower group into a unified, balanced whole capable of sustained cooperative action. We can view this task as physical, that is, structural, or we can see it as integral in the psychological work contracts leaders and followers make. As such, spiritual leadership asks us to trust our followers and to try to be worthy of their trust.

Trust is an always present, but often overlooked factor in our group and organizational relationships. Unless followers feel confidence in the leader's fairness and trustworthiness they will not continue to follow (Vanfleet and Yukl 1989). Spiritual leadership can operate only when trust among members in relationship is high. Trust is a critical element in defining spiritual leadership or the communities that sustain this kind of leadership. Indeed, it is a key ingredient in all human interaction. Daily living requires us to trust those around us. Organizations also require members to trust each other to function at all, let alone attain excellence.

Trust is central to leadership based on spirit because followers are people who elect to follow leaders. They are not forced to do so. The trust of followers allows leaders to lead. In situations where trust is low, followers reduce their willingness to volunteer to follow. Low trust cultures necessitate the use of control mechanisms to secure member compliance. That is, low trust cultures force us to manage, not lead.

Trust, therefore, is central in understanding the pull of spirit on individual member actions. It is central to the culture the leader creates that allows us to behave with varying levels of assurance that certain actions or events will produce known results. It also prescribes our willingness to trust others. One culture may allow us to trust others more or less than another culture, but without the constraints imposed by the culture we could not exercise trust at all.

Trust is a prerequisite to any attempt by the leader to transform his organization (Sashkin 1986). Vision setting and dissemination depends on trust in the leader. Carrying out vision-based programs requires trust. Trust is the salient factor governing effectiveness in most relationships, and it makes interpersonal acceptance and openness of expression easy. Trust is a conscious realization of one's dependence on another person. It is a central factor in understanding the community's impact on group members.

To trust our leaders means we expect them to assume a stewardship relationship toward those who follow them. We expect our leaders to work for us and to assume this obligation as a primary responsibility. We can identify several dimensions or attributes of trust that help define and delimit this basic foundation of human interactivity. First, trust is both an expectation and a personal debt to be authentic, trustworthy, and reliable. In law, trust is a fiduciary relationship in which one person, the trustee, holds responsibility for the benefit of another in a steward-ship capacity.

Second, common values build trust, and trust is the foundation of cooperative action. The kind of leadership that grows out of shared val-ues only flourishes in a climate within which individuals can accept the individuality of others without sanctioning all of their behavior or words. In a climate of trust, individuals can give open, candid reactions to what they see as right or wrong. In trust cultures there is little ma-nipulation, few hidden agendas, no unreasonable controls, and no sac-charine sweetness that discounts real problems. Instead, there is a congruency in concepts, conduct, and concern; a unity appropriate to group membership that does not risk individuality. Without trust, our collective values can become strictures, impeding individual and group progress.

Defining Trust in Spiritual Leadership

Trust may be the first principle of human interaction. It is the foun-dation of success in interpersonaal relationships. It is central in spiritual leadership. Trust lets us act as if information is true without solid evi-dence. Trust lets us act as if the people we work with are competent before they prove to be. Trust lets us act with faith that a future event or a distant place or a past event are real, actual, and sure. Trust places obligation on both the truster and the person in whom we place our trust. It is constraining to both. It is also a principle of action. Because we trust someone or something we act with assurance, even when all the information is not available. And, finally, trust is a principle of power. It lets the trusting person function in an otherwise ambiguous and risky situation.

Trust is a governing part of all human exchange. It allows organiza-tions to form. It sustains them. Without trust the individual has no de-pendable power in relationships. We cannot expect to exercise control over other people not actually in sight save for the presence of trust somewhere in the relationship. Trust lets us expect that others will do what is asked of them in the absence of direct supervision.

Trust is the cement holding the organization and its programs and people together. It is the prime mechanism for group cohesion. In fact, no leadership can take place without interpersonal trust. And, no leader can ignore the powerful element of trust as they go about creating and managing their organization and persuading stakeholders to behave in needed ways.

We can define trust as reliance on the integrity or authenticity of a person or thing. It is a logical, thoughtful hope in the reality, the au-thenticity; in a word, in the truth of that person or thing. That is, we base value, trust, on a given level of truth. Trust becomes both an expectation and a personal obligation to be authentic, trustworthy, reliable, which is provable by ensuing experience (Fairholm 1994a). Seen in this light, trust is one of the values supporting spiritual leadership that helps define how and in what degree members value others.

Trust is the foundation of success in any interpersonal relationship. Past leadership theory assumes, but largely ignores the idea of trust. It has been conspicuously absent from most discussions of leadership. Nevertheless, it is integral to that set of interpersonal relationships.

Success in our social or organizational life is based on trust in someone or something however intangible and ambiguous it or they may be. Without at least some assurance that the unknown information, actions, and events are real, trust is extremely risky. That kind of trust is, in fact, not trust at all, but foolhardiness. The fact is that all life (i.e., personal as well as institutional life) is always more or less unknown. Trust represents our best guess—and hope—that things are in truth as they appear to be.

Trust is transforming. It is the prime tool spiritual leaders can use to help their followers grow and develop to their potential. Having trust in a person or something (we believe to be true) impels us to change. It lets us act out of our trust. Properly placed trust empowers us; misplaced trust spells defeat. Some level of trust is essential, and present, in any given group. However, the exact level and nature of the trust relationship impacts on that group's capacity to change.

The Process of Trust

Trusting others is not simple or fast. It takes time to fully trust a person or group. It is an incremental process. Each successful attempt immediately reenforces the trust. Successive positive experiences with another cumulate until we fully trust that person. Negative trust experiences produce the opposite result.

Leader trust and trustworthiness are closely related. The less trusting a person is, the less others will trust that person. And the reverse is also true; the more we trust, the more others trust us. Trust is a learned capacity and the best teacher is example. The bottom line appears to be: if you want someone to trust you, you have to tell them the truth, act on that truth consistently, and then patiently wait for the relationship to mature.

Trust is a unifying and coalescing idea. Without it the idea of joint, cooperative action would be unthinkable, let alone practical. Because trust and truth are interrelated concepts, the essential truth we come to believe about another person or event is the basis of our trust. Trust becomes more powerful than charisma, blind faith, the threat of punishment, or the promise of reward in getting others to act for us. Organizations with high trust levels are more competent and unified than other organizations. And this unity eases leadership and vision accomplishment activities of leaders.

The emotional state of both leader and led impact the level of trust in the group. Feelings of apathy and alienation present in the larger society sometimes bleed over into the work community and cause similar emotions among the workers there. Personal self-interest may hamper development of a fully trusting culture. And, too, the personal and institutional risk of loss or failure to meet necessary goals may constrain full trust. Past events also have a powerful affect on our willingness to trust. In these situations an enduring trust relationship may be hard to create.

Trust and Commitment

Personal commitment is dependent on our willingness to trust and our own trustworthiness. This assurance comes from a sharing of spiritual values. People trust whose whom they honestly believe to be committed to the common purpose. It is difficult to scientifically define "commitment," and a precise measure of someone's level of commitment is hard to prove. Nevertheless, commitment is nothing more than doing what everyone can do, but usually doesn't. Commitment is a personal attitude or value that excites us to do whatever needs to be done because we see the need.

Commitment is more than mere identification of intent, it is *doing*. The attitude of commitment flows out of our deeply held spiritual beliefs and values and is part of our (and others') definition of who we are. The spiritual values that shape our personal and social-institutional life and around which we commit our lives are matters many find hard to speak about. While we can recite some traditional shibboleths, their application in our life is less sure (Alfano 1985). But when we find someone committed to values we also espouse, we trust them almost implicitly.

Tocqueville (1956) notes that Americans' habits of the heart are more powerful in describing their individual and group self and behavior than the physical dimensions of their communities, natural resources, or formal institutions. History would lead us to believe that our ancestors connected self and community values in ways that made being true to self synonymous to being true to the community. Today we do not find it easy to commit equally to each level: to individual self-interest and to a community interest. It is hard to commit to both simultaneously. Without resort to our common spiritual foundations, we compartmentalize our commitment. Those seeking to trust us can become confused as they see us behave differently in these two contexts.

The problem is the idea that the sum of individual benefits equals the community benefit. This mind-set has led to a depressing focus on single issues. On the level of the work community the stress between individual and organizational values and goals is great. It has contributed to the decline in commitment and a deterioration of trust in our social systems and our community leaders.

Commitment is a decision of the heart to follow one course of action rather than another. It asks us to select and then to act on that selection and not others, which may have many positive qualities as well. Commitment is a matter of what we pay attention to and use as the basis for action rather than randomly following ideas and actions that may appear tantalizing when considered alone. Commitment is focusing on one set of cultural values to the exclusion of any other value set. It is a decision process that selects one course of action, one attitude of mind, one set of values, one culture to the exclusion of all others.

Commitment is both limiting and liberating. The decision to commit to one course of action forecloses other possible decisions to guide our life. It limits our allegiance to one course of action, ideas, or attitudes. It allows us to govern our actions via known and understood values and models and thus frees us to be our best self within this accepted construct.

Dedication to one value system defines us and prescribes our actions in all of our life situations. When we commit to one partner, other possible partners are out of bounds. When we commit to one value system we cannot honestly measure our progress in terms of another system of values. We should be anxiously engaged in the actions of our times at the peril of being adjudged not to have lived at all. Commitment to life is part of the irreducible formula for living. Not to commit places us on the fringe of life.

Commitment defines in part our spirituality. It gives us focus and identity. To remain "free" and uncommitted, denies us definition. We don't know who we are, nor does anyone else. Being on the fringe forecloses significant action to affect our lives or our social groups. Only committed people play controlling roles in our organizations. We reserve the benefits of membership for the committed. We each need something at the core of our life to which we can devote our whole heart. Something which permeates all phases of our activity. All that we do must relate directly, be influenced by, and be subservient to our central spiritual values.

THE SPIRITUAL DYNAMIC OF INSPIRATION

Inspiration is the name of that influence under which we may be said to receive extraordinary guidance. This definition implies several ideas.

First, it involves a confirmation in the hearts of the believer that the common message (vision) of the group is true. It connotes the idea of guidance to individual believers in their group relationships. Inspiration also is a means of full understanding of the inspiring vision. Inspirational messages are a way for the believer to have communion with other believers. It impels us to do good. It carries with it a feeling of rightness. And, finally, inspiration is a way to teach others.

Inspiration means to enliven, exalt, animate another person. It is akin to motivation in that when we feel inspired we want to act on that feeling. As leaders learn to inspire their followers they can produce more focused action directed to their (or to their organization's) goals. Inspiration goes beyond motivation in appealing to a collective spiritual need. Inspiration appeals to a need to be part of and engaged with others in lofty enterprise.

Inspiration grows out of the interchange between leaders and followers and the community in which leadership takes place. Inspiration is a particular relationship between an individual leader and a group of other people that enlivens the group and impels them with new insight, new emotions, a new sense of spirituality, and new directions. Inspiration is not so much a quality in the leader (the inspirer) as it is a function of the spiritual needs of the inspired.

The Process of Inspiring Others

To inspire someone the leader must appeal to them on a different level than mere motive (internal drives). They also must connect at the level of the spirit. Inspiration is more than rational; it is extrarational. It appeals to the spiritual self, to the supernatural dimensions of personality. Someone inspires us when they take us outside (beyond) our routine ways of thinking and behaving and leads us to another higher level of interaction and focus.

Spiritual leaders inspire followers and provide a helpful setting for this interactive relationship. They provide the climate and conditions within which the leader's personal needs and the particular personal needs of the follower group can be juxtaposed in ways that let the one inspire the other. The community the leader creates provides a broad basis of consensus around spiritual values, the vision guiding group and individual actions, and the ways group members can and should interact with each other.

A central task of spiritual leadership, then, is to create the conditions in the organizational surroundings that ease the leaders' task of inspiring followers to accept and act upon their vision, values, and spiritual longings. Inspirational leaders have high self-confidence, dominance, and a conviction of moral rightness. They transfer these qualities to followers

(See Bass 1987, Peters and Waterman 1982, Maccoby 1976, Nixon 1982, and Burns 1978).

Inspiration is a strong tool in the hands of the leader to reenergize followers and to commit and bond them together in the joint enterprise. Spiritual leaders find opportunities to use this technology frequently. Inspiration has always been either an actual or potential tool in leadership. It is a new concept in the leadership literature. This accounts, perhaps, for its infrequent mention as a legitimate leader technology. Nevertheless, leaders report that inspiration is a tool in values leadership (Fairholm 1991).

Preparing the Follower to Be Inspired

Craddock (1985) says that because inspiration is more a function of the readiness of the group member than of the leader, creating a community high in mutual trust is essential. The leader can only inspire others when those others trust what the leader says and does to be true, right, and appropriate for them. For Craddock, this cultural foundation is a matter of shared history, mutually understood emotional needs, and shared vision.

Past joint relationships provide a history of shared understandings and a reservoir of group emotions. Just as one's personal prior history defines that person, so does the shared past of the organization define the organization. As leaders shape that joint history via culture creation and maintenance, they can help prepare the stage for inspirational relationships.

Shared meanings developed from past associations and past events help the leader understand followers and appeal to them more directly and more personally. From an inspiration point of view, shared past events are most important for the meanings the group attaches to them than for the details of the event itself. They define meanings, important values, and an integrating context that lets both leader and followers trust each other.

Getting in touch with followers' understanding of their joint past allows the leader to appeal to followers on an inspirational, more than rational level. Working from this shared past cultural base, the leader's vision and other messages have greater authenticity. Because of their common cultural experiences with their leaders, followers can more easily recognize both the leader's vision and the meanings it carries. We enhance the strength of the vision or other message communicated to followers by reference to the cultural meanings we attach to our shared experiences together.

Working from the base of a common history of shared cultural values and history leaders can get more fully in touch with their followers' spiritual needs. They can better develop programs and assignments that satisfy followers' personal motives and needs while in the same process accomplish the leader's desires. The symbiosis, thus achieved, pays off for both the leader and those who are led. Indeed, the connection between the leader's message and the personal psychological needs of followers is the essence of inspiration. One is inspiring precisely because what one says impels another to do something out of that person's personal spirituality.

Actions or words by the leader are inspiring because they clarify and vivify what is already in the hearts of followers. In visioning, leaders only articulate latent dreams followers share. Visions become inspiring because of this and because leaders have touched powerful inner emotions and desires shared by others in the organization.

Inspiration is a forceful tool in the hands of the leader to reenergize followers and to commit and bond them together in the joint enterprise. Inspiration is what many in the world call motivation. They mistake the inspirational, emotional element in some leader behavior for motivation from without. The only true motivation, of course, is self-motivation. Motives come from within the individual. When someone else, through their behavior, actions, or words, induces the individual to act they engage in inspiration as defined earlier in this chapter.

What another person does, is, or says, may trigger action to get us to behave in ways they want us to in one of two ways. First, they may induce us to act via coercive means. This is not motivation because it comes from outside the individual. Nor is it inspiration because it involves coercion. Second, they may induce us to feel it important to do what they ask. This is also external force, but a force of ideas triggered by commonly held values. This is inspiration, not motivation.

To inspire means to influence through emotional, even supernatural forces or methods. To inspire is to enliven and animate others. Inspirational leaders stop doubt. They impel people to act without thinking. They refuse the facts by putting words to people's dreams and hopes and giving them purpose and direction. Inspiration is articulating the felt needs, values, and visions of the group. Inspiration is fundamentally a power activity. Leaders use physical and ideological symbols to inspire others. There is an extrarational (spiritual) quality about inspiration.

Chapter 12

Spiritual Leadership Visioning

Values, the leader's and those others helping to define the nature and character of the group led, determine the nature of the leader's relationships with his or her followers. The values shared by all members of the team define not only the character of the corporation, but the kind of relationship that exists among them. Shortell (1985) suggests a model of high-performance organizations consisting of ten characteristics, including a culture that features a willingness and ability to stretch members by appealing to the whole person. Leaders of these organizations maximize learning, take risks, in short, exhibit values-based transforming leadership. This kind of organization and these leaders reflect deep inner spiritual values.

American organizations face challenges in the future, including fundamental changes in goals, forms of authority, core technologies, and marketing strategies. High-performance organizations offer an eclectic particular model for firms seeking to improve their own performance. High-performance organizations do not necessarily exhibit all of Shortell's ten characteristics, but they rate highly on many of the criteria and are aware of all of them. They are vision-centered, and they are concerned with the inner needs of leaders and followers.

Rue (1994) identified seven traits of high-performance companies based on a McKensey and Company study. He concluded that leaders, not managers who relentlessly pursue a vision, drive these companies. They are intense, performance-driven, and demanding. They develop simple structures, provide world-class training, value people skills, and are entrepreneurial within the parameters of their vision. Such organizations and their leaders exhibit a well-defined sense of the importance of people keyed to values and to a vitalizing vision. They reflect, says Shortell, a basic spirituality.

These new spirit-sensitive leaders exercise a bias for action around the common vision. They create a kind of chemistry among top leaders that bonds them to each other and to corporate vision-defined tasks. We often need a particularly spiritual leader at the time of the birth of an organization and at the time of severe crisis. These leaders cope with ambiguity and uncertainty and exhibit a loose coherence around common vision aims or methods.

We cannot confine such crises to global or national problems. A Scout troop can be having a crisis as well as a multinational corporation. At times of stress those involved need a powerful leader or teacher. In such situations they need a leader who goes beyond what is required and who is visionary enough to see the needs of the people around him or her and engages anxiously in a balance of directive and participative leadership (Maxwell 1973).

THE VALUES BASIS FOR VISIONING

More and more organizations are learning to lead on the basis of values-laden visions rather than management by objectives. Before there can be purposeful participation, people must share certain values and mind pictures about where they are trying to go (Senge 1990). Values are the settled beliefs we have that are true or good or beautiful for us. They guide our actions and judgments of what is good, right, and appropriate. Values that work are those that trigger the most intense feelings or rightness in both the leader and group members.

Our values represent those truths all or most members of a community share and know they should seek (whether they do or not) because they are good for them and will result in greater material, moral, or spiritual development. Commonly shared values are the foundation of trust among individuals. Shared values also form the basis for mutual trust among groups, whether nations, communities, or organizational work teams.

As values shape our communities, so too do they shape leadership. The style of leadership adopted (though not necessarily consciously) grows out of the leader's ideas and feelings about the nature of human beings. Some agree with Thomas Jefferson that some—the managers among us—see followers as children and love them with paternal affection. Others—leaders—see followers as adults whom they can prepare and then leave to govern themselves. For still others, either of these views looks excessively optimistic. Yet experience with self-governance teaches that people respond to training, sitting in counciling with their leaders, and the opportunity to lead themselves (Fairholm 1991) with greater trust, loyalty, and commitment.

Leadership by values rather than management by objectives restores people to the fullness of life, especially if we are authentic to our spiritual core values. The best way to lessen the domination of the zealous manager is to enhance the community and the strength of its moral suasion. The spiritual leader or would-be leader is at the core of this approach to leadership (Nair 1994).

We must be willing to openly discuss the spiritual aspect of leadership. Spiritual values are at the heart of our being. We rely on our values when we consider developing our own leadership potential or evaluating the leadership of others. When we believe that service to others is the way to spiritual truth, how can we avoid giving the very best service to our followers and customers when we try to lead them?

Values permeate organizational life. They define organizations and all other interpersonal relationships. They are a main cause of the sense of permanence most organizations enjoy. They also are a prime cause of the difficulty many people—leaders and workers alike—experience in attempting to change organizational structure, process, or systems of work. Yet, most people ignore inner values in their analyses of organizational life. We need, and some organizations are providing, a unified, but this time nonhierarchial, vision of what is an increasingly complex world. We are coming to see a new myth of teams and communities that can lead themselves (Koffman and Senge 1993).

Values define the organization, prescribe its purposes, and provide the basis for measures of success. Values are powerful paradigms prescribing organizational visions and the rules and regulations governing worker actions. Values are enduring beliefs that a specific kind of conduct or a particular state of existence is personally or socially preferable. We prize and cherish them. They are part of a repeated or repeatable pattern of behavior. Individuals freely choose values from among alternatives after reflection. We act on the basis of those values we positively affirm.

Our guiding values typically are part of a system, or set, of variously rated values that guide our life and actions and that make that action conventional, predictable, and useful to us. Most people's values are similar to those of the people around them and in their community. Values form a network of known and shared understandings and norms that we take for granted, and they provide a substrata of commonality in organizational life.

Values guide day-to-day activities in organizations. Ott (1989) equates values with beliefs, ethical codes, moral codes, and ideologies. For Ott they mean the same things as organizational culture. Also Deal and Kennedy (1983) suggest that organizations become meaningful to members only after leaders infuse them with values (see also Selznick 1957). Viewed in this way our values define and describe who we are and why we think we are in life. They are part of, and defining of, our sense of self, our spiritual center.

CENTERING SPIRITUAL VALUES THROUGH VISIONING

Values are an important part of human experience. They can be personal, professional, organizational, societal, or spiritual. Values define both what *ought* to be and what *is* in our lives and cover a wide range of topics. At the core of our corporate spiritual beliefs is the values system of its top leaders. These values often find voice in a vision statement or commonly accepted focus around which the organization and its leaders act.

The vision is the leader's values version of what the organization is and what it should do and become. It sets the direction and limits of the organization's capabilities. It is the crux of the leader's core beliefs about the work, the workers, and the organization's possibilities. The leader's vision, therefore, is a spiritual statement more than an operational one. People commit when leaders appeal to them in terms of their values, needs, beliefs, customs, and practices. The vision encapsulates a common set of values binding people together in a community. Conversely, conflicting values among employees affects work behavior and attitudes. They disrupt and may even destroy community and team structures.

The central unifying theme around which leaders work to accomplish is the vision they create and announce to the group. Vision setting is the most important leader function. It, as no other idea, distinguishes leadership from management. Bennis (1989) suggests that we can summarize the difference in the leader activities of vision and judgment versus the manager activity of efficiency.

Vision is a mental image or understanding of the past, present, and future of the organization. Vision setting is a capacity to see what others do not see. It is a purposeful activity closely connected to the leader's self and institutional image. A vision is the reality in the mind of the leader. It is a truth that is not yet revealed to others in the group. The vision is a source of power for the leader. It is expressed in enthusiasm, desire, and energy directed to activities.

The leader's inner strength does not come from charisma, but from his spiritual self—that is, from what he really is and believes as shown by action. Vision setting is taking some of what the leader is, thinks, and does and sharing it with the organization. The vision comes after the leader learns to know himself or herself and gains confidence from that knowledge. Visioning is the central leadership activity. It sets the boundaries of the possible (Fairholm 1991). Vision is understanding the history and the future as one entity. Vision is goal plus energizing passion. The vision is a reality in the mind of the leader. The task is to make it real to followers.

The vision empowers the leader. Creating a vision engages the leader in a variety of tasks (Bennis and Nanus 1985). One is foresight for achieving a vision that fits the environment. Another is hindsight to ensure the vision is compatible with tradition and culture. Vision also asks the leader to have institutional depth perception to delineate the vision in detail, scope, and peripheral vision so the vision can respond to the aspirations of all stakeholders over time.

Creating a vision asks the leader to create a worldview that interprets current developments and trends affecting not only the local community but also other communities. It is both global and specific. Finally, visioning asks the leader to engage in periodic re-vision to synthesize the vision according to environmental changes. The leader needs the qualities of balance and perspective for vision setting.

Assuming the accuracy of the above summary of the value of vision, it is the capstone of the organization's culture. The vision the leader creates becomes the basis for all other interactivity in the organization. It is the repository of values, the future anticipated, the measure of interim activity and the foundation stone of the community the leader heads.

Creating the Vision

Visions are the guiding principles of the organization (Fairholm 1991). The spiritual leader's success in large part depends on his or her ability to institute a base of loyal, capable, and knowledgeable workers. The leader's task is to generate momentum among these workers and then to preserve that momentum. Much of this momentum comes from the vision the leader sets of what the organization is and ought to be. Strategy, structure, and system are important, but the guiding process is vision setting. Vision articulates a realistic compelling view of the future of the organization. It is the bridge between now and tomorrow.

Creating a vision involves leaders in several specific activities and tasks. The first, and perhaps most important task is self-preparation. Leading on the basis of vision does not come naturally to people. It takes a specific mind-set, specific skills, and specific knowledge. Nanus (1992) identified four skills leaders need to lead on the basis of vision: management of attention, meaning, trust, and self. Gaertner and Gaertner (1985) describe this process as intention setting. Vision setting is a strategic change technology using spiritual foundations to interpret current work processes.

Self-preparation to be competent in these kinds of activities and attitudes asks the leader to be optimistic, confident, assured, and to know what exactly the organization should become. Setting visions is a risk activity, one requiring a secure, confident leader who finds the vision, the tasks, and the organization an extension of self. The task is to define from all possible futures the one that fits the leader at this time. It also should fit the organization, which can be seen as an extension of the leader's personality, goals, and values.

Visions are an amalgam of past, present, and future, but they prioritize the future. They come from the leader's and the organization's cultural traditions. They reflect the combined talents and capacities of the organization including the leader's, and they adhere to the inner spiritual values guiding both leader and led over time. On this base, vision creation assimilates features of the present situation including present capacities, constraints, and limitations as well as new community values, standards, and resources.

The vision's future focus builds on the present and past, and probes, tentatively at first and then forcefully, the possibilities for the future. Small pilot changes in system, process, or program can help lessen the risk of implementation of a new vision for the organization. These experiments begin the new vision culture. They allow for controlled application of the vision in ways that let the leader make midcourse corrections and to refine long-term forecasts.

The genius of leadership visioning is in the leader's ability to assemble a variety of information and form a coherent, values-laden statement of the future *being* of the organization. Leaders realize this goal as they answer questions (Bennis and Nanus 1984) about who has a stake in the organization, possible results of continuation of present or alternative actions, possible value indicators of performance, and actions needed to realize vision goals. Answers to these kinds of questions reveal patterns that may suggest a possible vision.

Vision setting is a process where leaders integrate both inner- and other-directed community factors affecting the team (Pascerella 1984). It is a process of bridging past and especially the present and future potential of the organization. It is an integrating process of uniting cultural values with present interactions among stakeholders. Vision setting makes those values driving forces moving both leader and led to the same future, employing the same methods and measures of success along the way.

Setting the leader's and the group's vision is a simple process, but it's of critical importance to leader success. It asks leaders to create the future for their organizations rather than letting the future just happen. Vision setting is most easily done in entrepreneurial environments because they encourage taking personal authority and responsibility. They encourage enlightened self-interest, and they allow individuals to hone and use behaviors that increase personal and organizational interests. Entrepreneurial organization cultures emphasize authentic tactics and living by example. Bureaucratic organizations, by contrast, emphasize organizational (not individual) self-interest, employ manipulative tactics, and overuse political behavior.

Visioning involves seeking and understanding the forces for change in the organization, community, and broader cultural environment. It seeks answers to questions about individual and organizational roles, service fields, and legal, moral, and social constraints from the extant and possible future cultures. Developing an effective vision requires that leaders know and understand complex economic forces, know the technological state of the art, and be conversant with applicable political policy and processes. Vision setting also asks leaders to be futurists, molders of opinion, and teachers. The task also challenges leaders to create trust cultures where organization members feel free to expose something of themselves without undue risk of attack.

The vision flows out of the ferment of these tasks. The vision thus created becomes the basis for the organization's mission statement. It is a clear statement of what leaders and followers alike wish to be. It is not necessarily what they now are; it is a statement of what the purpose, the dream, of the organization is.

Vision setting requires empirical knowledge of the firm, its stakeholders, and its leaders. Visions deal with change, should be incorporated into goals, and should center on people. The vision must extend beyond the leader to followers or it is ineffective. An organization's vision statement reflects an organization's core purposes. It articulates a practical and a challenging goal that has a significance beyond immediate work goals. Vision statements alter the nature of the relationship among the leader and team members and provides a common purpose for all. The vision is, simply, the reason for being for the group's activities. It serves as a standard by which the organization reaches decisions and makes clear the directions of the group—their horizon outcomes.

Vision statements have a stretch quality about them. The leader must secure member understanding and then tie it to members' specific work tasks. It is a process of securing member trust and commitment to the common goals, processes, and values supporting both goals and methods. In the final analysis, vision setting is the duty of the leader. Members can help, but the task belongs to the leader, who must create or confirm a group vision and to articulate, interpret, and apply it to all aspects of the organization's work.

The vision setting task takes time, thought, and creativity. Preparation is necessary to ensure effective, directed action. Leaders need to prepare by being clear about the purposes of a vision statement and have ideas in mind before they begin to develop a vision statement. They need also to prepare the members of their leadership cluster and other members of the organization who may participate in the vision setting process.

The process involves identifying what the organization does for its employees, clients, the total organization, and society. Selection of the central activity of the organization is not always easy. Even current mission and goal statements may be misleading, often they tell us what we want to do, not what we are. We need to look beyond routine activities to focus on the nature of the organization's tasks, the technology used (or possibly could use), the technical proficiency needed, and the relative abundance or scarcity of resources.

Assessment of personal interests, skills, and areas of commitment is part of this process as is identifying the organization's clients/customers, and matching external client needs and internal personal capacities and interests. Preparation of a formal, written vision statement must await this preliminary assessment work.

The vision statement is a mental image of desired future states that incorporates the central reason for being and the guiding values of the organization and its central leader(s). The vision statement should describe the central purpose for being of the organization, engage people's emotions, be simple and memorable, and provide meaning for all work done in the organization.

A final step in the visioning process is to determine the relationships of the vision statement to various interest group concerns. Members need to see all relationships and how important the statement is to the organization, its customers, and individuals and teams before they will personally buy into it.

Communicating the Vision Intention

A key task is communicating the vision to all stakeholders. Often transmitting this vision message requires judgment, intuition, and creativity. Leaders often communicate the vision by metaphor and models. The task requires enthusiasm, emotion, and passion. Group members need more than just task instruction or even goals. They need a central, guiding purpose toward which they can bend their mutual efforts. Visioning is comparable to setting the superordinate goals that Pascale and Athos (1981) discussed or what Bradford and Cohen (1984) called overarching goal setting. It is, at heart, a challenging, unifying, unique, and creditable statement of what the organization is and can become.

Visioning engages the emotions and the spirit. Visions are value laden statements, not rational statements. The leader's vision carries the strong message that the future will be different. It must be a flexible, overarching tool for harnessing change and making it work for leaders and their organization. The strategic vision ideally should encompass the whole community, the immediate work team and its related units, but wherever the leader is in the organization using a powerful spiritually authentic vision can help him play his role better.

Most vision statements are articulated in a few words that summarize what is unique and special about the organization. It is a guideline all employees can use to focus their individual and collective attention on what the organization stands for. For example, one personnel department decided to focus on providing training and procedures that would enable managers to "manage sensitively in a global culture." A payments department manager selected a vision to "work with clients with an attitude of solving problems with originality."

By themselves these statements can be meaningless. It is only when the leader believes in and constantly talks about them and uses them in all his or her interactions with followers that they come to life, that they become inspiring visions of the present and future for organization members, for the leader, and for followers.

Vision setting is a process of intention setting (Gaertner and Gaertner 1985). Vision intentions are activated by proactive decision choices. There are three levels of intention setting. First is the visionary level, which simply defines what is important, what the leader expects, and how to do the work. The second, the strategic level, communicates the global picture. It is strategic rather than tactical thinking. Use of institutional memory is part of this phase. The third level is the goal setting, which means translating the strategic vision into short- and midterm goals and purposes. Goal-directed behavior is more efficient than nongoal–directed behavior.

Bennis and Nanus (1985) studied organizational leadership to answer the question: How do organizations translate intention into reality and sustain it? He reminds us that before we can translate an intention into reality, we must express it convincingly enough to attract and motivate participants. It must be compelling. Leaders express their vision in ways that achieve two goals: to take an organization to a place it has never been and to have the capacity to permeate all levels and divisions.

Vision is the compelling intention or plan to build creative, long-term linkages from the present to the future, so as to transform the organization's processes in ways that positively affect its capacity and productivity for the future (Bennis 1989, Sashkin 1986). The compelling vision is made up of symbolic forms expressing a tapestry of intentions that gives what goes on in organizations a sense of importance and, notably, connects the organization with the larger world of ideas and actions. Leadership is truly effective when individuals place symbolic value on these intentions and their expression via the vision statement.

This kind of involvement with the whole world motivates and empowers others.

The vision once created must be communicated. Leaders sell the vision by acting on what they talk about and believe. Spiritual leaders use their vision as the primary motivating force for self and others. And they must communicate it continually. The leader's vision becomes the basis for all leader action. It is, in effect, an internal contract with employees to encourage trust, commitment, and innovative effort to realize the shared vision. It is the inspirational basis for the leader.

USING THE VISION

Making a vision statement is one thing, using it is another. The vision is only valuable as leaders work to the vision continuously after they introduce it to the group. Leaders need to use the vision by giving it continuous attention in their words, pictures, speeches, training, promotion decisions, pamphlets, posters, plans, and by their every action to help realize the vision aims. Leaders enhance group trust as they are authentic to their vision.

Sharing the vision unleashes the discretionary power of the workers. Sharing the vision involves motivation, inspiration, and empowerment of others. Acting to make real the vision and not another goal, object, or purpose is the final test of visioning. Visions focus leader attention and the workers on shared goals, methods, and values. The vision is successful when leaders reflect the vision in every choice and action of the entire leadership team and the larger workforce.

Chapter 13

The Spiritual Leadership Dynamics of Servanthood

The secret of leadership founded on spirit is that the leader is a servant first. Many of the problems we have as leaders, or in working with other leaders, result because we often reverse this order. That is, we concentrate too much on controlling others—making them do what *we* want—instead of serving them by helping them be the best they can be in their work with us.

We cannot separate service and leadership. Those who would be leaders must be servants. While a seeming paradox, that is the key to the kind of leadership based on the leader's (and follower's) spirit self. Leadership is really servant leadership (Greenleaf 1977). By virtue of their position leaders have more information and control more resources than followers. They must provide these resources if followers are to be successful. The emphasis in this task, however, is on growth of the people we work with, not just programs conducted without problems. Leadership focuses on the *process* of interaction, not just the results of that interaction.

To be a good leader, a person must first have learned to be a good follower (Litzinger and Schaefer 1982). Thoughtful people in all fields have long recognized this idea. The philosopher's idea of master and slave points out that there is not only followership in the leader, but leadership in the follower. Leadership must assume a spirit of followership when both leader and follower alike are held to obedience to defined principle. Many good leaders—such as Churchill, Bismarck, Caesar, Stalin, Hitler, Mussolini, and Ghengis Khan—were excellent followers, not always of societal norms but of their group's norms.

In the context of an organization, the leader is its obedient servant. The acceptance of common values in an organization forms the link between obedience and command, and leaders cannot break this link without destroying the legitimacy of their rule (as did, for example, Richard Nixon). Followers hold power over their leaders because followers grant authority by either giving or withholding their obedience (Barnard 1938).

America is becoming very suspicious of leaders (Steller 1995) in part because they have not linked leadership to followership. Leaders relate to followers on the basis of their style. For example, transformational leadership is a style of leading in which leaders encourage and develop ideas from all levels. This contrasts with transactional (managerial) leadership. Transforming leaders must serve their followers' interests in the context of the group purpose. Transactional managers serve their own version of the group's interests. Thus, different styles of leadership call for different styles of followership.

Followership is not a second-class grade for those who will never make it to the top. A good leader who accepts also his or her follower role can choose an appropriate followership style. It is a fundamental skill that should be a part of any effective leader's training. The idea of servant leadership suggests that people lead because they choose to serve one another and a higher (organizational) purpose (Koffman and Senge 1993). We all have to lead and follow or get out of the way.

SERVANT LEADERSHIP

Servant leadership appeals to the spiritual and wisdom side of people. It appeals to their intrinsic common sense (Greenleaf 1977). Servant leaders take people and their work very seriously. They value human beings for their own sake, not merely as "resources." They focus on doing good, even if it doesn't pay off immediately (or at all) at the bottom line.

Max DePree (1989) describes the following characteristics of servant leaders:

- Integrity
- Vulnerability
- Discernment
- Awareness of the human spirit
- Courage in relationships
- Sense of humor
- Intellectual energy and curiosity

- Respect for the future and regard for the present
- Predictability
- Breadth
- Comfort with ambiguity
- Presence

Becoming servant leaders engages us in personal, internal self-change and changes our outward behavior—we must become self-leaders. Servant leadership models self-leadership. It encourages self-set goals. It asks the leaders to create positive thought patterns, develop self-leadership through appropriate reward and reprimand systems, and to promote self-leadership through teamwork. And, finally, servant leadership asks leaders to create and promote a self-leadership culture.

Work requires people to perform it and people require work to fully realize their potential. The business exists as much to provide meaningful work to the workers as it exists to provide a product or service to the customer or profit for owners. Given these intrinsic truths about our work lives, truths many people ignore until they are called to their attention, leaders of the effective organization of tomorrow must articulate goals and inspire trust. These leaders will have to learn to listen and take their lead from co-workers as well as lead themselves. They will heal, rather than hurt. Servant leadership is self-effacing. Leaders who see themselves as servants first are stewards, not masters of self, the organization, and their followers. They rely on foresight, use positive feedback effectively, and emphasize personal development.

Servant leaders take their people as well as their work seriously. Kiechel (1992) suggests that these leaders act on the principle that human beings have intrinsic value and that work exists as much for people as people for work. Leaders who recognize the spiritual side of themselves and their followers listen and take their lead from the workers. They intuitively understand that answers lie in the people closest to the work end of the product. Persuasion is the critical skill of the service-oriented spiritual leader.

The foundation of effective leadership comes from the desire to serve and leadership by example (Bethel 1989). In many modern situations, the most appropriate leader is someone who can lead others to lead themselves (Manz and Sims 1991). Employee compliance is not enough. Leading others to lead themselves is the key to tapping the intelligence, spirit, creativity, commitment, and unique potential of each soul for the spirit in us strives to be free to choose for itself. Servant leaders recognize this fact and develop relationships with their followers that serve this follower interest.

We base servant leadership on the idea of *primus inter pares*, first among equals. These leaders involve workers fully in setting organizational goals. They lead by serving subordinates and all stakeholders. They take risks and are creative. They are enthusiastic, and they are driven by ideals and values focused in a mission statement. They use individual gifts and talents, not just skills—all the resources of the collective group.

THE BASIS OF SERVANTHOOD

In one important respect most team members are lay members; they have little specialized expertise in team affairs. Because of this, members accept responsibility to serve in one or more of the jobs required to operate the team including the myriad social and interpersonal roles all teams display. The observer can look with awe at the dedication, commitment, and sacrifice literally millions of team members exhibit daily as they take responsibility for making the many corporate teams successful by serving their fellow team members.

Examples of the service role of the leader is available in most teams. Surely any person holding a leadership position can be inspired by the example of Washington, Jefferson, Churchill, Colin Powell, Martin Luther King, Jr., Norman Schwartzkopf, Lee Iaccoca, and many others. They offer powerful patterns of effective leadership. Their lives and their work provide valuable insight into how we can better accomplish our stewardship by serving our followers. Literature, scripture, professional writings, and theories all may serve as the basis for any discussion of servant principles of leadership. They focus on the importance of leadership and the need to concentrate all of our talents, time, attention, and energies on our responsibilities as leaders of other people. The message is clear: if you would lead the charge the need is to serve others and to do so unreservedly.

Our task is to serve self, the team needs, and our fellow workers with all our heart and our mind and to do so with all of our effort. Three ideas describe the total person: (1) our full spiritual self (our heart); (2) the full faculties of our intelligence (our mind); and (3) in either dimension of self, the challenge is to exert all of our physical energy and skill (our effort).

The team expects its leaders to be diligent and productively occupied. Being idle does not simply mean that we are not willing to perform manual labor. Idlers refer also to team members who are not diligent in the performance of their obligations or responsibilities. It is critically important, therefore, that wherever we serve as leaders that we serve with all our talent, energy, and skill. Leadership is like a calling, and our calling is to serve with our full spiritual, emotional, mental, and physical selves.

SERVICE ASKS OUR BEST: BOTH OUR HEAD AND OUR HEART

Traditionally, we defined leadership in terms of the institutional head. For many the head of an organization is a leader. Many think leaders are those who carry out a program of activities, make assignments, and prepare reports to be delivered on time. This conception more accurately defines our managerial role. All heads of organizations assume a management role involving control over others' behaviors and actions. Not all organization heads can mobilize the spirit and emotions, the values and ideals of their followers.

For most people a position of leadership centers around the management role, its tasks and techniques, in short its technologies. It conjures up the following ideas:

- Controlling interpersonal relations
- Making decisions
- Aligning individual member actions and perceptions with organizational goals
- Directing the effort of the several followers engaged in the work with us
- Ensuring that group activity is timed, controlled, and predictable.

Lumping these operational tasks under the name *leadership* has some merit. One part of leadership has to do with accomplishing organizational goals and with development of the behavioral skills to get others to do the organization's work. It is helpful to the team for the leader to give attention to managerial detail. We should be scrupulously accurate in computing costs or ensuring strict adherence to the intent of the law. While important and needed, there are, however, more significant matters than the mere letter of the law—like judgment, compassion, and faith—that leaders also need to give attention to.

Management tasks are intellectual and skills-based tasks asking the team leader to learn how to manage others and know the laws, rules, and procedures, and the tools, needs, and requirements for program success. There is merit in understanding these control tools and the life experiences that systematize them into strategies that guide action. The managerial mind of leadership is critical to day-to-day success. Some techniques work better than others. Knowing these tools and becoming expert in their use is important. Knowing which rule to follow, which tool to use, can help us attain success in a given situation.

We need to do more than just getting the work done and reporting promptly—difficult as this sometimes is. While important, management is only one part of the leadership role. Spiritual leaders who focus too much on these physical and technical aspects of leadership are in error. More important is the heart, the spiritual dimension, of leadership. Spiritual leadership is the part of leadership that has to do with what individual leaders believe, value, dream, what they focus on, and what they commit to. Our vision, translated to the organization we head, defines its unique place in the larger corporation and in the lives of its members.

The heart shapes the mind of leadership. That is, a leader's philosophy about life and leadership are given substance and meaning by the internal system of spiritual values focused on. These values become a vitalizing vision of the possible. This spiritual heart-vision, in turn, drives the mind and shapes the behavioral—managerial—tools we use. Our behaviors, in turn, reflect and reshape the heart and the mind in an interactive, continuous, developmental dynamic.

Together the heart and mind (our philosophical values and our intellectual skills) shape our behavior—our decisions, actions, and relationships. Leadership is a complex of spirit, intellect, and physical skill in action, and leader acts out of this complex. We can summarize the special characteristics of leadership versus management in the following kinds of statements taken from current literature on the spiritual dimensions of leadership. This list serves only to point out the essential differences in these two concepts as one of focus on people, not task.

- Leaders are to be people-focused trustees and not just task-focused administrators. The challenge of leadership is to be of service.

- Leaders are to be servants of those with whom they serve. They are not to follow the typical pattern of having subordinates serve their managers.

- Leaders focus on others; their orientation is outward, not toward self-aggrandizement and pride. Present conventional wisdom counsels us to look out for self. The spiritual leader, on the other hand, counsels unity and cooperation, a feeling of oneness.

- There is more to leadership than reporting and budgeting. These management tasks are important, but the constant development of those with whom we work is more important. Spiritual leaders would chastise modern managers for too much attention to details of administration and not enough to matters of individual importance to team members as people.

THE LEADER AS SERVANT

Often attempts to analyze leadership fail because the analyst misinterprets the issues. Too often we fail to deal with the leadership task and service orientation, but, rather, with the leader's charisma, power, or wisdom. Some leaders enjoy these qualities but they are not the essence or spirit of leadership. Leadership is the accomplishment of program goals through others and, in the process, helping followers become their best selves.

An orientation toward people, their needs and spiritual maturation, not just on the details of organization, internal cohesion, the punctuality of staff meetings or other administrative matters marks the true leader. While these aspects of the leadership function are important in one sense (they can be very helpful in achieving a spiritual, growth-facilitating atmosphere), they are not the purpose of leadership. Leaders have a profound opportunity by their attitude, actions, and example to help their followers to mature in their talents and their commitment.

Spiritual leaders help their followers. In the work of team leadership, spiritual leaders find many opportunities to enter a helping relationship with team members. The principle purpose of this helping contact is to aid the one helped to appreciate more, to make more fundamental use of his or her latent talents and abilities. Leaders act out the role of Pygmalion. What we expect followers to do and what we help them to learn and know and do, they will tend to continue to do. The leader places ideas and expectations in the minds of followers and helps them make these thoughts (about their capacity) real. People grow in their thoughts first then through actions.

Several aspects of this service role are important. First, our job is to prepare followers for their service in and for the team. In doing this, we act to prepare and then empower them to be of service. The second facet of the job is also to provide help to those whom we have prepared as they do their work. Leaders are facilitators of the work of others via personal help, providing resources, training, or encouragement, or in any of a myriad ways that enhance follower capacity and resources.

A third principle of leadership is that we need to foster growth among team members. Our role is one of transforming self, followers, and the team to achieve the common vision in unique and creative ways. A critical role is to create and articulate this clear and uniquely focused vision of what our organization is and can become. This vision becomes the focus around which all joint action is directed. Fourth, the spiritual leader's role also is to empower followers to lead themselves within the constraints of shared cultural values. This kind of leadership is enabling. It seeks to expand the scope of personal control that followers enjoy in working collectively in the team.

Fifth, leaders maximize follower choice. Leaders set the guidelines and boundaries—by example, precept, and by the values implicit in the team's special version of the corporate culture—of acceptable follower behavior and train followers to conform. That is, we teach correct principles pertaining to each follower's duties and the organization and program that the follower needs to be successful. Then we let followers make independent choices. Leaders do not abridge followers' freedom to make choices.

Finally, spiritual leadership asks us to know ourselves more fully. It is knowing how we "fit" in the team. It is learning how best to serve to promote the work of others instead of doing it ourselves. Leaders are not workers. Leaders do not provide direct service, supply those who do, file papers, or regulate commerce. Nor do they manage, direct, or control these activities as a central part of their duties. Others in each leader's team do this. Leaders do something else. Our leadership job is to pay attention to the central ideas, the vitalizing values, and the guiding visions of the future of our priesthood or auxiliary organization. Our job is to focus attention on the group's central ideas, values, needs, and priorities so cluster members can watch and copy our interest.

To act in this role, we need to change our attitudes toward followers and toward our leadership skills. Leadership is a technology of face-to-face guidance. True leadership is personal and intimate. It is many small acts involving the leader and individual followers in joint action that both value.

THE FOCUS OF THE SPIRITUAL LEADER'S SERVICE

The aim of spiritual leadership is change in the individual. This purpose requires all of us—leaders and followers—to change. In truth the individual leader can do little to impact for good the vast numbers of workers in the typical modern corporation. But, the conventional misconception is that we leaders should try. In truth, the idea of spiritual leadership has most direct meaning to the leader in its application in the team as they try to provide help and service to their portion of the firm's work force.

We often focus on the wrong targets in our leadership. Many spiritual leaders think they have a personal direct stewardship over every worker in the corporation, all of its customers, and stakeholders. A more limited focus is implied—even described—in practice. Surely the corporate CEO has a responsibility toward all people in the corporation. But so does each vice president, director, and unit chief. If we look at who the leader interacts most with, we see a more workable picture of stewardship: leaders interact most often with a relatively small core of immediate followers and colleague leaders—the supervisors and workers making up a leader's team. The leader's prime task is to serve this relatively small number of individual members, leaving them to serve the rest.

We should strive to develop the latent talents of each of the individuals under us so these followers of the leader can also practice the skills and attitudes of spiritual leadership. As followers mature in their work, leaders pull back to allow them more freedom to exercise independent action and to develop their skills and their agency in their assignment and within the overall standards set for the team's work.

Serving Others Involves Earning Their Trust

Implicit in this factor is the idea of mutual trust. Trust is vital to any organizational action. It is the grease that allows all parts of the organization and all individuals to interact smoothly (Fairholm 1994a). Our followers must trust us if we are to lead. We must rely on the good will of our followers to do what is needed. Force, authority, formal structural roles, and other negative sanction systems cannot substitute for basic mutual trust relationships.

Trustworthy people are dependable and deserving of our confidence. Trust implies predictability and stability of position. Followers will only follow us as we prove to be trusted servants. Trust is the basis for the character of leader-member relations, perhaps the most important of our challenges as spiritual leaders. Our spiritual leadership is keyed to the confidence we inspire in our followers. Our followers must trust us before they will follow us. Trusting relationships are empowering to both the leader and follower. Being trusted is motivating, enervating, and exciting.

As leaders we more and more are called upon to develop trust relationships with our followers. Such a relationship is built on many things, among them is the need to articulate clear goals, sound policies, and a basic love and respect for others. Spiritual leadership takes place in a culture supportive of factors like these, factors that are sensitive to the needs of both the followers and the leaders. Leaders care for their followers, they respect them, and like them as friends.

Caring behavior demonstrates trust. Spiritual leaders give their followers as much autonomy as possible given the nature of the work relationship existing in the organization. Spiritual leadership involves trust relationships among co-workers. This is caring behavior. Trust implies predictability, reliability, and mutuality of concern. It integrates the organization into a team. The task is to broaden the scope of trust relationships. Leaders must manage the levels of trust and the scope of trust relationships in the organization as much as they do any other factor of culture.

SPIRITUAL LEADERSHIP IS SERVICE

Spiritual leadership has to do with serving our followers. It is a service. Our job is to prepare followers to provide high-quality, excellent service to the customers we jointly serve. One aspect of our service role is similar to training and education programs managers and leaders have been doing routinely. If there is a difference in these activities associated with spiritual leadership, it is in the effort to prepare the follower to be of service on a wider front. Leaders are facilitators of the work of others. Facilitation in this sense means easing their tasks and energizing and inspiring them to unified action to increase and maintain spiritual services and programs.

The service role casts leaders as stewards in relationships with followers. The stewardship role asks leaders to hold in trust the organization, its resources, its people, and the common vision of the future. In this stewardship role leaders set goals and plan, inspire, and train others to carry them out. Once trained and committed, leaders also share their stewardship responsibilities for action with their followers. In effect, leaders prepare followers, provide facilitating help, and then allow followers to lead themselves within the constraints of the shared vision.

Leaders prepare the way so followers can participate fully in doing the work that needs to be done. People want to make a difference, and if leaders let them and help them do it they (the leaders) gain followers. Spiritual leaders have prepared themselves to assist others in their efforts toward service excellence. This perception of leadership casts leaders as "in service" to others. When leaders see their leadership role as that of servant to their followers they, in effect, go to work for the follower. They provide necessary authority and the physical, operational, and psychological resources and services the follower needs to be effective.

Chapter 14

Emerging Spiritual Leadership Technologies

The movement today is from the age of producing to an age of thinking (Marquardt and Reynolds 1994). Results come more from the heart than from the mind. Tomorrow's organizations will engage the mind and heart (the soul) of workers, indeed, all stakeholders (Pinchot and Pinchot 1994a). The organization that will replace bureaucracy will grant their employees more of the rights and freedoms we now consider normal for citizens in their relations with the larger society and its institutions. These rights include freedom of speech, freedom of press (and e-mail), the rights of free choice and alliances, and the right to make democratic agreements. It assumes workers are thinking contributors, not just physical extensions of the manager's capacities, ideas, and creativity.

There is a move away from the culture of uniformity and rote work to a civilization of knowledge and customization (Pinchot and Pinchot 1994). Europe and Japan are ahead of the United States in this effort. They have moved from faith in centralized power to faith in the self-organizing systems of the marketplace and democratic control. The recent experience in Eastern Europe has shown that centrally planned economies don't always work. But neither do all centralized systems. Many free enterprise organizations are characterized by preplanned economies and they don't work either; that is, they are becoming less competitive in the global market. Something more is needed than just decentralization.

A similar transformation is taking place in America and it is beginning in our workplaces. It holds the promise of revolutionizing the workplace, leadership, and the relationships among leader and led. Commentators are suggesting that our workers are greater assets to organizational success as independent actors than they are as mere cogs in the industrial machine. Especially, as unskilled work disappears, corporate leaders are coming to realize that employees will have to continually use their intelligence, education, and experience in making the decisions that guide their work and determine organizational success.

We need radically new organizational structures to meet the challenges of a more complex and turbulent business world (Mitroff 1994). While we can see some evidence of this change in present-day leadership theory, current application is spotty. For example, William Ouchi's Theory Z, is a popular management approach based on Japanese management systems. Theory Z principles include developing a work culture characterized by long-term employment, unhurried evaluation and promotion processes, and wide career paths. Theory Z leaders involve co-workers in consensus decision making, control work effort through implicit controls of trust and egalitarianism, and demonstrate a holistic concern for people.

As with any other leadership idea, for these principles and processes to work they must first be imbued by top management who can then effectively pass the organization's goal and process aims down through the company. A participatory structure, with appropriate forums, is a necessary and basic element of Theory Z. Also critical to the success of this theory is a strong belief in people and a commitment to excellence. Theory Z ideas run counter to traditional management theory; they partake more of holistic, spirit-based ideas described in this book.

Historically, however, we design organizations around such largely independent, self-contained, and traditional functions as accounting, finance, human resources, strategic planning, law, and marketing. While these functions remain important, today's business environment calls for organizational structures that also address crisis leadership, issues management, global competitiveness, total quality management, environmentalism, and ethics and moral values. Some organizations also are coming to recognize worker needs for recognition of their central spiritual self as part of the dynamics of organizational relationships.

THE EMERGING TECHNOLOGY OF SPIRITUAL LEADERSHIP

It is more helpful today to think of organizations in terms of force fields (Wheatley 1992). Organizations, rather than being characterized by fixed boundaries, can helpfully be viewed as packets of energies leaders can use to gain their ends (Osborn 1994). Spiritual leadership goes beyond the narrow confines of traditional organization theory to merge the values of the larger communities, of which they are only a part, with the work team. Leaders create organizations out of and as part of the hierarchy of cultures that describes modern society. The work organization helps shape and in turn is shaped by the values and ideals characterizing the parent culture.

Accordingly, leadership is a task of culture creation and maintenance, primarily within the corporation, but tangentially in the larger culture as well. The challenge is to build cohesive teams that include workers and supervisors, create and communicate effectively a strategic vision, institute strong intracompany support systems, and create a participative organizational structure recognizing workers' innate needs and desires as well as company needs.

Our programs will stall unless leaders give up their restrictive authority-based power over people. If leaders want to build a better society, the way to do it is to raise both their own capacity to serve as well as their performance as servants of existing institutions, and their co-workers. For something great to happen, there must be a great dream (vision). Spiritual leadership deals with the reality of great vision in everyday—its legitimacy, the ethical restraints upon it, and the beneficial results that leaders want to attain through its proper use.

Human values have a common heritage in our humanity. These values include faith, hope, trust, and love. These core human values are very practical business values as well. If we don't lead spiritually, problems occur. Giving people power is a good idea, but we must couple this grant of power with helping them perfect their competence and conceptual capacities within the confines of the shared vision. When we get into spirituality we risk treading on other people's religious orientation, but the alternative of ignoring core human values in designing and building organizations is equally risky. This philosophy must be made to fit the culture or it may run into trouble.

As we enter a new era of spirit-based transformational leadership, leaders will need to become specialists in a variety of new leadership technologies. While not yet taught in most professional schools, we can see the basis for these spiritual transformational skill areas. These general spiritual leader technologies are reviewed in the following sections. They constitute foundation features of organization and leader orientation upon which spiritual leadership can be practiced. The most crucial new technologies are dealt with more fully in separate chapters.

Developing a Healthy Organization

Most management fads, and no modern leadership technology, will work in an unhealthy organization. Yet, most corporations buy into these approaches without considering the organizational health of their corporation. Healthy companies have a certain vitality and spirit—deeply held feelings of shared humanistic values at the core of the company (Rosen 1992). These values are the anchor holding the organization together. It is a holistic environment, one that nurtures, stretches, and empowers people. Unless these qualities are present attempts to add on new technologies are bound to fail.

Thus, the first duty of the spiritual leader—before attempting to introduce spiritual concepts and relationships on the job—is to ensure that the organizational community is healthy. The key values in healthy organizations include several, perhaps obvious, characteristics. For example, healthy organizations are committed to self-knowledge and development, their corporate cultures include a firm belief in individual decency, and they manifest a basic respect for individual differences.

Healthy organizations exude a spirit of partnership. They have in-place mechanisms to encourage flexibility and resilience, and they place high priority on individual worker health and well-being. Healthy organizations place equal priority on products and process. Review of the literature and observation reveal several specific characteristics of high-performance organizations. These include a willingness and ability to (Shortell 1985):

- stretch themselves,
- maximize learning,
- take risks,
- exhibit transforming leadership,
- exercise a bias for action,
- create a chemistry among top managers,
- manage ambiguity and uncertainty,
- exhibit a loose coherence,
- exhibit a well-defined culture, and
- reflect a basic spirituality.

American organizations face challenges in the future, including essential changes in goals, forms of authority, core technologies, and marketing strategies. These characteristics of high-performance organizations offer an eclectic approach for any institution seeking to improve its own performance. High-performance organizations do not necessarily exhibit all of the characteristics, but they rate highly on many of the criteria and are aware of all of them.

Creating a Sense of Spirituality and Moral Rightness

Three elements are missing from today's organizations: (1) a sincere desire to love each other in a friendly way, (2) an ability to assimilate spiritual values into their work, and (3) the ability to do something physical together. Workers are concerned that their employers prevent them from balancing work and personal life. Employers who ask too much of their people without also giving them a sense of their spiritual selves unwittingly risk eroding employee commitment.

Kostenbaum (1992) developed a four-part leadership philosophy that enriches leadership with a philosophical depth not typically explored in business literature. He says business is a vehicle for accomplishing something worthy and noble to achieve personal and organizational greatness. Leadership requires the marriage of individualism with community—teamwork. Leaders express team greatness in thought and action through vision, reality, ethics, and courage, which make up the four points of his leadership diamond. Each point of the diamond is defined further in terms of professional, social, psychological, and philosophical levels of understanding. The psychological level speaks to the universal human condition. The others deal with work skills, social skills, and the realm of intuition.

Mary Parker Follett, perhaps America's first female behavioral scientist, said progress implies respect for the creative process not the created object. Whether or not we are aware of it, we have left the era of things behind. The era of intangibles is on the rise. Leaders who are conscious of the spiritual force guiding all people can expedite this change. These kinds of leaders create knowledge, give attention to work flow, and interpersonal processes, create the right organizational environment, and they do not neglect the human side of change.

We cannot manage people into battle. We can only lead them to engage in life-changing activities (Flower 1991). Involvement at this level takes a different kind of courage—the willingness to change and grow in order to serve one's organizational goals and values. We cannot solve our problems with the same mode of thinking that we used to create them. Yet, people are still trying to change the wrong things; they want to change content, not context.

Content deals with symptoms, the cosmetics, the surface issues that we can see, hear, touch, and smell. Context, on the other hand, concerns the things we cannot touch; it is about the things we feel. Context shifts in the organization will not occur unless those who are influential in the system go through their own personal transformation and raise their own consciousness. This is the rising task of leadership in the twenty-first century.

The workplace is moving from physical objects to ideas; from the material to the creative. We will begin to see the quality of work life improve as our attention shifts from just profits to the process of work and our relationships within the work setting. The true leader can see situations in different ways and then bring alternatives to consciousness so people can appreciate them. The real goal of enterprise is the mental and spiritual enrichment of those who take part in it (Nirenberg 1994). Hence, the popularity today of empowerment programs. Leaders use empowerment programs to enable followers to engage more of themselves in the work of the firm. In this way they convert the organization to a team-based culture. They reengineer a new matrix structure and companywide cultural change (Bechtel 1994). They bring about a true transformation—a shift in context.

Fostering the Intelligent Organization

Employees are called on more and more to run their areas of work like small businesses. Workers will be far more efficient if they have a hand in designing their own work than if management designs it and hands it down for compliance. Teams can work only if their customers are free to choose between alternative vendors, alternative products, alternative methods of production, sales, and use. They must be informed to be free. The intelligent leader and work force is the key ingredient in successful spiritual leadership.

Tomorrow's intelligent organization will be characterized by choice (Pinchot and Pinchot 1994). Expertise in independent decision making and a work environment that aids freedom to choose is essential to workers in intelligent organizations. Worker free choice will require an organization characterized by widespread well-informed people who know the truth and have and exercise rights to its unrestricted use in doing the organization's work.

The intelligent organization worker will be a kind of entrepreneur—deciding when and how to do needed work independent of tight control and managerial oversight. They will function as free enterprise entrepreneurs working alone and in liberated teams. The movement we see is from control to collaboration, from top-level control to individual responsibility for the whole. The focus today is on the caring community, a community of common concern and rules of fair play.

Individual (not group) equality and diversity, the absence of fear, flattery, and power-based office politics (Fairholm 1993), and adoption of voluntary learning networks will predominate in tomorrow's workplace. It will be a culture of democratic self-governance, of limited corporate government where workers will have the information and intelligence they need to make independent choices to move the corporation ahead individually, unrestricted by a management overburdened with detailed rules, regulations, and procedures and policies imposed from above.

Freedom is the product of people's capacity to go to the core of their self and evoke new and ennobling patterns of meaning and significance. Tomorrow's intelligent organizations will be communities that develop their people within the freedom of responsible communities (Pinchot and Pinchot 1994a). They develop their intellectual capacity to execute their missions effectively, and they experiment with new forms of self-rule.

Global Facilitation

Leadership is necessary globally in the geographic sense, but also globally in terms of the whole person as team member. According to Bennis (1994) we can characterize international leadership by technologies of coaching, stewarding (stewardship), empowerment of all concerned, and alignment with a common vision. The same ideals are needed within teams. Leadership also requires routine technologies and skills like language ability and other cross-cultural skills. Advancing business globally asks leaders to create a learning, inquiry-based, and reflective culture. It is a matter of heart, not head.

Facilitating organizations from a global perspective may require leaders to abolish formal organizational structure and substitute teams. Undeniably it asks them to cut across boundaries and form strategic alliances with a variety of new people and groups. Leading global organizations asks leaders to use their own ideas to gain a broader perspective of the work they do, to create borderless satellite systems of partners who are even free to sell to competitors.

Leading in a global culture asks leaders to connect with others, whose support may be vital to their individual as well as the group's success, on a basis more deeply held than system, structure, or even, culture. It will require leaders to connect with others in terms of their deeply held values and sense of their spiritual self. These aspects of self ultimately form the motivational basis for human action. Leaders who aspire to lead culturally different people must first come to understand them at the level of their core self. Then, leaders can accommodate differences of procedure, language, and system. But until we make the connection between spirit and practice, these surface differences can become insurmountable.

Enabling Workers

The key to spiritual leadership lies in the idea of enabling followers. Empowerment is not mere delegation of some of the work to a follower. Nor is it an attempt to make followers happy. Empowerment is *enabling*, it is enabling followers to be and do their best. It invites more of a person's heart and mind to the common work. As leaders enable followers by giving them more autonomy and more opportunity for eternal progress (continuous improvement) of their work practices, they must deal with the spirit in others. The foundation of enabling rests on leaders' belief and inner commitment that followers are valuable and will magnify their job without undue control.

Enabling followers does not mean giving away leadership power. Rather it involves adding to the capability of co-workers by developing their capacities for action. Enabling followers appeals to their innate values of independence, self-reliance, and individualism. It allows people to actualize their inner capacities for good through interesting, challenging, and responsible assignments. Enabling others involves creating situations where followers can be self-motivated and not intimidated. There are three fundamental steps in enabling others. Leaders must (1) take action to maintain follower self-esteem; (2) listen and respond with empathy; and (3) seek follower help in solving problems, making suggestions, and contributing ideas and information.

The soul of enabling is to offer help to followers without taking over their responsibilities. Serving others is in reality a process of enabling them to do what they can and often want to do because leaders have given them a new vision and released some of their ability to decide for themselves. Enabling is a continuous process involving explaining the purpose and importance of the job, showing how it is done, observing the follower as they do the work, providing specific feedback, expressing confidence in the person's ability to be successful, and mutually agreeing on followup activities. People want to make a difference, and if leaders let them (help them) do it they gain followers.

There is some risk inherent in enabling others, in releasing the power potential in followers. It requires leaders to have faith in the essential goodness of their followers—in their talent, commitment, and capacity to do work independently and in different ways than we would do the work. This is a different mind-set than secular leadership or management. It requires us to be a teacher of others as we communicate understanding of and commitment to a common vision of the organization's future.

Empowering others begins with goals. Empowerment requires that we set the vision, communicate it broadly, and provide information to all followers about the organization, its purposes, processes, accomplishments, and its shortcomings. In effect, we become a facilitator of the work of others. The leader goes to work for the follower, providing all necessary authority and the physical, operational, and psychological resources and services the follower needs to be effective. And, we must be prepared to have the work done in ways different from how we would do it. It is possible that the work will be done better. It is conceivable, at least in the beginning, that it will be done worse. It will almost always be done differently. Acceptance of the need for flexibility in method and even in results is part of our preparation to enable our followers.

Creating Healthy Workers

Whether we address the spiritual side of people head-on, as some CEOs are now doing publicly, or whether we mask it in wellness and employee assistance programs, business is giving more and more attention to the other side of workers' needs—to their inner spiritual needs. Many corporations developed fitness programs originally to counteract financial losses to the company due to health-related expenses (Aguilar and Crossley 1982). Leaders are finding, however, that these programs increase morale and commitment as well.

Whether the programs deal with career development, personal wellness, or they involve flexible benefits, compressed work weeks, flextime, or telecommuting, they undeniably focus on the whole person. The payoff in personal need satisfaction and personal control over work lives far exceeds the material advantages touted for these programs.

Recent research provides information on the assessment of employee benefits relative to participation in a corporate fitness program. The potential benefits most highly rated by workers themselves include the following factors.

- A chance to learn new skills
- Participation mentally shortens the workday
- Wellness programs break up the daily routine
- They help employees develop self-confidence
- They help employees make new friends
- They improve employee emotional health

It is remarkable that employees found significant these nonproductivity aspects of the programs, elements that their managers were unaware of.

Both participants and nonparticipants gave high ratings to the improvement of physical health, the relief of tension, the increase of mental alertness, and the betterment of health and education. Given low ratings by both groups were ideas related to time management, competitive advantage, and, even, improvement of leadership ability. From these findings it is evident that economic savings is not the only benefit of fitness or wellness programs. Wellness programs feed emotional and spiritual sides of employee personality as well as physical ones. They may help improve morale, motivation, and overall satisfaction.

Creating Esprit de Corps

Esprit is having a positive experience with corporate purpose (Channon 1992). Unfortunately, there is little experience of esprit in most corporations today, and we can say the same things about the larger community. Increasingly expanding and complex communications technologies have atomized our social culture. There is little opportunity anymore for individuals to talk together without a specific purpose. Yet we need this kind of nonspecific, informal interaction in order periodically to fine tune the group for greater cooperation later during times of distress.

In ancient times tribal councils provided this need for communication to build community spirit. Unfortunately, there are few organizations who provide for employee councils where institution-building (as opposed to task-accomplishment) dialogue can take place. Today's quality councils or circles get at some of this lack in modern culture as, perhaps do, self-governing teams. But, unfortunately, few modern corporations make room for these team spirit-building councils in their normal work day.

Today's business meetings ignore the traditional features of councils that encouraged a sense of esprit. Where traditional councils provided an equal chance for each participant to set the tone, today's meetings do not. They focus too often only on information transfer. It is no longer typical to use business meetings to vent members' spiritual, emotional, and cultural proposals. Nor is full disclosure of the truth without retribution a characteristic part of today's business meeting and policy councils.

Success in today's organizations will involve leaders and followers in more interactive meetings where the topic of discussion is what goals to seek, how members will work together to achieve these goals, and how they can be happy and satisfied in doing the work. Workers will not stay in jobs any longer where their leaders do not overtly recognize and use their individual talents. They will not stay unless their leaders give them opportunity to participate fully in these kinds of corporate decisions. Leaders will need to pay attention to the spiritual side as well as the technical side of employee competence.

Building esprit involves seeing each follower, customer, or client as an original. It is leadership that relates to each follower in ways that enhance that individual. This kind of esprit leadership requires the leader to adopt a mind-set that values people. It requires specific behavior that actualizes people's values. These leaders will find ways to let followers—all stakeholders—become involved in institution-building dialogue. It is in this way that leaders build esprit and get followers to commit to the work community.

This behavior is, perhaps, best illustrated in the counciling-with relationship (Fairholm 1991). Spiritual leaders sit-in-council-with followers in joint action to accomplish group goals and to define and value the corporation as an institution and as a vehicle for producing needed goods or services. That is they *council-with* as well as *counsel* followers. Counciling-with is a sometimes neglected interaction relationship between leaders and followers where followers act as a kind of advisory council, collaborating with leaders on matters of policy, strategic decisions, and overall work guidelines.

Building esprit involves leaders in counciling-with relationships in contacts with individual followers, not just with committees. Leaders seek out opportunities and systems to share planning, decision making, and work methods determinations with team members as individuals on a more or less equal footing. Perhaps we can summarize the most significant definitional characteristic of leader behavior in the idea that leaders respect others enough to council with them in much of what they, the leaders, do. This is caring behavior.

Caring behavior includes common courtesy toward others, listening to understand, and otherwise showing respect for the ideas, actions, and opinions of others. It is seeking out stakeholders and asking their counsel as part of the communication process. Leaders who value those they work closely with have a penchant for close interaction with them. This technology builds quality, but, more importantly, it builds a sense of common spirit.

The sitting-in-council-with relationship puts the leader and follower together on an equal, sharing basis. Both—either—may propose the agenda, present ideas and methods to solve group problems, or suggest new or altered program plans. Counciling-with relationships operationalize the idea of esprit. Counciling-with is the mechanism for spiritual leadership, and it describes a mutually affecting relationship in which leaders and followers engage in joint consultation, deliberation, and advice-giving, a by-product of which unites the group in strong bonds of love, caring, and respect.

Setting Vision

Leaders create the future for the firm. They develop and articulate a corporate vision. That is, they articulate a clear, attractive, compelling prediction of what life, the firm, and the individuals involved can and should be like. Spiritual leaders continually communicate that vision, focusing member attention and energies on attaining this desirable future state of being. They bring a sense of continuity and significance; they help the group see the present in the past and the future in the present (Bennis and Nanus 1985). This technology is essential to spiritual leadership.

Celebrating Successes

Building corporate spirit involves leaders in activities that increase the mutual bond among employees and between employees and the corporation. Part of this task is creating meaningful experiences for individuals, groups, and the full corporate body. The intent is to motivate, inspire, and recommit individuals to agreed upon tasks, methods, and visions. Leaders should present important ideas (visions) passionately and spiritually if inspired action is to result, and they should celebrate any success in reaching toward that vision.

Frequent group gatherings whose primary object is to recognize and honor the individual performance of stakeholders help create and maintain this mutual bond. Celebrations take time to acknowledge a job well done and the success of the organization or individuals. Celebrations bind the followers to the common cause. Experience suggests that celebrations need not be elaborate or formal affairs, but they need to be heart felt and directly pertinent to known behavior by an employee that is in line with the vision, values, and culture of the organization.

Celebrations can take place at any time. Often they are rewards at the end of a period of hard work on a project. Leaders can reward (in celebrations that deliver the best regards of top management) their employees whenever groups or individuals exhibit exemplary behavior in hard work, creativity, imagination, or foresight. They mark employee activity in going beyond the call of duty. Rewards given at these celebrations are often simple and fun, but leaders need to relate them to the actual interests of the people involved. Reward celebrations are a way to dramatize the leader's commitment to the organization vision and the acceptance of that vision by individual workers.

Putting Spiritual Values to Work

There is a pressing need for stability and spiritual values in America today (Garton 1989). Leaders should seek out people who place more value on the spiritual side of life than on materialistic values (Walker 1989, Miller 1992). Spiritual leadership is also a matter of values and ethics. The ethical dilemma is in leading in this transition period from material to spiritual values.

Being ethical is the role of the leader as a trustee of the future. Being ethical is a challenging task that cannot be measured only by productivity, profitability, or product sales. It is a function of positive, helpful relationships among the people making up the organization. Primarily, leaders who take charge, set the moral and spiritual climate, and who are accountable for actions and results, manage the business of being ethical.

Ethical behavior flows from the ability to distinguish right from wrong and the commitment to do what is right. Being ethical creates a climate of ethical expectation. The best way to teach ethics is to practice them. As a society we have realized the powers of Genesis, but have the ethics of Faust. The new ethic requires the growth of those who do the work. Moral standards such as the Golden Rule have been a part of civilization from the beginnings of human community. This moral code is a part of many societies besides those governed by Judeo-Christian ethical values. For examples, the Mayan civilization version of the Golden Rule is "I am another yourself." The Iroquois Law of Leadership is that "in every deliberation the great leader considers the effects of his decisions on his children, his children's children and unto seven generations."

Any organization involves an exchange of values. Spiritual values are present in people and are part of the exchange people make with the organization. These core values include inner peace, truth, right-conduct, nonviolence, and reciprocal love. Becoming more spiritual is a process of learning to respect others as we respect ourselves. The social problems we confront at work—or in other social contacts—are the result of not learning to get along with each other. In the material world we don't make much progress without planning and work. In our spiritual development we need to do the same. We can't expect much progress without setting up goals and ideals.

Given the above, a legitimate question is: Whose values should leaders teach and use? Some values seem to me to be self-evident. They are reflected in the everyday experience of people of goodwill the world over. We commonly include them in lists of core values in America and in most other societies in the world. Perhaps we can begin to establish an ethical foundation for leadership that appeals to the inner soul of people with the following list:

Noboby considers it moral to abuse children.

Nobody considers it moral to rape.

Nobody considers it moral to steal.

Nobody considers it moral to commit murder.

Nobody considers it moral to discriminate.

Nobody considers it moral to be disrespectful.

Nobody considers it moral to lie.

Nobody considers it moral to be dishonest.

On the other hand, most people think it is right and proper to:

care for and love family and friends
treat all people fairly

respect the right of all to free moral choice

be bone honest in our dealings with others

conduct our lives so others will see us as trustworthy

Leadership sets the standards for performance and ethical behavior, and leaders enforce these standards by both edict and expectations. When our collective will is to peace and justice, conflict will no longer be an option. Successful teams have an expectation that their relationship with their customers will be personally satisfying, that allowing people to be all they can be and not worry about struggling day after day will produce the best bottom line both for the company and for its people. People in organizations need to be truthful, open, and respectful with each other. When they are, both the organization and the individual prosper.

Chapter 15

Building Community and Individual Wholeness

Leadership means building a responsible workplace community. The work organization is really four communities. It is a system of structured relationships. It is also a network of human resources integrated into a complex of work tasks. Work organizations are political entities, engaging members in a series of competing power relationships. And, perhaps most importantly, the organization is a culture with its own symbols, mythology, rites, and dominant people. Work cultures act to attract or repel workers to the group's purposes, methods, and goals. Workers choose to associate themselves with these work cultures, to engage actively in actions to further the group purposes, or to withdraw. Whatever action workers take is in part, at least, dependent on the strength of the sense of community instilled in them by the leader-created cultural community.

The task for leadership in the coming century is transforming work organizations into viable communities capable of attracting workers with needed skills and talents. Building attractive workplace communities counters present trends to worker anomie and alienation. A sense of community invigorates workers' lives with a sense of purpose and a feeling of belonging to an integrated group doing something worthwhile. Leadership is in large part about creating an arena in which competing interests come together and through negotiation strike a deal, as long as that deal does not intrude on what the organization stands for symbolically.

The recent quest for personal freedom—stemming perhaps from 1960s philosophies—has led workers to devalue many or most of their group commitments in the mistaken hope that it will liberate them. In fact the record is clear that the overfocus on independence has deprived us of the richness of shared community. It has devalued the mediating institutions in society—home, family, religion—that best foster personal development and real independence. And it has reduced leadership to mere coordination of factional groups, each of which is responding to a different, but equally acceptable, social agenda.

This situation makes real leadership impossible. Leadership takes place only in a context of mutual trust based on shared vision, ideals, and values. Leadership is in part the task of building harmonious, collaborative teams as well as the task of leading them. Few present local, regional, national, or global organizations can boast of these qualities and characteristics, hence the dearth of authentic nationally recognized leaders. Leadership happens within a context where both leaders and followers can be free to trust the purposes, actions, and intent of others.

We do not develop a trust culture as a byproduct of routinely developed and changed work programs. Trust is not a "new program" nor is it the result of a series of new programs. People will not continue to offer their commitment to leaders who continually present new programs, which are really versions of the same basic paradigm, to accomplish the same task. Rather, a trust culture is best illustrated by member actions that implicitly or explicitly prioritize values and are conducted consistently in terms of those values.

Rather than seeing the leader as a facilitator of the independent actions of individual members or subgroups, the true leader is a creator of community. Leaders create cultures to bond members in joint action based on the shared values of members. The central task of leaders, one essential to its practice, is to select one vision and one set of values to support that vision from the many possible future directions the organization might take. Leaders make one unit or group out of the many individuals. The task for leaders is to focus the group. It is a tack of reducing the possible courses of actions, methods, and outcomes, not enlarging them.

Leaders relate to the organization as a community. They build a sense of oneness by creating cultures consonant with the shared values of group members. Leadership is reductive; it makes one (team, group, organization, family, town, club) out of many individuals. Leadership focuses on one vision, one product or service mix from the many possible objects of joint activity.

Leaders see the organization holistically as both an economic enterprise and a human system. They work harmoniously with others in mutually beneficial interaction. They do all that they do in ways that bring both self and others satisfaction and peace. They treat each person according to his or her individual needs, while maintaining an attitude of unbending intent. Leaders avoid factions within the group. They define new ceremonies and rituals that bring people together.

The present resurgence of interest in flexibility, cultural inclusiveness, and full acceptance of difference in individual group members is antithetical to community—and to leadership itself (Fairholm 1994a). While emotionally attractive, it is operationally toxic. Leaders build group relationships, not just membership. They create bonds that fulfill deep individual needs and the purposes of the organization. They create corporate spirit, a spiritual force that honors high performance, compassion, empathy for others, and individual contributions. But, it is a focused force that builds wholeness and drives out factions. Both leaders and followers must serve both task and human needs. The current increase of interest in unrestricted acceptance of diverse groups is destructive of the community leaders need to practice their leadership. Group diversity destroys community and without community coordinated action is impossible. We follow leaders who care for us, empower us, represent desired goals, methods, or objectives. We follow people whose values and ideals match our own. In the absence of shared reasons that let followers volunteer to enter a relationship, leaders must manage and control followers in what most people would describe as restrictive, punitive ways.

People do not follow because of an imposed structural relationship. They do so out of choice because they think the relationship will strengthen them in some definable ways. The organization head can practice management based on externally imposed control and compulsion, as is most often the case in work organizations, but this is destructive of community. The key to effectiveness is in an organizational context where leader and led share values and vision.

This kind of community is a powerful force. It directs the life of members both as individuals and in their relationships with others within the organization. The communities in which we have membership act as emotional paradigms that can block acceptance of alternative cultures (Barker 1992). Community values can isolate the individual member from other cultural associations. They also can unite individuals into strong coalitions of mutually interdependent teams. The key to attaining this latter result is the strength of community the leader builds.

Finding a values basis for community building is the preeminent challenge of leaders today. However, the task is not so daunting as it may appear. As noted in Chapter 14, the fact is that most people share certain principles and truths in common. These principles and values transcend culture, race, religion, and nationality. They represent something more than mere preference or belief. They deal with the central self, the spiritual self. They provide a common bond upon which we base our trust of other people and a measure by which we can rate their actions. These common core values provide the foundation for building community in the team and for helping team members find personal integrity and wholeness.

BUILDING COMMUNITY

Holistic, spiritual leadership is no longer a choice. It is a need in today's world (Pinchot and Pinchot 1994). It is leadership, not management, that makes the differences we need to cope with this changing, global, complex world. The problems that many American organizations now face are not due to temporary downturns in the economy. Rather, they are a vivid testimony to earlier, now obsolete, ideas and principles of organization and management (Mitroff, Mason and Pearson 1994).

The time has come to employ new organizational designs. We need to focus on interactive communities of enabled, moral leaders and followers. We need to engage the people making up these communities in meaningful work, in work that ennobles them and their colleagues and customers. Our workplace are communities in which many of us live much of our productive lives. We need, therefore, to know what we can about how to make work communities not only productive, but personally inspiring.

Bureaucracies no longer can do this. They so segment responsibilities that work becomes a departmental, rather than a universal, responsibility. We need new structural forms and new relationship patterns. Today's challenges are beyond bureaucracy; we need corporate communities. Such communities use the full capacities and intelligence of workers by letting those closest to every problem have responsibility for finding solutions and acting. The work (or other) community serves as the vessel of vision, values, and mutually helpful connections that guide individuals and firms. The role of leadership in community is to change the people.

Service to a sense of community plays a critical role in the development of spiritual leadership potential. The central task of the leader, therefore, is to be a creator of community. This task counters the tendency to worker anomie and alienation. These corporate spirit communities are characterized by a willingness and ability to focus on group member development—to stretch them. Community members typically engage in continuous learning or development. They take risks to attain desired personal and group goals.

DEFINING COMMUNITY

Community is from the root word *commitos*, meaning *with unity*. Community-focused organizations operate at the level of heart, the central moral self. Community develops out of shared vision, beliefs, and values. Leaders build workplace community by providing this common vision. No community (society) can function well unless most members behave most of the time because they voluntarily heed their moral commitments and social responsibilities (Etzioni 1993). Leaders focus on this kind of unity in their organizations. They strengthen and use organizational culture and they define new ceremonies and rituals that bring people together to form communities. In sum, leaders transform work organizations into communities.

We can define the corporate community by ideas of authority, bureaucracy, competition, power, and profit. After all, the work community is a formal organization like any other organization. The sense of community, however, adds thoughts of consistency, democracy, cooperation, interdependence, and mutual benefit. Modern corporate organization and social theory and practice have separated us from traditional communities—family, farm, the land, the neighborhood. The family and the small social neighborhoods of the past recognized and legitimized spirit. Modern artificial social and work structures have divested the modern organizations of a place for our spirit or soul.

Free individuals require a community that backs them up against encroachment on their sense of independence by society's formal institutions including economic ones. The resurgence of the idea of community is a reaction against a controlled social process that robs people of their sense of self and substitutes a senseless conformity to sterile, abstract, and spiritless systems.

Pinchot and Pinchot (1994) say workplace communities serve as the mutually advantageous connections that guide individuals and teams. Community is intimate control by the team, not control at a distance, which may be amoral and gives little attention to the quality of life of the local people or their long-term future.

People want involvement with the group. They want to share in plans developed, decisions made, and actions taken. In one study of why people leave their jobs, the top items were related to this need to be an integral part of a team. People apparently move to work situations characterized by open communications. They want to be in work communities that give proper emphasis to personal and family life considerations. People want to be full members and to be considered whole people. And they want meaningful work that advances the overall good. They want their individual needs met for development and growth.

Community means caring about members' lives, their growth, their competencies, and their happiness as inherent values, not for just what they may do for motivation and, eventually, the bottom line.

A workplace community, as opposed to an organizational unit, allows for work to be creative. Creative work is work with a deep sense of life-purpose. It is work that lets people feel they are making a difference, producing meaningful results, and living fully. It is work that allows people to live with integrity and develop a sense of sacredness in their relationships. This kind of work turns the organization into a community where everyone can learn and grow.

CORPORATE COMMUNITY

Sometimes responsibility to society is a counterpoint to business success. Not everything that counts can be counted, and not everything that can be counted counts. Yet, business based on these values is creating the culture and the community today in which our children will grow up (Gaster 1992). As people come to recognize the power of the corporation to shape not only their own lives but those of their children, they are forcing business to change—to be more accommodating to spiritual values.

For this generation, the search is for soul, self, and meaning wherever we can find them. And the workplace is not out of bounds. People are looking today for who we are as people, and the meaning of work in our lives. The number of managers who feel that the key to the future depends on developing a value system emphasizing cooperation and the improvement of the total community has more than doubled in the past ten years. Knowledge and intelligence are the new basis of wealth (Handy 1994).

The time has come to attend to our responsibilities to the conditions and elements we all share, to the community. The corporation may be the modern community. The modern workplace has evolved into a community of sorts that satisfies the need for belonging to a larger group. It continues to evolve into one where people can exercise their soul along with their expertise. We should not confuse this search for the spiritual in our work with the idea of business operating as religious institutions. Rather, it is a movement back to community as a source of values that honor intimate personal aspirations to be the best we can be not simply corporate goals.

Half as many people paid twice as much as producing three times as much may be a formula for productivity, but it is not very exciting for the half who were downsized (Handy 1994). Available evidence suggests that the working half are experiencing symptoms of stress. As a reaction, there is a movement toward the idea of the corporate village. The central feature of the corporate village is that it effects not just a limited narrowly defined set of economic values. It is a social entity where employees, customers, and stakeholders get both value and values to give direction and meaning to their lives. Leaders of the corporate village are instruments by which all stakeholders can define the values important to them.

A key skill in leadership of community is in developing a vision. Vision implies imagery. It is a continuing process that is almost tangible. It is a feedback relationship, and it shows the flow of the links of value from the heart of the business to the customers. It is part of corporate/ leader wisdom—the ability to see the world from different points of view.

Another key is communicating that vision. Communicating the vision involves vision, applicable business principles, a specific situation, and the individual leader. With the vision as reference leaders use the situation to illuminate an element of the vision by explaining the business principle involved. Leaders need skill also in managing their own performance by their vision. They need to commit fully to a situation, be sensitive to context, and keep a balance in their work and personal life.

DEVELOPING INDIVIDUAL WHOLENESS IN THE TEAM

Science and religion both teach that we are all interconnected and thus interdependent (Ram Dass 1994). Unfortunately, science has usurped the place of faith in the last years of this millennium (Begley 1994). Science, like few secular quests, approaches the sacred more authentically. In fact, some have gone so far as to say we can integrate science into an existing religion, a personal philosophy of life, or new beliefs. In some respects that is the current state of affairs in work situations. Overreliance on system, structure, and strategy has overshadowed our former reliance on faith and the innate goodness of people. According to all available evidence, this modern science-religion is failing to bring individuals what they want—peace of mind and happiness.

When sensitivity to the oneness of life dawns, there is openness and humility, there is relaxation and competition and conflict, there is an easy grace to relationships (Thaker 1994). To fix matters outwardly is useless if we do not fix what we are within (Weaver 1994). There is no reality except the one within us. That is why so many people live such an unreal life. They take the images outside them for reality and never allow the world within to assert itself (Hesse 1994).

Holistic leadership is not an option in today's world, it is a necessity (Pinchot and Pinchot 1994). Many of the most important choices we make—that make life happy or sad—are not individual choices, but group choices. We have come to know (again) that the important, meaningful circumstances in life cannot be attained alone. We need other people to help us become our best self. We need, therefore, to know what we can about how to make productive communities because this is where we make ourselves.

The power of all institutions is limited; every member has certain in-alienable rights that take precedence over the power of rulers. Among these are free speech, the right to associate with others, and individual and/or group ownership as a means of support. When people lose the sense of meaning and purpose in their lives their productivity declines (Adair 1985). Leaders need to bring back community within the orga-nization. People are looking to the job to find what other social institu-tions have not provided: spiritual confirmation. Here spiritual leaders can develop entrepreneurial firms inside the organization. They can help create borderless satellite systems of partners who are free to excel.

Societies with a deep respect for the truth outperform those that ignore the truth. Societies that treat people according to the Golden Rule per-form better than those whose members are habituated to acts of cruelty against one another. Religious tenets that support good treatment of fel-low members form the foundation of social relationships. Extending the right of choice broadly characterized democratic societies and these groups outperform those that restrict choice. Societies with a unifying common vision outperform those whose dream is dim. Putting your life and your money where your values are is the only way to lead in the new world toward which we are headed.

Organizational Citizenship

Culture is the social organization within which members interact—the way they express mores, customs, and values. The kind of culture that is supportive, adaptive, appreciative, and enhances performance is a community (team) culture. This kind of culture also promotes self-leadership. It is a culture where each member is responsible for getting himself or herself to wherever the community is going. Each member looks to himself or herself—not only to the leader—to determine what to do. Every member knows the direction of the team (set by the leader). Sharing the common direction makes assuming leadership easy, and every member is willing to assume leadership when the team needs it.

Today most Americans relate more to their work relationships than they do to any other social grouping with the possible exception of the family. They value their organizational citizenship sometimes more than they do their citizenship in the state. This fact impacts how they act, what they value, how they measure themselves and their actions. Control of environmental stimuli, therefore, becomes the key mechanism for con-trol over worker performance. Controlling—managing—the organiza-tional culture becomes the central managerial task. This is, at heart, a values displacement activity.

The values that define citizenship relationships also dictate work actions in our teams. The organizational value system is replacing larger context political and social theory. Large-scale organizations now provide an important experiential arena within which individuals learn to behave in society. Organizations are more-than-rational instruments of efficient human interaction. They also provide members with a sense of social values, which once was the task of sociopolitical systems. As organizations move beyond mere associations of people and take on the coloration of social institutions, they infuse members with values. Organizations become valuable not only as tools for accomplishment, but as sources of personal gratification and vehicles of group integration.

Leaders choose, if only implicitly, organizational values. It is only as members come to accept and act in terms of these values that the organization transforms from work mechanism to community. These modern communities—organizations—become the repository of social values driving human performance. The leader's task in all this is to generalize acceptance of these community values.

Leaders do this in several ways. They provide a core of people who accept the organization's institutional values. They communicate a shared vision that operationalizes the organization's values and that attract members as coparticipants, and leaders reorient or replace members who will not or cannot accept the central value system. The measure of acceptance of organizational values is the level of personal commitment and involvement in organizational actions. This acceptance creates community.

We cannot buy people's citizenship in the team. It is voluntary. Freedom of action (autonomy) is a value implicit in organizational citizenship. Too much exercise of leadership authority will hamper individual commitment. The use of authority must fall within the employee's zone of acceptability or group members will resist it (Barnard 1938). We can define organizational citizenship as acceptance of organizational values set by the leader. The association is either ethical or it is contractual, economic, or social. In either case we can define the association not by mere membership, but by acceptance and commitment shown by action to the organization's values.

Similarly, obligation, consent, and participation are also elements of organizational citizenship. Individuals have rights the organization must honor. They also have responsibility to the organization to be involved, committed, and supportive. Organizational citizenship is a mutual relationship with opportunities and duties on both sides. Whether the relationship is total or limited to task, organizational citizenship asks both leader and follower to accept common values and act according to them. Values become the adhesive of citizenship in the organization.

Commitment

We can define community and our citizenship in terms of commitment. Meeting the challenge of leadership first requires an understanding that people commit, not to measurable goals, but through trust, integrity, innovation, and similar ideals. Commitment is a binding process that is built by recognizing small victories along the path to total commitment. Letting people take action and make choices builds commitment. Helping people want to commit and a committed leadership also build commitment.

Commitment comes in the beginning, unifying organizational members and making them a community. It increases their capacity to succeed. Individuals join organizations when what they think they will give equals or exceeds what they think they will receive. Individuals accept organizational membership (citizenship). They give up some personal freedom of action when participation helps them gain some or all of their own goals. Leadership is, in part, helping individuals see the possible payoffs for joining and facilitating (not directing) commitment to citizenship in the organization.

Leaders need to realize that followers have other dimensions of their lives than that part committed to the work organization. Unless the organization respects the individual's nonwork life, members will not commit fully to the organization's work goals. Leadership must recognize this fact and authentically value the idea of respect for liberty and the quality of life implicit in its living. Notwithstanding this, we should be totally committed. The challenges we face ask for our best. This means with our head, heart, and hand—with our intellect, spirit, and energy.

How can we strengthen our commitment? How do we prepare to be of service? Commitment means doing what everyone can do but usually doesn't. Commitment is not professing, but doing. Commitment gives us self-definition and self-identity. Commitment is example leadership. It is a binding principle on the person. Commitment changes us.

Commitment is a process of self-denial of anything alien to what we are committed to. Commitment keeps us in the center, not on the fringes of life. Fringers want the advantage, not the work. When we have two standards we are trying to live we are double-minded. A double-minded person is unstable and erratic. Full commitment is essential to excellence. Full commitment means single-mindedness. Our decisions in life—short-term and long-term—will be dictated by a shift from one standard to the other and will make us unstable.

SUMMARY

Spiritual community is a basic change in the way one thinks about work and all life. A community is one that has undergone a fundamental shift in orientation from the individual and collective belief that people must merely cope with life and are powerless, to the conviction that they are individually and collectively empowered to create their future and shape their destiny. Leadership in a community stems from the leader's soul rather than from his or her behavior.

Community leaders are the custodians of the organization's values. This kind of leader empowers and coaches others to create what they want. In doing this they structure rewards and incentives. They specify personal and organizational values and belief structures and the energy these values create: habits, the free flow of information, and the physical work flow and management systems work flow processes.

Chapter 16

Spiritual Leadership: Setting a Higher Moral Standard

Most of us spend most of our lives in work. And the work we do has a moral dimension. Individuals want to work for the common good. Every individual wants to do good work and to contribute to the success of the organization. Unfortunately, in too many work situations we have been led to believe that there is one standard for private morality and another for public (business) morality and conduct (Nair 1994). Not so. Morality argues for one standard, applicable in personal, social, economic, and all other aspects of life. Our morals and ethics come out of our values as individuals and as communities (cultures). If we ignore our values at work, it is likely that the moral tone of the rest of our lives will decline.

People are, by and large, consistent in their morality in all dimensions of their lives. Leaders recognize this as they interact with followers on the job. They couch their relationships with followers in values terms, in terms of the prevailing moral and ethical tone of their work (or other) community.

Leaders must consider the whole person—their moral center, the range of their capacities, and the height of their aspirations. Leaders need to learn to nourish and respect the spirit. They need to integrate profit and respect for the people who create profit. The purpose of the company should be to create a positive impact on its community, rather than using profit as the sole motive.

Including a moral dimension in our choices and actions as leaders will help us think and act beyond narrowly defined business and political interests. It will force us into the realm of the spirit itself. Such leadership will give meaning and purpose to our working lives. And, arguably, this is the only way we can attract tomorrow's workers to our vision and our goals.

Some jobs ask us to sacrifice what is fundamental in self-definition at the altar of what is expedient. Unfortunately, too often we have come to accept a lower public morality as necessary to get things done in the real world of business or politics. Politicians ask us to judge them on their policies, not their personal conduct. Social activists claim high moral ground for their programs and sometimes use violence to obtain their ends. Business executives do not want their conduct examined, but ask instead that we evaluate them on their bottom-line performance. Journalists may maintain a personal commitment to truth but often succumb to the pressure to be first, and rather than wait for the whole story, publish half truths, they print their biases as the truth.

Arguably, much government regulation of business is a result of business leaders not accepting personal responsibility to serve their clients. Some organizations encourage a spirit of violence by rewarding executives who achieve economic goals by humiliating people and motivating them through fear. A society driven by responsibilities is oriented toward service. One motivated by rights is oriented toward acquisition, confrontation, and advocacy.

We lose respect for our leaders if we do not approve of their personal conduct—public or private. This loss of respect impacts the leader's ability to command our trust. Our central standard of right conduct comes from our core values. We form these values in the family and in religion. If leaders don't give these core values a place at work we lose our moral center. And without this moral and ethical standard we demean life.

Many people measure the operational manifestation of our core spiritual values by the Golden Rule: treating other human beings as we want to be treated. Leadership is a process not just an objective. Leadership is love in action. We cannot be successful over the long term unless we base our relationships with those assigned to assist us in work on processes that consider differences of opinion, on human worth, on impartial analysis and scrutiny, and on caring for our followers. Both the ends and the means of accomplishing the leader's program goals are important.

All people have multiple needs, only some of which the organization can deal with. Today's workers want more balance between their own needs and the organization's (Ruppert 1991). They need to be active in the several dimensions of their lives: love, family, faith, self-confidence, and other dimensions. These qualities animate and qualify life. Leaders need first to make sure that they serve other people's highest standards of personal and group conduct.

For many, the goal over the past forty years has been peace of mind, higher consciousness, personal transformation, or self-esteem. Caring for the soul is a way to uncover the sacredness that arises from things like cooking, music, and the family. Some seek wisdom. Others see the need to connect their lives to something larger than self. Czech President Vaclav Havel sees the coming of a new global politics based on "global spirituality." He says we must recover that which modern man has lost: his transcendental anchor.

As we enter the twenty-first century it is apparent that leaders are acquiring a new language of leadership, one where it is again okay to use all of the operative "S" words—soul, sacred, spirit, and sin as well as structure, strategy, and system.

SPIRITUAL WHOLENESS

Organizations are not working well (Wheatley 1992). They are overly complex, and they fail to achieve significant results. The organization does not function well when honesty and responsibility atrophy, particularly at the top. We can define ethical leadership as a process both of inquiry—asking questions about what is right and what is wrong—and a mode of conduct—setting an example for others about the rightness or wrongness of particular actions (Kouzes and Posner 1992).

The soul of ethics and spiritual leadership is love. It constitutes the basis of ethical leadership. It accesses the healing and energizing powers of spiritual leadership, recognizing foremost that leadership is a reciprocal relationship with constituents. Leading with spirit means that the leader's love is demonstrated in compassion, service, and support. Love is the source of the leader's spiritual courage. Leaders love their organization's products and service, and the people with whom they work.

Leaders create corporate spirit, a spiritual force that honors high performance, compassion, empathy for others, and individual contribution. They deal with follower contentment, capacity, equanimity, detachments, and connectedness. It is illogical, therefore, to assume that people coming to work in our organizations leave at home their innermost core values and beliefs; that they will be content to focus for ten or so hours on mundane tasks and ignore the profound needs of their inner selves. If leaders are to capture the heart of their workers and reveal their highest capacity for service, they must concern themselves with the need followers have to reflect their spirit forces at work along with their experience and expertise.

When we lose the spiritual content of our leadership, we lose our commitment to help the less fortunate, our need to be of service, our respect for those who are different. Leadership based on our inner search for what is serene, that which will sustain us as we go through life, will always endure. Spiritual leadership instills the principles and ideals of leadership quality and excellence into the soul of the organization.

Caring about someone is different from taking care of someone. To care about someone is to recognize him or her as someone who has independent ideas, values, and the ability to create, develop, and grow on his or her own. Caring about employees has replaced taking care of them through benefits and laws to protect them.

In the context of a person's life, caring has a way of ordering his or her other values and activities. When this ordering is comprehensive there is a basic stability in life—she or he is "in place" in the world. We live the meaning of our lives through caring about certain others. In the sense that we can ever say a person can be at home in the world, he or she is at home not through dominating, explaining, or appreciating, but through caring and being cared about.

Some leaders appear to proceed through life insensitively. They apparently believe that in this life we fare only according to the individual management of the physical creature, and that everyone conquers according to his or her genius or strength. To the "strong," this seems ideal, but what of the conquered and subdued? Injustice multiplies like insects in the sunshine (Maxwell 1990).

We are warned on every side of a waning of traditional values in our organizations today that has not been followed by a solid affirmation of new values. Nothing is filling the vacuum. The 1970s and 1980s turned vice into virtue by elevating the unbridled pursuit of self-interest and greed to the level of social virtue (Etzioni 1993). Leaders who are sensitive to the nonphysical suggest we need to return to a society where some things are beyond the pale. All people, including our co-workers, want a set of moral virtues, some settled beliefs and values that our communities can endorse and actively affirm—and beyond which we will not allow our self or others to go. We see this in the move to be drug free. We see it in the demand to return to values of hard work for a fair day's pay. We see it in the call for all to treat others with the same basic dignity with which we wish to be treated.

How do we remain spiritual on the job if our leaders are dishonorable to the trust we invest in them? We need to learn to know good leaders from profane ones. We have the inalienable right of free moral choice. The irrevocable law of the harvest—restore good for good, evil for evil—operates in our work lives too. We feel better when we do what is right. We need to put the emphasis on we—values *we* share. We need a balance of self-interest and self-expression and commitment to common rights and responsibilities. Developing character without attention to sharing spiritual values is like trying to develop the muscles of an athlete without having a particular sport in mind.

This applies equally in work and in other aspects of our personal life. When "the economy" becomes the main and engrossing concern of a society and its leaders, the economy will self-destruct. When leaders are more concerned with the bottom line, they begin to wallow in pride, envy, strife, malice, even murder. Note the sequence: first we are pleased with ourselves because of our wealth, then comes the game of status and prestige, leading to competitive maneuvers, hatred, and dirty tricks, and finally the ultimate solution.

Where wealth guarantees respectability, principles melt away as the criminal element rises to the top. Given full reign to these vices, the society ends in utter frustration and total insecurity as morals and the market collapse together and the baffled experts surrender (Nibley 1989).

We must have leadership in this nation whose voice will be clear; whose virtue, clarity, and uncertainty will give us the assurance that the course the government pursued under their leadership is right (Moyle 1952). Then we can put our whole heart and soul back into our business and government, support those who lead, and feel toward them even as we do toward those who we believe to have been specially chosen to guide and direct us in our religious affairs.

MORAL LEADERSHIP

Spiritual leaders are moral leaders. Moral leaders realize that they cannot compromise some ideals. They must defend them. Moral leaders may prefer not to compromise, accommodate, or collaborate in areas where their core values are at stake. Rather, they may prefer to compete with opposing ideas. Thus, spiritual leaders may sometimes be assertive and deliberately confrontational of alternative value systems. Spiritual leaders affirm the superior value of the spiritual over other systems or leadership models. While traditional functions and roles taken may be similar, spiritual leaders apply them in overtly moral ways.

Leadership entails principles of action, motivated by spirituality. Sixty-three percent of those responding to my survey found spirituality a core basis for their values, beliefs, and ethics (see Table 7.1). This source of individual ethics is also recognized in the recent quantity of leadership literature dealing with values-based transformational leadership (see, for example, Burns 1978, Covey 1991, DePree 1989, Fairholm 1991, 1994a, Greenleaf 1977, Lee and Zemke 1993, Vaill 1989). The application of ethics in work situations compels a spiritual orientation that centers on moral conduct. It is a task of doing good while doing well.

The higher leaders climb the greater their burden of responsibility and their need to reevaluate themselves and their spiritual roots. The root of spirituality is service. The infrastructure of spiritual leadership is an idea of moral leadership focused on service. It is uncompromisingly committed to the higher principle of selfless concern for others. Spiritual leadership rejects coercion to secure desired goals. It does not interfere with human freedom and choices, though these choices may entail some painful decisions and shifts in priorities.

Following is a list of some of the elements of moral spiritual leadership.

Common Ethical Values. Spiritual leaders inspire a sense of shared ethical values. Common values shared by group members provide the basis for the sanctions systems that define the team morality and determine *its* ethical sanctions system. A leader must find or inspire in his or her constituents a common basis of values. Moral leadership inspires this sense of shared values.

Sharing Meaning. Spiritual leadership is about the sharing of intentions. Effective leadership, a pattern of actions calculated to influence change in groups, is more likely to be helpful when it comes from people of strong character. Spiritual leadership attends to choices made by all persons in relationship with the leader. It is about persuasion, about right or wrong. It is about finding shared meaning, not about coercion or force.

Leadership is the integrating capacity in complex social interaction. The leaders we select to head our business organizations will set the goals and determine the values by which we measure accomplishment. But these values also define acceptable process methods of interrelationship. They integrate the needs and activities of the pluralistic constituencies that look to the business culture for support, assistance, and meaning. They tie together the disparate goals, measures of success, and strategic policies that govern our work lives.

The leadership task is more than physical structuring of people or function that has occupied business managers for over a century. It includes formal relationships, but, more importantly, the leader provides values, meaning, and focus to that structure. It will be leaders (not managers) who will focus the power present in work relationships. Leaders will shape the cultural surround within which the organization and its people operate. They will provide direction, incentive, inspiration, and support to individuals and groups.

Spiritual leadership is an approach based on ideas of defining meaning for the group and for individual members. It is about what leaders think about and value and how they apply those values in doing the group's work. Spiritual leadership focuses on those aspects of the relationships and purposes of the organization identified as spiritual. Spiritual leadership adds belief to system. It adds meaning to formal structure and roles. It aims to secure commitment and form team relationships that bind co-workers into a unified whole.

Influence and Power. Followers confer leadership. Until followers choose to accept the leader's power, the leader cannot lead (Barnard 1938). This acceptance comes out of the relationship, not out of formal structure or system. The measure of leadership is not structural, but attitudinal (DePree 1989). Spiritual leaders have no desire to manipulate others. They help followers feel powerful and able to accomplish work on their own. They show people how to evaluate their power bases and use their sources of power as sources of leadership. People underestimate the amount of real or potential power they have in areas of position, task, personal, relationship, and knowledge power.

The measure of leadership is not the caliber of the head, but the tone of the heart (DePree 1989). The model of spiritual leadership is not command and control. It is confer and network. The leadership is an influence process aimed at transforming both people and systems (Fairholm 1993). Success in the coming century will depend on how well we understand the role, the technology, the values, and the orientation of spiritual leadership. For leaders are power users. They are influential in the group and with its members. Leaders typically influence those people immediately around them, the general society, and the institutions they serve. Power is the ability to get others to do what the power user wants them to do, even in the face of opposition. This definition is strongly reminiscent of that of leadership itself. The results of power use and of leadership is the same. The purpose of each is to get others to comply; that is, to get others to behave in desired ways.

Power is the extra element in interpersonal relations that lets the leader influence others and secure their willing compliance. At one level, all interpersonal relationships are power relationships. We are constantly moving from a directive to a follower position in our contacts with others (or vice versa). The leader's words and actions combine to influence all stakeholders to desired levels of performance by making full use of individual abilities, interests, and capacities. The leadership task is to teach stakeholders to do without the leaders. Leadership teaches people to lead themselves (Wildavsky 1984).

Risk Taking. Spiritual leadership is active, and action involves risk. Leaders need to challenge existing work and team processes (Kouzes and Posner 1987). They do not simply accept current work systems or existing structural relationships. Rather, spiritual leaders are pioneers. They try to produce real change that meets people's enduring needs regardless of the risk. For Kouzes and Posner, spiritual leadership engages the heart. The spiritual leader's role is to change the lives of followers and of institutions in ways that enhance both. Spiritual leaders convert, change, and transform followers into leaders.

Risk taking challenges the process (Kouzes and Posner 1987), not simply the existing structural relationships, but the value system underpinning it. Moral leadership is active, and action involves risk. Moral leaders try to reduce the risk to employee and business psychological health, well-being, and safety. Additional benefits of moral (spiritual) leadership include enhanced production and improved operational efficiency, improved morale through employee teams, greater coordination across functional areas, and enhanced relationships within the larger community and society.

Service. Spiritual leadership is servanthood. The spiritual leader is a servant committed to the principles of spiritual relationships defined earlier in this chapter. This kind of moral leadership is the reverse of much of past leadership literature. Rather than attempt to dominate followers, spiritual leaders go to work for them, providing everything necessary for follower success. The leader's job is to encourage and sustain high-quality service to all those who have a stake in the group's work. They do this partly by managing the organizational culture and teaching core values and patterns of behavior. It is attained as the leader models desired morality in relationships.

Two aspects of this service role are important. First, the leader's job is to prepare followers to provide high-quality, excellent service to clients, customers, and citizens. In doing this, leaders act to prepare and then empower followers to be able to be of service. This aspect of the service dimension is similar to training and education programs leaders (and managers) have been doing routinely. If there is a difference in these activities associated with moral leadership, it is in the effort to prepare the follower to be of service on a wider front. Morally focused leaders see merit in helping followers broadly develop their capacity of be of service.

Second, leaders service their followers. The leader's job is not only to encourage and sustain high-quality service to customers, but to provide service to all those who have a stake in the group's work. Leaders are facilitators of the work of others; they serve co-workers as they have needs so they can accomplish their set tasks. Leaders serve followers in ways that ease their tasks and that energize and inspire them to unified action to increase and maintain high-quality services and programs. Leader service to followers can be in the form of personal assistance, providing resources, training, or encouragement, or in any of a myriad of ways that enhance the capacity and resources of the follower.

The service role casts the leader as a steward in relationship with co-workers. The stewardship role asks the leader to hold in trust the organization, its resources, its people, and the common vision of the future. In this stewardship role leaders set goals and plan, inspire, and train others to carry them out. Once trained and committed, the leader also shares stewardship responsibilities for action with followers. In effect, leaders prepare followers, provide facilitating help, and then let followers lead themselves within the constraints of the shared vision (Greenleaf 1977).

Transformation. Spiritual leaders are spiritually transforming. They enhance people's moral selves, help confirm others' beliefs in their own inherent self-worth, and, in the process, they help create a new scale of meaning within which followers can see their lives in terms of the larger community. Spiritual leaders create meaning for others. They engage the heart (Kouzes and Posner 1987). The spiritual leader's role is to change the lives of followers and of institutions in ways that enhance both. Spiritual leaders convert followers into leaders.

Moral (spiritual) leadership converts followers into leaders. Moral leadership asks only one thing: surrender everything you have and follow. Successful leadership implies influencing change in the values, attitudes, abilities, and behaviors of others. In this sense it is transformational of the people and their organization. Transforming leaders try to elevate the needs of the follower in line with the leader's own goals and aims. In doing this leaders pay attention to the individual by understanding and sharing in the realization of followers' developmental needs. Influencing others to change involves trusting them to do their best.

A moral organization is not attained without a congruence of each of the factors noted above. In the attainment of these goals, all three groups of corporate actors (leaders, followers, and customers) are improved, developed, and matured. Moral leadership is a change process that transforms stakeholders and the institution itself into something better than they were before. This transformation takes place in a consciously created and managed culture that prioritizes morality and focuses on the spiritual side—the heart—of the individual stakeholders.

Integrity. Integrity means having the courage and self-discipline to live by your inner truth. Integrity is a function of feeling whole and perfected. It involves the idea of goodness, human decency, fairness, kindness, politeness, and respect. Moral integrity involves a willingness to say what needs to be said, and not needlessly saying what may hurt another. It demands self-discipline, strengthening the self in terms of inner prompting.

Living by inner truth means putting truth into practice. People work harder when there is mutual trust, respect, and concern for each other, and mutual integrity among the group members as human beings. These ideas are appropriate for the chief executive of the organization as well as the worker. Morality demands integrity of all who govern their lives by high moral standards.

Moral Judgment. Ethical behavior flows from our ability to distinguish right from wrong and the commitment to do what is right. Fundamentally, there are two standards to measure moral judgment: "How would I want to be treated in this situation?" (the Golden Rule) and "How will the decision or action read on the front page of the newspaper?" Our spirituality is always with us if we are aware. It is the activating mechanism of our moral character. It is part of our self-analysis as we observe and reflect on our actions and judgments of events. It is a part of all aspects of life. Our spirituality is what sustains us through long periods of emotional drought in a crumbling universe. It is a shield in a corrupt and oftentimes disappointing world.

MAINTAINING HIGH MORAL STANDARDS

Spiritual leaders empower followers to build and use a personal belief system that reflects their innate goodness, ethics, and morality and to live it. This kind of credo accepts life, reveres it, and gives it dignity. It means listening to one's inner self and doing no harm—doing nothing to make matters worse. It recognizes our debts, mental or material. It puts a ceiling on desires because our desires constrain personal freedom. A personal belief system awakens our inner goodness and activates our character. It strives for integration, wholeness of self. The Greek word *ethos* means more than just obedience to rule. It is also about reputation, how one feels about oneself (Blanchard 1992). Being ethical means being moral. It means doing the right thing, doing the best for the greatest number of people. It is a matter of personal and professional character. Character is a cluster of related ideas that include morality, ethics, honesty, and humane values. Character means knowing that the actions we take are right, that is, acceptable to ourself. Moral leaders learn to know good from evil. They understand that all people have the inalienable right of free moral choice. And they know that the irrevocable law of the harvest—restore good for good, evil for evil—operates in our lives.

Moral leadership has been seen as a process both of inquiry—asking questions about what is right and what is wrong—and a mode of conduct—setting an example for others about the rightness or wrongness of particular actions (Kouzes and Posner 1993). Being moral means creating a climate of ethical expectation. The best way to teach ethics is to practice them. Especially recently, business morality has received increasing attention in practice and in classrooms.

Business needs to be more moral. Some corporations try to enforce moral action through formally adopted codes of ethics. Others schedule time to formally discuss moral issues and practices. Primarily, the business of being ethically moral is managed by leaders who take charge, set the moral climate, and who are accountable for their actions and results. Leaders set the standard for performance and morality within their group, and these standards are enforced by expectations. Operationally, morality involves following ethical standards and patiently sticking to one's purpose. It means feeling good about one's self and reflecting on the ideals of current business questions, but also thinking about one's actions in terms of inner standards of right and wrong.

There is some gamble that leading on the basis of moral standards may not work. Asking leaders to foster a specific moral dogma entails risk. The risk is that members will accept only the outward form, not the inner conviction necessary for true moral change. That is always a risk—that members will accept the tenets as an outward show; not have it written on their hearts. Inner conviction, patience, and predictable moral actions will ensure the leader's success as a moral guide for the organization and its people. If leaders remain focused, if they are seen as authentic, success will come.

Love constitutes the soul of moral leadership. It is the source of the leader's courage. Spiritually moral leadership accesses the healing and energizing powers of love. It recognizes that leadership is a reciprocal relationship with constituents. Leading with love also means that the leader's passion comes from compassion and that, ultimately, leaders serve and support their followers. Moral leaders are in love with leading, in love with their organization's products and services, and in love with people.

There is a pressing need for stability and spiritual values in America today (Garton 1989). Living by our inner truth involves strengthening personal and organizational integrity (Hawley 1993). Honesty is essential for moral leadership, but so is giving attention to our spiritual needs. All who hold positions of leadership—chief executive officers, teachers, supervisors, heads of families—should feed the spirit and nourish the soul (Hinckley 1967).

MORAL LEADERSHIP: CHRIST'S MODEL

Someone will always lead. The question is, what factors rule or govern leaders. The Hartwick Humanities in Management Institute's case, "Jesus and the Gospels" (1993), outlines the moral model of Jesus as depicted in the Gospels. Jesus is an inspiring example of leadership and service. His was an absolute moral leadership. There is a clear correspondence between Jesus' model of conduct and that of the Suffering Servant mentioned in the Old Testament book of Isaiah. Many believe Jesus was that servant.

He was uncompromisingly committed to a higher principle of selfless love and concern for others. He refused to rely on coercion to obtain desired goals. He showed serene willingness to accept whatever the future may bring because it will vindicate everything he represents. His was the rule of God (adherence to a higher standard than that of one person), which is moral leadership.

Jesus' credo was, "In everything, do to others what you would have them do to you." His moral leadership will not interfere with individual freedom and choice. These choices may entail some painful decisions and shifts in priorities as people decide to respond to his kind of leadership, but the right to choose remains inviolate. Moral leadership asks followers to devote everything humanly possible to the enterprise of absolute moral leadership.

Moral leadership is assertive and deliberately confrontational of alternative value systems. Moral leadership is a competing personality. It asserts a superior kind of moral leadership over other systems or models. Moral leaders may prefer not to compromise when such accommodation might jeopardize their moral standards.

Moral leaders serve others. Jesus "modeled the way" (Kouzes and Posner 1993). He gained others' trust with his congruent words and deeds. Moral leadership is not subordination of self-interest, but rejection of it. Moral leadership is directed by the moral framework the leadership develops.

Jesus' model of absolute moral leadership involves a qualitative change. The best example of Jesus' moral leadership is during his trial. He could do nothing to defend himself because moral leadership is not in any way motivated by self-interest. Moral leadership is the reverse of much of past leadership literature. Here failures succeed, losers win, and the servant leads.

Moral leadership asks us to reject altogether the enterprise of human leadership. Past leadership models are focused on self-interest. These secular theories honor values that are not considered ultimate to the moral leader. In their relationship with their community, secular leader models are influenced by ambitions of power, wealth, and prestige.

The transcendent values of moral leadership entail a complete renunciation of self-interest. Its values are ultimate and focus on ultimate ethical leadership values, the rule of God, and transcendent spiritual leadership. These values include:

- *Mercy.* Doing good things indiscriminantly on behalf of the people. Helping the undeserving and expecting nothing in return.
- *Righteousness.* Promoting those who show the same moral leadership Jesus showed.
- *Noncoercion.* Refusing to impose our will on others who contest it.
- *Justice.* Demonstrating good toward others through personal example.
- *Love.* Unbiased love, establishing relationship with persons as persons, regardless of their status.
- *Forgiving.* Willingness to forget the past and accept resulting losses in order to risk a new relationship basis of leadership.

• *Trust*. Security in the belief that our mission will succeed even if we die before it happens.

In their relationship with their community, moral leaders are motivated by a rejection of self-interest and by serving others. It is servant leadership because people are serving a higher purpose that stands behind the transcendent values.

Chapter 17

Stewardship

We observe continually that people with a sound value system, a moral orientation, and a stewardship concept of their leadership role can be effective though their technique or style is unorthodox. As we bring spirituality to the work place, a new idea of the individual-in-the-group emerges, an idea called classically (and revived recently) *stewardship*. The idea of ownership is shifting to stewardship (McMillen 1994). Ownership connotes possession, control, and proprietorship. Stewardship connotes holding work resources in trust for a temporary period. In a stewardship organization, power is inherent in each steward to help accomplish the stewardship unit's—not just the steward's—ends. Stewardship is a collective idea. It is by sharing equally all power that we become one.

Stewardship is a conception of organizational governance that connotes initiative and responsibility without the baggage of control behaviors, direction, and knowing what is best by others. Many business people no longer accept the responsibility of stewardship, which is, at the very least, to leave their community no worse off then they found it. They see no reason to go beyond mere profit to furthering self or corporate enhancement or to serve as trustees of social undertakings. It is consensus building in the process of developing vision and mission statements.

It has to do with how we identify ourselves in that part of our lives, that community, called work (Lee and Zemke 1993). Peter Block (1993) calls stewardship the willingness to be accountable for the well-being of the larger organization by operating in service, rather than in control, of those around us. Stewardship is accountability without control or compliance. Stewardship is less prescriptive. It has more to do with being accountable than it does with being responsible for what's been created than it does with defining, prescribing, and telling others what to do.

Block says the real issues are power, control, and choice. Stewardship is not a single guiding principle but a part of a triumvirate that includes empowerment and partnership along with stewardship. The principle of stewardship brings accountability while partnership balances responsibility. It is a sharing of a governance system where each member holds control and responsibility in trust for the group as a whole. It is a relationship system based on accountability.

Stewardship and service are intimately related. Servant and steward may be more similar roles than they appear on first thought. *Servant*, in ancient Greek, means one who is dedicated to service on behalf of another. The Greek root of *steward* means a household servant, one who superintends a household. Stewardship means being accountable without control or forced compliance. Block (1993) sees leadership without stewardship as relegating the leader to the role of parent—caretaker, supervisor—and is demeaning to the follower.

STEWARDSHIP

We base stewardship on self-directed free moral choice. The steward has the power of self-governance. Every steward has the same rights and is subject to identical limitations in the exercise of self-direction. This sharing of power preserves harmony and good will. The leader is a steward also and subject to the same limitations and advantages of other stewards. Leaders ensure every steward has a single voice in sitting in council with other stewards and a single vote in the power of consent. Stewardships preserve oneness by procedures that enhance common consent. In this way each steward is protected against unjust or dominating leaders.

The steward-leader is servant first. The leader's sense of stewardship operates on two levels. The first is a stewardship for the people they lead. The second is a stewardship for the larger purposes or mission that underlies the larger enterprise. The steward-leader demonstrates these critical skills: building shared vision, surfacing and challenging mental models, and systems thinking. Steward-leaders build corporate vision from their own personal vision. They challenge current thinking by making clear the distinctions between espoused theories and theory-in-use, and they focus less on day-to-day events and more on underlying forces and trends of change. They see interrelationships, move beyond blame, focus on areas of higher leverage, and avoid symptomatic solutions.

Both ends and means are critical to stewardship. How we do work is as important as what we do. Stewardship is a conception of organizational governance that connotes initiative and responsibility without the baggage of control behaviors, direction, and others (the leader) "knowing what is best" for followers. Instead, stewards have self-directing authority over their stewardship within the stewardship unit. The only limitation is that the steward's claim on the stewardship unit resources must be just—all claims are equally subject to overall stewardship unit resource limitations.

Steward leadership is operating-in-service-to rather than in-control-of those around us. It is less prescriptive. It has more to do with being accountable than it does with being responsible for what the group creates or with defining, prescribing, and telling others what to do. The principle of stewardship brings accountability while partnership balances responsibility. It is a sharing of governance system where each member holds control and responsibility in trust for the group as a unit. It is a relationship system based on mutual accountability.

Organizing for Stewardship

To expect people to live out their personal spiritual beliefs without a shift in the governance system is to assume we can fool them into adapting cheerfully to their haplessness. A fundamental change in the structure of governance in the corporation is essential to adopting spiritual leadership ideas and ideals. Stewardship requires a cooperative, not a contentious (competitive) environment. As such, the team becomes a more logical structural arrangement than does the traditional hierarchial formations we are used to.

Contention limits freedom and is never helpful. Arguing never benefits the hearer. Rather love opens doors. Contention is not and never will be an ally of progress. Stewardship ideals bond leader and led in the same mind-set and of the same moral judgment. Stewardship avoids contention, division and strife, even on the smallest issues.

The test of the steward-leader is not how much work is done, but how well we spread the word so that all who *will* hear and accept may do so. Contention builds walls and leads to disunity. False information arises and people reject their leaders. They ignore past practices and thus open the way to spiritual ruin and renunciation. The principle of authority counters contention. As followers turn to the authoritative statements of their leaders, oneness results. Two people at odds cannot both be right.

Elements of Steward-Leadership

A steward role asks leader and led to risk losing class distinctions and privileges in the pursuit of living out a set of values and creating an organization where members personally reclaim the institution as their own. Stewardship operates at the whole-person—spiritual—level of existence and interrelationship. It includes ideas of team work and individual free choice.

The Stewardship Team. The team is a prime institutional focus for stewardship ideas. Members can take ownership of the team and participate at a level beyond consensus and compromise. At this level, one member does not merely support another member's position, rather that position becomes a course of action all members accept and foster.

The team—stewardship unit—is critical in stewardship ideas. In the spiritual leader model we base relationships on shared values, habits, and practices that assure respect for others' rights. Stewardship is integral to ideas of corporate community. Membership in a stewardship team asks spiritual leaders to lead the stewardship team but also play a role as a member of the team community.

Moral voices reflecting community values gain their impact mainly through education and persuasion, not coercion. Schools should begin again to teach moral values. Adults need to inform themselves on major social issues. Can we then blame our government leaders for the evil done by a nation, or our corporate leaders for the alienation, anomie, and corruption we find in our work? No. Members still come to their work free and able to make moral choices.

The Role of Free Choice in Stewardship. Personal liberty—the capacity to make free choices—is integral to the idea of stewardship. It is also important to community. Freedom to choose was the second most often identified value of surveyed respondents (see Table 8.6). The expectation that we can be free to make our own choices in our groups is fully American. Americans feel an unalienable right to free choice. One cannot sustain human existence or individual liberty for long outside the interdependent and overlapping communities to which we all belong (Etzioni 1993).

Many of the most important choices we make are not individual choices, but group choices. A stewardship community lets members make free choices about whom to partner with, what products or services to buy from internal or external suppliers, how to spend discretionary funds and time, and how to serve their customers. Letting people choose independently builds commitment. Spiritual leaders serve the choices made by persons in their stewardship.

Learning to lead by letting others in the team make important choices asks steward-leaders to learn new competencies, be responsive to today's concerns, and at the same time be forward thinking (Reynolds 1994). Team members will not follow unless they trust their leader's ability to move the group forward. Steward-leaders need a proven track record. They need the ability to grasp relationships, to see the big picture.

Steward-leaders see to it that the corporation knowingly does no harm. They guide the corporation between profit and humanity, between capitalism and societal conscience, between the shareholders and the community at large. They build profit with society's needs in mind. They build moral cultures. Stewards must be able to affect change, avert crisis, and plan for an increasingly unknown and unknowable future.

THE STEWARDSHIP TEAM

The idea of a stewardship orientation to corporate governance is new. Many leaders have no operational experience with this concept and, therefore, cannot immediately visualize their steward-leader role in the corporation or their part in building stewardship teams. While the idea may be appealing, many don't know how stewardship works in practice. The following explanation may help operationalize what is, for many, just a good idea.

Stewardship is an expectation of production in proportion to what is given. It involves accounting. It involves no interference with the steward until the time of accounting. The stewardship team is based on decentralization. Both ends and means are critical to stewardship. How we do it is as important as what we do. It is based on principles of self-governance. It recognizes, uses, and honors the agency of stewards. It is based on equality of class, free moral agency, interactive esteem, personal growth, and shared power.

Stewardship teams eliminate class distinctions. All team members—stewards—are equal, and all have equal opportunity for managing their stewardship. All have equal access to available rewards for a well-done stewardship. The steward-leader is a steward also and subject to the same limitations and advantages of other stewards. Every steward has a single voice in the power of council and a single vote in the power of consent. This balance is preserved by the law of common consent. Each is protected against unfair stewards.

Stewards are allowed to use their moral agency—the innate capacity to make moral choices. Stewards are self-directed, not other-directed, within the confines of the team vision and operating values. Stewardship is based on agency. The center of initiative in deciding what to do lies with the steward. He or she is a self-directing agent and has the power of self-governance.

All stewards are esteemed equally. Their contribution to the team is not measured in terms of differential recognition. Status and hierarchial distinctions are absent. No one member is more important to the team than any other. Loss of the contribution of any one member diminishes the team and jeopardizes its success because the team is not whole without all members.

Members play roles that give each an equal opportunity for personal growth. They have equal access to the resources of the team in accomplishing their assignments and magnifying their stewardship for both personal and team purposes. Every steward has identical rights and is subject to identical limitations in the exercise of self-direction.

Power is the authorized ability of each steward to help accomplish the stewardship unit's ends. A stewardship unit is a set of interrelated positions aimed at achieving certain goals. Each has self-directing authority over this stewardship within the stewardship unit. The only limitation is that the steward's claim on the stewardship unit resources must be just—no claim is given privilege. All claims are equally subject to overall stewardship unit resources limitations. It is by sharing equally all power that we become one, united as a stewardship team. Harmony and goodwill are preserved when authority is shared.

The Stewardship Team Structure

The basic entities of the stewardship unit are the individual steward, the stewardship leader, the unit membership that forms a council of the unit, and a high-level council. The power of each entity is limited by the right of council and consent to preserve each member's free agency.

The Role of the Steward

All stewards are equal with all others in the stewardship unit. Four ideas are part of this role. First, each steward has the right to exercise the power of counsel and consent in forming the particulars of his or her stewardship within the stewardship unit. Each has the right of choice to be the center of initiative and decision in carrying out his or her stewardship. The process of accountability takes place between equal people who share the desire to be authors of life for self and the other.

The individual steward participates in deciding what his or her stewardship will be. The center of initiative and decision resides with the steward. The steward-leader retains the power of counsel and consent. Appeals go to the stewardship unit council or to the high-level council.

The Role of the Steward-Leader

The leader's role is that of servant rather than master. By assisting stewards to achieve to their potential, steward-leaders multiply the contribution they otherwise could make. Their role as servant encourages feedback from those they serve. They foster cooperation not competition. The steward-leader is required to counsel and obtain the consent of the stewardship unit in giving direction to the unit. By so doing they gain the use of the best experience in the stewardship unit and the maximum creative energy and wisdom of the unit.

The stewardship team council must have the leader's consent. They cannot compel the steward-leader in the direction of the stewardship unit. Steward-leaders are in a relationship of equality with each steward over whom they preside and with the team council. Communication is easier in this relationship. It avoids the isolation leaders so commonly feel in leadership.

Because each steward determines his or her own resource needs, the steward-leader is relieved from the troublesome task of allocating resources. He or she is relieved from the many personnel problems stemming from greed, jealousy, and rivalry. Leaders give only general direction to the stewardship team with respect to administrative matters. They help determine the nature of each steward's stewardship. They receive each steward's accounting and judge whether he or she has been discerning and steadfast. They share the power of determining the uses of the resources of the stewardship team.

The Role of the Team Council

The resources of the team are allocated by the team as a council. They make decisions based on the principle of common acquiescence. Assuming the resource allocator is faithful and wise, they settle important disputes among the stewards and the steward-leader. Each stewardship team membership is equal in all things. The goals of the stewardship team council and the team itself are to develop each member into his or her best self while attaining team work outcomes.

The Role of the High-Level Council

High-level councils settle important disputes that arise in the various stewardship teams. They also help administer team resources, especially when shortages occur.

The Stewardship Organization Structure

A diagram of a typical stewardship team can be developed showing formal relationships among these four actors in the stewardship leadership model. Relationships and key responsibilities are shown (Figure 17.1).

The Principles of Stewardship

Stewardship-leadership is founded on several spiritual principles, including the principle of service, the principle of independence and initiative, the principle of counsel and consent, and the principle of accountability.

The principle of service relies on the idea that leaders are servants first. Equality is preserved through a hierarchy of service and team mem-

Figure 17.1
Typical Stewardship Team Structure

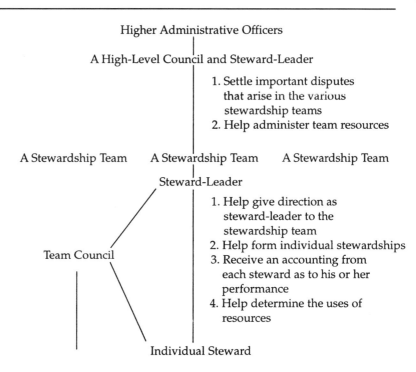

Higher Administrative Officers

A High-Level Council and Steward-Leader

1. Settle important disputes
   that arise in the various
   stewardship teams
2. Help administer team resources

A Stewardship Team   A Stewardship Team   A Stewardship Team

Steward-Leader

1. Help give direction as
   steward-leader to the
   stewardship team
2. Help form individual stewardships
3. Receive an accounting from
   each steward as to his or her
   performance
4. Help determine the uses of
   resources

Team Council

Individual Steward

1. Counsel and consent of
   membership in the general
   direction of the stewardship
   team.
2. Voice and consent in uses
   of team resources
3. Voice and consent in the
   selection of steward-leader

1. Participate in forming his or her
   own stewardship
2. Decide how to carry out his or her
   own stewardship, which includes
   the right to employ needed
   available resources
3. Participate as an equal in
   stewardship team affairs as a
   member of the team council

bers (including the leader) as servants of each other. Free choice is preserved because through service one can assist directly in the personal development of others without violating their rights of moral agency. It is only through service that the domain of people's legitimate activity is enlarged.

The principle of independence and initiative builds on the idea that each person is essentially, unalienably free. While this freedom brings an essential aloneness and responsibility for one's actions, it is also liberating. We are free to act and not to be just acted upon. Stewardship teams are formed by spirit-centered leaders to allow followers a field of independent action and initiative that will not be interfered with. Each steward is free to accept the duties and responsibilities of this stewardship or leave it.

Independence is preserved by noninterference in another's stewardship by the leader so long as the steward is functioning in useful ways. The locus of initiative is with the steward rather than the steward-leader. Decisions as to what is needed must be made by the steward. That is, resources needed to operate a stewardship are set by the steward within overall resource limits of the stewardship team.

The principle of counsel and consent governs the interaction among member-stewards in a stewardship team. It preserves the right of action in a steward's own domain. Though the locus of decision may reside in the steward, the power of consent in the steward-leader preserves the right of counsel. This lets each be an essential actor in the ensuing action for themselves and for the other person. It gives life to the idea of equality among members and promotes brotherhood among them. It fosters genuine service interaction between the steward-leader and the steward. It provides feedback, which corrects organizational defects or insufficiencies.

Finally, the principle of accountability is based on principles of agency and a willingness to conduct one self on the basis of law. Four factors must be present in a proper stewardship accounting. First, stewards possess the power and opportunities of agency necessary for self-governance. That is, they have the power to make things happen. They are unconstrained in what they do and how they do it within the context of the team vision. They are the center of initiative and decision.

Second, stewards are obligated by that law to conduct themselves in a certain way and for certain ends. The team's vision and its related rules and regulations provide the framework of possibilities for action. It is the basis for self-governance. The law, therefore, must mean something important to the stewards. Third, the stewards are answerable for their conduct according to their position as agents and their knowledge of the law. Fourth, they are subject to the requirements of justice according to their acceptance or rejection, obedience or disobedience in relation to the law.

Accounting consists of people who are equal in esteem and power working together in a spirit of mutual concern to achieve a set of mutual obligations. Accountability requires that the steward be under the obligation of the law. That is, the steward has been counseled and has given his or her consent to the adequate definition of the authority, powers, and responsibility associated with the stewardship. Within the domain of the definition of his or her stewardship he or she is not interfered with except at times of accounting. That is, independence and initiative has remained inviolate. The resources (including knowledge) are available to him or her and are commensurate with the responsibilities associated with the stewardship.

In the course of accounting the steward establishes a claim to the resources of the team by proving an account of what he or she is doing and setting forth future plans that relate to the team. As long as the steward is faithful and wise in his or her conduct of the stewardship, he or she has claim on needed resources. Only as the steward is deemed perfidious and/or imprudent is he or she subject to the judgment of the steward-leader and the team council (in the case of a need by either party for appeal).

A possible threat to the stewardship is the steward-leader, who are challenged by the possibility of exercising unfair power over stewards. As the steward-leader over-controls, the stewards may become other-directed rather than self-directed; his or her locus of control moves from self-governance to subordination.

Accounting also includes the idea of punishment for noncompliance with the demands of the stewardship. Deterrents to unwise behavior preserve the status of agency. That is, unwise and disloyal stewards incur punishment. In this way, steward-leaders allow the steward to become better.

Chapter 18

The Leader's Goal: Continuous Improvement

Spiritual leaders seek one superordinate goal: continuous improvement. They seek improvement of self, their core of co-workers, and all other stakeholders—customers, suppliers, consultants, and the rest. They seek to enlarge the pool of self-led leaders.

CONTRASTING SPIRITUAL AND OTHER LEADERSHIP APPROACHES

Many of the methods and styles defined in nonspiritual leadership literature focus on the science of leadership and management. They emphasize organization, authority, role rankings and formal relationships. Those experts who do focus on human relations aspects of leadership do so, often, from the perspective of reaction against the scientific methods and a disillusionment with hard science. Yet, even the human relationists focus on science as the path to truth about leading human beings. Nevertheless, scientific management methods have fallen short as a way to understand and relate to other people in productive ways.

The world has, of course, gained much knowledge and useful technology from the work of management scientists. Our physical, organizational, and emotional lives are fuller as a result of the application of the scientific process. The work of management scientists is useful, as are their insights and their dedication to seeking the truth. But, also needed, is the spiritual assurance that our relationships with our co-workers and our colleagues in leadership are complete and mutually beneficial.

Spiritual leaders recognize these intense personal and spiritual—human—factors in leadership. They direct their energies to, first, finding out as much as they can about their followers and their mutual interrelationships. These leaders also learn how interpersonal relationships operate within the team and with other elements of the corporation. On this base they can then practice proper relationships with those around them and especially with those in the team cluster they head.

The tendency to manage, not lead, has crept into the leadership of our business organizations. It is easier for many heads of corporations to focus on the immediate needs to build a product, deliver a service, put on an event or activity, or teach a class and forget that the real purpose of leadership is to help others change, become perfected, and assure that everyone will attain program results efficiently.

Command values have characterized the modern corporation for most of its modern history. The results of good management in the world are more power, prestige, and material possessions. The mechanism often is control of the people who work for and with us. Sadly, and too often, good hearted organization heads fall victim to this managerial style because it is all they know.

For spiritual leaders this is not true success. Success does not come from the control over and accumulation of things. It comes from the change, constant progress, and the transformation of people—leaders and those with whom they work. Spiritual leadership partakes of different values from managerial acquisitive leadership. Spiritual leaders think differently about their role as heads of their firms. They value people, programs, and policy differently. They have different expectations for followers and seek different results from individuals and from the group. Indeed, we are moving away from seeing leadership as merely coordination of work in relationships bounded by structure and system. Rather, we now are coming to see leadership as a kind of mutual aid contract in which the leader and follower agree to cooperate voluntarily.

The great criterion of leadership is that leaders can change other people's lives. The model of life is a personal change model. We move through this life according to a natural principle of evolution that lets people change physically, intellectually, and behaviorally. Individually, and as a species, we grow and move from life phase to life phase, evolving in the process. Whether the changes we make enhance our personal goals, or, even, our humanness, is up to us. Each of us will gain by this process according to our efforts and the makeup of our values and goals.

Spiritual leadership as described here consists of providing the right actions to produce right responses in our followers. It means getting people to respond and sacrifice when they are under no obligation to do so. It is a persuasive task, developmental, growth-producing, other-directed. It is a teaching, not a directive role. It is a service role, one that involves commitment and sacrifice by both leader and follower. And the results are change—transformation of self, others, and the larger communities within which we work and live.

THE PERSONAL TRANSFORMATION RESULTS OF SPIRITUAL LEADERSHIP

The goal of spiritual leadership is to change peoples' lives. Since Cain's encounter with the Lord, humans have known about the need each of us has to be concerned for, and a contributing part of, the development and growth of our fellows. Service to others is the primary mechanism for developing transformational leadership ideals within individual team members. Selfless concern for others is the mark of the spiritually mature individual. It is the prime measure of success for the spiritual leader.

In our work teams the leader's change and individual transformation orientation takes two forms. First, the team is really a community of leaders designed to encourage the growth of all members in knowledge and the practice of effective principles of human interaction. The focus of much of the work and the end product of team activity is to provide expanding experiences for the members in doing cooperative, productive work, work that is continually better today than it was yesterday. The role of leaders is to develop and implement programs designed to apply and interpret these productivity and people-growth team goals in the light of current problems and situations.

Second, spiritual leaders see the team as a prime environment within which the members can gain experience in creativity, innovation, and independent vision-directed action. The team is the most effective place to apply ideals of interpersonal relations, leader and led sit in council with each other to plan, organize, and carry out needed work. Here the leader can find opportunities to model desired standards as well as find opportunities to let others practice similar conduct under his or her watchful care. A position of leadership carries with it this dual goal structure. First to develop and conduct a variety of programs to help team members learn and find opportunities to experience effective work personally. And, second, to help the leader gain the experience of working with others as they provide a variety of goods or services for their customers.

Leadership asks both leaders and followers to change at the spiritual level; to behave toward others in more authentically helpful ways. We can do much to create a situation where concern for the individual freedom of the action of followers is a recognizable part of any work situation. As leaders we have a great responsibility to provide opportunities for service to those with whom we work—opportunities as spiritually fulfilling as our responsibility to seek growth-producing opportunities for ourselves. As our followers learn the lessons of followership and determine in what actions and which situations they grow most we (their leaders) also mature spiritually. We base spiritual leadership (and in all of our relationships with others) on this golden rule of relationships.

This kind of atmosphere of personal concern can exist in every interpersonal contact. In terms of some specific things we can do to make the results of our service more satisfying for the follower we can enumerate the following:

1. We should learn something of the need for personal and spiritual development of individual followers. As leaders we can then assign them to tasks and duties that will bring out their latent qualities and talents.

2. We can be alert to the problems resulting from the frequent changes in follower assignments. Followers need time to learn their duty fully and feel a sense of accomplishment before moving on to other assignments.

3. As spiritual leaders we can discuss openly aspects of the personal development potential that may result from assigned work. This can be a regular part of the agenda for individual performance evaluation interviews with followers, or it can be the subject of special team or individual meetings.

4. We should recognize that many of the interpersonal contacts followers have with any stakeholder are or can become training experiences for them in helping them relate better to their own team work. As we consider team member needs when we assign them to specific work tasks both inside and outside the team, they gain needed experience and confidence. By giving them tasks that let them practice behaviors and skills that need development as part of their team assignment, followers gain valuable experience that will aid them in their maturing competence.

5. Leaders can assign followers to work with others—other team members, customers, or clients—based on similar or complementary interests. Matching personality types will increase the learning potential of both individuals.

The more we keep our relationships with followers free of judgment and evaluation, the more this will permit team members to reach the point where they recognize that the locus of responsibility lies within themselves, not outside in the organization, with other people, or with an ephemeral "them." Only then can followers be really free to use their inner capacities independently. Change is essentially the goal of the helping contacts—help for the giver of help to assist the other to modify behaviors that both see and recognize as needing change. Change is up to the individual.

SPIRITUAL LEADERS PRODUCE MORE LEADERS

The substance of the leader's job is to produce more leaders, not more followers. Each of us over the years of our work life has opportunities to lead as well as follow the lead of others. We become more intelligent, responsive leaders if we have the experience of working under leaders who allow us to function freely within organizational and program constraints. As leaders ourselves, we will have more effective, more knowledgeable followers if they have had some previous leadership assignments. Spiritual leaders adopt a system wherein the individual serves in a task for a time and then moves on to some other position in the team, providing an opportunity for team members to gain valuable experience in both leadership and followership—in reality two aspects of the same thing.

In each of our contacts with followers, spiritual leaders can find opportunity to enter a relationship with the individual, the prime purpose of which is to help that other person to appreciate more, to make more functional use of, his or her latent talents and resources. These contacts can be the most meaningful contacts we can have with a follower. If leaders understand the nature and characteristics of these helping contacts as opportunities to aid follower growth, it helps them act responsibly in these interpersonal exchanges.

People change is basic to the purpose of all of the organizations and programs in team leadership. Spiritual leaders also have that goal. As we behave toward our followers in a warm, expressive way, as we are respectful of the individuality of our followers (and of ourselves), and as we exhibit an active attitude of affection toward others we probably contribute more to their self-realization than any other attitude or action we might take. As our followers perform the simple tasks we assign them, they will be transformed. As we continue to increase the scope and complexity of the tasks assigned, our followers will grow.

The net result is to help followers understand their innate capacity to govern themselves in their lives. Facilitating self-governance is an essential part of the goal of spiritual leaders to help followers become leaders themselves. Also critical is the need for the leader to address productivity questions of high-quality service and achievement of gospel and program goals. Like the secular manager, some spiritual leaders focus too much on the single goal of producing goods, services, and activities. Accomplishing these tasks is important to the expansion of a corporation's influence, but so is the need to help our followers become self-reliant, self-governing free agents.

With all else asked of them, spiritual leaders have the vital goal of helping followers to attain their personal self-development aims for independent action. Spiritual leaders create leaders out of their followers, each animated by similar values and ideals. As spiritual leaders we have the dual goals of producing high-performance and spiritually mature, self-led followers. These two interrelated goals permeate all aspects of our job. Spiritual leadership is a task of changing followers toward free use of their powers of choice.

The measure of success in any activity is in the outcomes it produces. In the last analysis, spiritual leadership success is about the leadership skill and experience we encourage in our followers. It is about attracting people to the team vision and then helping them to change their lives to conform to its precepts.

Spiritual leadership accepts improved performance as a desirable result of leadership behavior; however, it highlights the task of helping followers attaining their personal, not just corporate, aims. Leaders help followers increase their talents for the sake of both the team and the individual.

Spiritual leadership is an essential element in corporate governance. It is the most significant capacity required of the successful corporate head or team leader. As leaders we test our spiritual leadership continually through our own research and practice. For it is only as leaders incorporate these spiritual principles of leadership into their programs and activities that their true value becomes known. This challenge has always been at the heart of spiritual leadership and of our constantly evolving progress.

SPIRITUAL LEADERSHIP IS A HELPING SERVICE

Changing lives is a service. Spiritual leaders play a servant role. Spiritual leadership is first and fundamentally a call to service. All positions of authority in the corporation and on its teams are helping ones. Fundamentally, our leadership position is to help those with whom we work—our colleagues in leadership—and to help the organization's customers. It is not geared to using people as cogs-in-the-industrial-machine as much so-called scientific leadership literature suggests.

Spiritual leaders help team members to grow and mature to their full human potential. Our goal as leaders is to move the team's work forward with diligence. The essence of this task, however, is on people's growth. Our work is to assist others—and, through this service, ourselves—to develop into fully functioning team members. A part of individual development and evolution comes as we apply ourselves and our capacities to our work in the team. In these aspects of followers' lives, leaders have a profound opportunity, by their attitude, actions, and example, to help followers to mature in their talents, understanding, and commitment to the team vision.

Leaders challenge their followers to excellence. Thus, they create opportunities to inspire and motivate followers toward their best efforts and increase the value of the programs or services delivered and the learning experiences of followers. In doing this, spiritual leaders learn and then rely on the strengths of their individual followers. Armed with this information, they can provide tailored opportunities to let followers accentuate their strengths and develop in weak areas of their personality through their actions in the team. This work is, perhaps, the most significant service a leader can provide.

Spiritual leaders help three groups of team members to grow and mature to their full spiritual potential. First, as leaders we need to be concerned with helping ourselves become good leaders. Next, we should focus on the body of customers we serve. The third group we need to help is the other team members under our specific direction. The keys to success with each target audience are the same. Successful spiritual leaders are spiritually seasoned, self-disciplined stewards. They influence others through persuasion, are inspirational, are teachers, and lead through one-on-one joint counciling-with relationships with followers.

It is not enough to have successful programs, a well-made product, an interesting class, or fruitful planning meetings. A mutually supportive relationship between the leader and his or her followers that helps them both gain and maintain a sense of personal worth and importance is also required. As we learn to know intimately where we are in this pattern of testing and growth we can effectively gear our actions to the acquisition of needed disciplines of physical, emotional, and spiritual control that qualifies us for service as spiritual leaders. And as we prepare to serve before offering service, we act out of our deepest sense of self toward others in the team.

Our leadership task is to watch over the people making up our stewardship and to strengthen them. We do this not through our direct efforts so much, although direct service is expected of us and is appropriate, as in providing opportunities for followers to strengthen themselves through successful action within the organization. The basis of spiritual leadership is the free will choices we let team members make. The task of life, in which the leader is a key participant, is to assist people to learn and then guide their lives in terms of ageless principles of human conduct.

TO CREATE A VITALIZING VISION FOR THE TEAM

Spiritual leadership is based on wholeness, shared values, and concern for the human side of life, rather than the materialistic pattern typical of past models. Spiritual leaders seek a capacity to build consensus and lead democratically. The mechanism for this consensus is the leader-set vision. The vision provides the group a base of values for commitment.

Vision setting implies integration of values that honor and sustain the individual. Values like respect for life, personal liberty, justice, unity, and happiness (Fairholm 1991) let people grow. Visions based on one or more of these core values provide the culture foundation for more operational values like excellence, high-quality service, innovation, and empowerment. Visions reflecting these founding American values form the basis for most of our social interaction and the basis for personal development.

The vision represents common values intrinsically held and to the realization of which most people devote their energies. Leaders set the vision for their organization and all stakeholders. They are continually engaged in displacing incompatible workers' values with desired ones. The result of vision setting by the leader is the creation of an ethical substructure guiding leader and member actions and defining group success. Vision setting requires thinking through the organization's ethical core and defining and establishing it clearly and visibly.

Visions synthesize, vocalize, and translate the aspirations of the group. Visions transcend the prescribed or commonly perceived goals of the group; they are future-oriented, ethically based, and spiritually specific. Visions are revelations to the senses of something intangible, a moral method of seeing or conceiving the world.

Chapter 19

Epilogue

Doing business as usual is not a formula for success in the current state of crisis in which we find ourselves. Conducting business based on conventional theory and experience is to court failure. Business has now absorbed or replaced many of the occupations in which people formerly engaged to attain personal satisfaction. The workplace is a locale of our heart-thoughts as well as our economics. It would be a devastating blow if we found neither spirit nor inspiration in work.

As we move into a new era of interpersonal relationships and need satisfaction using the workplace as the prime site, researcher and practitioner alike must deal with several issues, the resolution of which will define corporate and societal life for the foreseeable future. The incongruence between our personal ideals and values and the traditional exploitation process in business has caused increasing numbers of concerned people to question their behaviors and to call forth new paradigms based on the human spirit. Both practitioner leaders and scholars must consider together several issues as they complete the evolving model of spiritual leadership. This chapter discusses some of these issues.

A CRISIS OF MEANING: RELIGION VERSUS SPIRIT ON THE JOB

For most of human history no one had to search for the spiritual in their lives. At the core of every culture was a religion, with sacred times and places set aside for public rituals. For many today, these holy places are less and less familiar. Nevertheless, spiritual and religious values and those of a free democratic society go hand-in-hand (Lee and Zemke 1993). Workers are much more than a bundle of skills and knowledge, as some managers think. People also come to work armed with a spirit, a life-giving principle that involves higher moral qualities.

There is, however, a clear difference between spirituality in religion founded on sacred writ, and the spirit or soul of a person defined as body and spirit. Many people see spirituality to include a much broader range of experience than religion and faith. Religion and faith may serve to limit the discussion to experiences that arise in traditional institutions or ways of thinking (Vaill 1989). Spirit defines individuals in the context of their relationship with their surroundings, their past, and their understandings of their experiences. Defined this way, we all engage in work with our whole soul (self), whether or not management theory or managers take note of it.

Church and corporate life differ, but the committed corporate executive or worker, like the committed religionist, bring their passions with them twenty-four hours a day. Religions have evolved as structures or forms designed to support and perpetuate specific beliefs or dogmas about spiritual matters. These dogmas are expanding to include work-life concerns and relate spirit in business to ideas like empowerment, assigning meaning, and people-centered business practices (Autry 1992).

PROFESSIONALISM AND SPIRIT

Doing our best at whatever we do is intimately tied to our deepest sense of self and spirit (Jacobson 1995). Yet, academic or professional research and discourse rarely take seriously the term and the area of human experience described by spirituality. Spirituality in our society too often represents a retreat from the world of intellectual discourse. In many contexts spiritual pursuits are cloaked in a reflective anti-intellectualism that mirrors a view of spirituality as an irrational cultural residue, but circumstances are changing. Spirituality now includes issues of core values, transcendence, and individual subjectivity.

There is increasing current interest, however, in the integration of spirituality into secular leadership and organizational development (see Greenleaf 1977, Senge 1990, Vaill 1989, Covey 1990, DePree 1989, Lee and Zemke 1993). Spirituality is perceived to include a much broader range of experience, while religion and faith are seen as limiting the discussion to experiences that arise in traditional eleemosynary institutions or ways of thinking (Vaill 1989).

This significant connection between leaders' ability to have a transformational effect on the organization and their disposition toward spirituality is key. It may define more fully the leader role than past conceptions focusing, as they do, on position, personality, and partici-pation. Indeed, James M. Burns (1978) defines transformational leader-ship as a process in which leaders and followers raise each other to higher levels of morality and motivation. Transformational leaders find the language and values of spirituality to have significance for them in their self-understanding and in understanding their activities as leaders.

Jacobson's (1995) work records the transformational leader's defini-tions of spirituality in terms of several ideas, all central to understanding the person as an individual and as a leader of other individuals. My work confirms Jacobson's findings. It describes a new force in the work-place that up to now has been ignored. Placing spiritual ideas and ideals on the table opens up the field of leadership and organizational change and development. Spiritual leadership may redefine the work of orga-nization executives as dramatically as have the earlier ideas of values-based transformational leadership, applied power use, and cultural leadership. (For direct examinations of these seminal changes, see Fair-holm 1991, 1993, 1994a.)

Some may suppose that attention to the spirit side of self discourages education and professionalism (see, for example, Peters 1994). They be-lieve the two are antithetical, that it is education's purpose to dispel the mists and shadows of religion and free the human mind from so much error and delusion—like day and night, were either of them to gain mastery, the reign of the other must cease. In reality, human life is a duality of the spirit and the physical. Our inner self continues to have a life of its own that is an almost imperceptible fabric of feelings, thoughts, and actions that form the measure of our life, all that we really are (Gross 1995). We must invent professional relationships suitable to this whole-self reality. But we doom such efforts to failure if they do not grow out of something deeper, out of commonly held spiritual or moral values.

CORPORATE COMMUNITY: MAKING ONE OF MANY

In the past we have evolved cultures that separate our spirituality from our institutional life (Pascale and Athos 1981). The typical corporate cul-ture is antagonistic toward many of the values that drive the spiritual leader. Nevertheless, a condition of success in leading from a base of spirit is the presence in both leader and follower of shared ideals, cus-toms, and morals—on a mutually accepted and desirable culture. People want passionately to engage in work that lets them connect to these passions and make a difference. The new task of the leader is to become whole-makers, creators of oneness in people and in their groups. Every-one in the organization will be a leader sometime.

Leaders are mood setters as well as task givers. The leader's task is to first create a unifying culture and then nurture its values and customs among followers. The leaders' task is to bring this kind of unity to organizations. Leaders relate followers to organization goals. They build community. In doing this leaders build and use organization cultures to define and make special their core of co-workers. Without this community building, spiritually based relationships don't happen. If the act is not consistent with the culture, it may run into trouble. Giving people power is a good idea, but power to do without a unifying focus leads to chaos. We must couple enabling followers with community building to make spiritual progress.

VALUES FOCUS OF LEADERSHIP

Leadership based on spirit means putting your life and your money where your values are. This may be the only way to lead in the coming new world (Fairholm 1991). Leadership based on spirit requires people who are unafraid to offend, who bravely stand apart from the rest, and who willingly give voice to ideas that may run counter to the existing situation (Graham 1994). Spiritual leaders focus on individuals' values and expectations, not just task accomplishment. They set out to do the work by changing individuals' lives for the better, not just presiding over tasks or conducting meetings. They influence followers and constituent groups in a volitional way, not merely through formal authority mechanisms.

Before there can be purposeful participation, people must share certain values and pictures about where they are trying to go (Senge 1990). Creating spiritually oriented workplaces is a task of nurturing essential values among followers. Our central standard of right conduct comes from our core (often sacred) cultural values. We form these values in the family, in religion, in school, and in our other social institutions. More and more organizations are nurturing leaders who lead from spiritual values rather than management by objectives, TQM, or participatory means.

SPIRIT AND VISION

We are moving away from seeing leadership as a coordination of work in relationships bounded by structure and system. Rather, we now are coming to see leadership as a kind of contract in which the leader and follower cooperate voluntarily according to shared core values and a shared vision of what the organization is and can become. The vision defines the group's values-laden (spiritual) focus. The power of the vision comes from the inner strength of the values, experiences, and assumptions developed by leader and led over time. Group members need to feel related to the organization's vision statement to feel connected on a personal, intimate level. The true source of motivation is inspiration, not control. The new breed of leaders fulfill their role by providing spiritual visionary anchors in turbulent seas (Rasmussen 1993).

SPIRITUALITY AND LEADERSHIP

The essence of leadership stems from the leader's soul rather than from his or her behavior (Kiefer 1992). By focusing attention on a vision, the leader operates on the emotional and spiritual resources of the organization, its values, commitment, and aspirations (Bennis and Nanus 1985). The dictionary defines spirituality as the intelligent or immaterial part of humans, the soul or inner nature of humans. It does not apply to a particular religion, although the values of some religions are part of a spiritual focus. Spirituality in organizations refers to the inner values of the leader and the followers.

The retrogression of moral society and the growth of the global marketplace is causing people to search for spiritual and moral anchors in their lives and work (Covey 1991). Covey, describes seven habits of principle-centered leadership. These habits embody many of the key principles of human effectiveness. They include being proactive and taking responsibility for personal attitudes and actions. Effective leaders have a clear understanding of the desired direction and destination of their work and that of their organization. They organize and manage time and events around personal priorities. They seek mutual benefit for all parties, and they create a balanced, systematic program for renewal of self and others involving physical, mental, emotional, social, and spiritual considerations.

Spiritually guided leaders identify with a set of shared values that raises both follower and leader to higher levels of morality (Burns 1978). Morality is not self-starting. The ultimate custodian of moral conduct is a person's own conscience (Etzioni 1993). A spiritually guided leader engages in socialized rather than personalized power. Such a leader sacrifices for the benefit of the followers, not only for wealth or status. Spiritual leaders set vision, take pride in the vision, and use it in transforming the group. They recognize that change takes time. They are persistent and take the extra effort to distinguish what is really important.

We ennoble the spirit in the workplace by creating a sense of holism, of spiritual development, of feeling connected to the workplace, the environment, and relationships with one another. It is not the old work ethic, or the current self-ethic, but a new enterprise or bureaucratic ethic that is guiding spirituality in the workplace. It is a vision of work that includes belief in one's own abilities, a pessimism about dwindling opportunities, and an acknowledgment of the necessity of connecting with other people.

THE RISE OF BUSINESS POWER IN SOCIETY

Business may be the most powerful force in society today replacing both government and religion. Business is now entering center stage taking over from government or labor the power to shape society and its institutions. In the past it has been unconstrained by spiritual values. Money detached from values may be in truth the root of all evil. We continue to base mainstream economics on concepts borrowed from classical Newtonian physics. Contemporary economics is a static, predictable engine. Adding spirit to economics lets us see the economy as a self-regulating information ecosystem responsive not only to economic principles, but human ones as well.

Anita Roddick (1991), CEO of the Body Shop, sees modern business as a renaissance concept. For her, there is a spiritual aspect to business just as there is to the lives of individuals. Most of us have a wellspring of selfless love within us and spirituality is very much connected to this (Conger 1994). As, perhaps, the preeminent social entity, workers are looking to corporate America for this spiritual support.

THE POWER OF THE WORKER

Today's generation of workers reflects values that insist on a higher purpose in whatever it undertakes, and companies respond to these worker needs—demands. For example, Ben and Jerry's ice cream company has a generous employee benefits package that includes many particulars not directly related to money. Indeed, they deal with the higher motives people have. For example, they have a generous sick leave plan including parental leave. They sponsor a children's center, give benefits to unmarried partners, and offer sabbatical leaves and employee assistance programs. Additionally, they provide workers with free massages, health screening, smoking cessation classes, and a free health club.

Abraham Maslow (1962) laid an intellectual foundation for much of New Age spirituality in the workplace thinking we see in a growing number of firms like Ben and Jerry's and the Body Shop. Self-actualization is still the ideal by which many professionals measure the value of their work. It is part of a commonplace working assumption that each individual is profoundly (and mysteriously) connected to other people. Maslow suggested that self-actualization can lead to several dangers. For example, self-actualizers, by focusing on themselves, may take less responsibility for helping others. Surely, any discussion about meeting worker needs on the job may not see past their well-cultivated community vision to what employees in an expanding (or contracting) company really need. The emerging spiritual awakening may overcome these risks.

THE POWER OF CUSTOMERS

Customers, too, want a spiritual connection to their suppliers. People understand that their purchases are moral choices as well as economic ones. Common values and a shared sense of purpose can turn a company into a community where daily work takes on a deeper meaning and satisfaction. They are rejecting business ethics based on a sense of loss— loss of the ideal of self-actualization and loss of an unlimited horizon. They are calling for a community centered on the individual-in-relationship in what is turning out to be a chaotic future.

SEEKING DIFFERENT GOALS FROM WORK

For most of the history of modern management the highest goal of joint activity has been increased productivity, efficiency, effectiveness, and profitability. Spiritual leadership offers a more transcendent goal toward the attainment of which people collaborate: inner peace. The idea is that inner peace will produce more of the goals sought by organized interactivity. There can never be peace between nations or within work organizations until that quality of life is a part of our relationships and one object of our effort.

True peace is within the souls of men (Black Elk 1994). As leaders recognize this and respond through their interaction with their followers, they will attain their goal of inner peace, and can encourage it in others. Peace only comes as we carry out justice in our relationships with others. As we live the higher moral standard that is part of spiritual leadership we can have this peace. Peace comes on earth to people of goodwill as they act out of their authentic caring in their relationships with their fellows.

SUMMARY

Leaders in this quest for spiritual significance are surfacing from all points. The metamorphosis to a new business politics based on spirituality is not complete. Indeed, it is just beginning. The distinguishing features of this transitional period are a mixing and blending of cultures and a plurality or parallelism of intellectual and spiritual worlds. Our civilization has globalized only the surface of our lives. Our inner self continues to have a life of its own. It is here that we must invent organizational structures appropriate to the multicultural age. We doom such efforts to failure, however, if they do not grow out of something deeper, out of widely held spiritual core values.

Bibliography

Adair, John. "Leadership." *International Management* (Europe Edition) 40, no. 4 (April 1985): 78.

Aguilar, Teresita E., and John Crossley. "How Employees Benefit from Your Corporate Fitness Program." *Employee Benefits Journal* 7, no. 4 (December 1982): 32–33.

Anantaraman, V. "Evolving Concepts of Organizational Leadership." *Singapore Management Review* 15, no. 2 (July 1993): 17–32.

Autry, James A. *Love and Profit.* New York: Avon Books, 1992.

Badaracco, Joseph L., and Richard R. Ellsworth. "Leadership, Integrity and Conflict." *Management Decision* 30, no. 6 (1992): 29–34.

Bargal, David, and Hillel Schmid. "Recent Themes in Theory and Research on Leadership and Their Implications for Management of the Human Services." *Administration in Social Work* 13, nos. 3–4 (1989): 37–54.

Barker, Jack. *Future Edge.* New York: Marrow, 1992.

Barnard, Chester. *The Functions of the Executive.* Cambridge, Mass.: Harvard University Press, 1938.

Bass, Bernard M. *Leadership and Performance Beyond Expectations.* New York: Free Press, 1985.

Bechtel, Riley. *Toward 2001.* New York: Bechtel Corporation, 1994.

Begley, Sharon. "Science and the Sacred." *Newsweek*, November 28, 1994, pp. 56–59.

Bennis, Warren. *Learning to Lead: A Workbook on Becoming a Leader.* Reading, Mass.: Addison-Wesley, 1994.

———. *Why Leaders Can't Lead: The Unconscious Conspiracy Continues.* San Francisco: Jossey-Bass, 1989.

Bennis, Warren, and Burt Nanus. *Leaders: Strategies for Taking Charge.* New York: Harper and Row, 1985.

Berson, Bert. *The New Leaders,* Bonus Issue (Sterling and Stone, San Francisco) spring 1994.

Bethel, Sheila Murray. "Qualities of Leadership." *Executive Excellence,* December 1989, pp. 27–28.

Black Elk. *The Spiritual Athlete,* in *The New Leaders,* Bonus Issue (Sterling and Stone, San Francisco) spring 1994.

Blanchard, Kenneth H. "Faster, Simpler, Better." *Executive Excellence* 10, no. 1 (January 1993): 17–19.

(Interview with Ken Blanchard). "The Extra Minute." *Executive Excellence* 11, no. 5 (May 1994): 6–8.

———. "Maintain High Ethical Standards." In *New Traditions in Business: Spirit and Leadership in the 21st Century,* edited by John Renesch. San Francisco: Berrett-Koehler, 1992.

Block, Peter. *Stewardship: Choosing Service over Self-Interest.* San Francisco: Berrett-Koehler, 1993.

Bowman, James S. "Altering the Fabric of Work." *Business Horizons* 27, no. 5 (September/October 1984): 42–48.

Boyce, W. Duane. "The Ecology of the Soul." *National Forum, The Phi Kappa Phi Journal* (winter 1995).

Bradford, D. L., and A. R. Cohen. *Managing for Excellence.* New York: John Wiley & Sons, 1984.

Bradley, Senator Bill. Speech read at Business for Social Responsibility Conference, October 1993, Washington, D.C.

Brown, Juanita. "Developing a Corporate Community." In *New Traditions in Business: Spirit and Leadership in the 21st Century,* edited by John Renesch. San Francisco: Berrett-Koehler, 1992.

Burns, James McGregor. *Leadership.* New York: Harper and Row, 1978.

Cappelli, Peter. "Can this Relationship Be Saved?" *Wharton Alumni Magazine* (spring 1995).

Chakraborty, S. K. *The New Leaders* (Sterling and Stone, San Francisco) September/October 1994.

Channon, Jim. "Creating Esprit de Corps." In *New Traditions in Business: Spirit and Leadership in the 21st Century,* edited by John Renesch. San Francisco: Berrett-Koehler, 1992.

Chappell, Tom. Quoted in Rensch, *The New Leaders* (Sterling and Stone, San Francisco) September/October 1993, p. 1.

Chenglieh, Pan. "In Search of the Chinese Style of Management." *Practicing Manager* 7, no. 2 (April 1987): 5–7.

Cimino, S. M. "Nurses' Spiritual Well-Being as Related to Attitudes toward and Degree of Comfort in Providing Spiritual Care." Ph.D diss., Boston College, 1992.

Clinton, Bill. Quoted in *The New Leaders* (Sterling and Stone, San Francisco) March/April 1994.

The Compass Group. *Executive Summary of the First International Workplace Values Survey.* San Francisco: The New Leaders, 1994.

Conger, Jay, et al. *Spirit at Work.* San Francisco: Jossey-Bass, 1994.

Cound, Dana M. "A Call for Leadership." *Quality Progress* 20, no. 3 (March 1987): 11–15.

Covey, Stephen R. "10 Dilemmas." *Executive Excellence* 9, no. 1 (January 1992): 11–13.

———. *Principle-Centered Leadership*. New York: Summet Books, 1991.

———. "The Seven Habits of Highly Effective People." *I/S Analyzer* 29, no. 2 (February 1991a): 15–16.

Craddock, Fred B. *Preaching*. Nashville: Abington Press, 1985.

Deal, T., and Kennedy, A. *Corporate Cultures: The Rights and Rituals of Corporate Life*. Reading, Mass.: Addison-Wesley, 1983.

Dali Lama. "Purpose of Life." *The New Leaders*, Bonus Issue (Sterling and Stone, San Francisco) spring 1994.

DePree, Max. *Leadership Is an Art*. New York: Doubleday, 1989.

Drucker, Peter. "The Coming of the New Age of Man." *Harvard Business Review* (January/February 1988): 45–53.

Eckhart, Meister. Quoted in *The New Leaders*, Bonus Issue (Sterling and Stone, San Francisco) spring 1994.

Erteszek, Jan J. "The Common Venture Enterprise: A Western Answer to the Japanese Art of Management?" *New Management* 1, no. 2 (1983): 4–10.

Etzioni, Amatai. *The Spirit of Community*. New York: Crown Publishers, 1993.

Fairholm, Gilbert W. "Leadership: A Function of Interactive Trust." *Journal of Leadership Studies* 2, no. 2 (1994).

———. *Leadership in a Culture of Trust*. New York: Praeger, 1994a.

———. "Leading Diverse Followers." *Journal of Leadership Studies* 1, no. 4 (1994b).

———. *Organizational Power Politics*. New York: Praeger, 1993.

———. *Values Leadership: Toward a New Philosophy of Leadership*. New York: Praeger, 1991.

Flower, Joe. "Factory, Family, Jungle and Theater." *Healthcare Forum* 34, no. 2 (March/April 1991): 28–32.

Fox, Matthew. *The Reinvention of Work*, quoted in *The New Leaders* (Sterling and Stone, San Francisco) September/October 1994.

Gaertner, Karan M., and Gregory H. Gaertner. "Proactive Roles of Federal Managers." *The Bureaucrat* (fall 1985): 19–22.

Garton, Richard D. "The Business of Being Ethical." *Vital Speeches* 55, no. 14 (May 1989): 435–437.

Gaster, David R. "Business Is Creating the Culture and the Community Today in Which our Children Will Grow Up." In *New Traditions in Business: Spirit and Leadership in the 21st Century*, edited by John Renesch. San Francisco: Berrett-Koehler, 1992.

Goodpaster, Kenneth E. "Work, Spirituality, and the Moral Point of View." *International Journal of Values-Based Management* 7, no. 1 (1994): 49–62.

Goss, Tracy, Richard Pascale, and Anthony Athos. Quoted in *The New Leaders* (Sterling and Stone, San Francisco) March/April 1994.

Graham, John. "Prescription for Success Overlooks Today's Harsh Realities." *Business Realities*, January 1994.

Greenleaf, Robert K. *Servant Leadership*. New York: Paulist Press, 1977.

Gross, William H. "Row, Row, Row Your Boat," quoted in *The New Leaders* (Sterling and Stone, San Francisco) March/April 1995.

Hancock, Ralph C. "What Is a Mormon Intellectual?" *This People* (1994): 21–34.

Handy, Charles. *The Age of Paradox*. Cambridge, Mass.: Harvard University Press, 1994.

———. Quoted in *The New Leaders* (Sterling and Stone, San Francisco) March/April 1994a.

Harman, Willis. Quoted in *New Traditions in Business: Spirit and Leadership in the 21st Century*, edited by John Renesch. San Francisco: Berrett-Koehler, 1992.

The Hartwick Humanities in Management Institute. "Jesus and the Gospels." In *Hartwick Classic Leadership Cases*. Oneonta, N.Y.: The Hartwick Humanities in Management Institute, 1993.

———. "Mahatma Gandhi." In *Hartwick Classic Leadership Cases*. Oneonta, N.Y.: The Hartwick Humanities in Management Institute, 1993a.

Hawley, Jack. *Reawakening the Spirit in Work: The Power of Dharmic Management*. San Francisco: Berrett-Koehler, 1993.

Heerman, Berry. "Spiritual Core Is Essential to High Performing Teams." In *The New Leaders* (Sterling and Stone, San Francisco) March/April 1995.

Hertzberg, Frederick. "One More Time: How Do You Motivate Employees?" *Harvard Business Review* (January/February 1968).

Hesse, Hermann. Quoted in *The New Leaders*, Bonus Issue (Sterling and Stone, San Francisco) spring 1994.

Hickman, Craig R. "Soul of Leadership." *Executive Excellence* 6, no. 12 (December 1989): 15–16.

Horton, Thomas R. "Leadership of the Spirit." *AGB Reports* 31, no. 1 (January/February 1979): 51–64.

Howe, Susan E. S. "Exploring New Leadership Styles." *Pennsylvania CPA Journal* 65, no. 1 (February 1994): 14.

Hunt, Eugene H., and George R. Gray. "The Participative Approach-Time to Catch Up." *Management World* 10, no. 5 (May 1981): 30–31.

Hurst, David K. "Creating Competitive Advantage." *Academy of Management Executive* 3, no. 1 (February 1989): 29–36.

Jacobs, Devi. Quoted in *The New Leaders* (Sterling and Stone, San Francisco), November/December 1994.

Jacobson, Stephen. *Spirituality and Transformational Leadership in Secular Settings: A Delphi Study*. (An abridgement of an unpublished dissertation completed in 1994 and available through University Microfilm.) Goleta, Ga., 1995.

Kantrowitz, Barbara. "In Search of the Sacred." *Newsweek*, November 28, 1994, pp. 53–55.

Keifer, Charles F. "Creating Metanoic Organizations." In *New Traditions in Business: Spirit and Leadership in the 21st Century*, edited by John Renesch. San Francisco: Berrett-Koehler, 1992.

Kelleher, Herb, and Colleen Barrett. Quoted in *The New Leaders* (San Francisco, Sterling and Stone) November/December 1994.

Kiechel, Walter, III. "The Leader as Servant." *Fortune*, May 4, 1992, pp. 121–122.

Kimball, Edward L. *The Teachings of Spencer W. Kimball*. Salt Lake City: Bookcraft, 1982.

Koffman, Fred, and Peter Senge. "Communities for Commitment: The Heart of Learning Organizations." *Organizational Dynamics* (autumn 1993).

Kostenbaum, Peter. *Leadership: The Inner Side of Greatness*. San Francisco: Jossey-Bass, 1992.

Kouzes, James, and Berry Z. Posner. *Credibility: How Leaders Gain and Lose It*. San Francisco: Jossey-Bass, 1993.

———. "The Credibility Factor." *Healthcare Forum* 36, no. 4 (July/August 1993a): 16–24.

———. "Ethical Leaders." *Journal of Business Ethics* 11, nos. 5–6 (May 1992): 479–484.

Kübler-Ross, Elizabeth. Quoted in *The New Leaders*, Bonus Issue (Sterling and Stone, San Francisco) spring 1994.

Kuritz, Stephen J. "A Holistic Approach to Process Safety." *Occupational Health & Safety* 61, no. 10 (October 1992): 28–32.

Leavitt, Harold J. "Educating Our MBAs." *California Management Review* 31, no. 3 (spring 1989): 38–50.

Lee, Chris, and Ron Zemke. "The Search for Spirit in the Workplace." *Training*, June 1993.

Litzinger, William, and Thomas Schaefer. "Leadership Through Followership." *Business Horizons* 25, no. 5 (September/October 1982): 78–81.

Maccoby, M. *The Gamesman*. New York: Simon and Schuster, 1976.

Magaziner, Elmer. "New Thinking, Not Just New Insight." *The New Leaders* (Sterling and Stone, San Francisco) January/February 1994, p. 6.

Manz, Charles C., and Henry P. Sims, Jr. "SuperLeadership." *Organizational Dynamics* 19, no. 4 (spring 1991): 18–35.

Marquardt, Michael, and Angus Reynolds. *The Global Learning Organization*. New York: Irwin, 1994.

Maslow, Abraham. *The Further Reaches of Human Nature*. Harmondsworth, England: Penguin, 1971.

———. *Toward a Psychology of Being*. 2nd ed. New York: Van Nostrand Company, 1962.

Maxwell, Neal A. *A Wonderful Flood of Light*. Salt Lake City: Bookcraft, 1990.

———. *Wherefore Ye Must Press Forward*. Salt Lake City: Deseret Book Company, 1977.

———. *Deposition of a Disciple*. Salt Lake City: Deseret Book Company, 1976.

———. *A More Excellent Way*. Salt Lake City: Deseret Book Company, 1973.

McGregor, Douglas. *The Human Side of Enterprise*. New York: McGraw-Hill, 1960.

McMillen, Kim. Quoted in *The New Leaders* (Sterling and Stone, San Francisco) September/October 1994.

Meher, Baba. Quoted in *The New Leaders*, Bonus Issue (Sterling and Stone, San Francisco) spring 1994.

Meister, Eckhart. Quoted in *The New Leaders*, Bonus Issue (Sterling and Stone, Corte Madere, CA) spring 1994.

Miller, Margery. Quoted in *The New Leaders* (Sterling and Stone, San Francisco) May/June 1994.

Miller, William C. "Put Spiritual Values to Work." In *New Traditions in Business: Spirit and Leadership in the 21st Century*, edited by John Renesch. San Francisco: Berrett-Koehler, 1992.

Miller, William. *Quantum Quality: Quality Improvement Through Innovation, Learning & Creativity*. New York: AMACOM, 1993.

Mitroff, Ian I., Richard O. Mason, and Christine M. Pearson. "Radical Surgery: What Will Tomorrow's Organizations Look Like?" *Academy of Management Executive* 8, no. 2 (May 1994): 11–21.

Mollner, Terry. "Developing a Relationship Oriented World View." *New Traditions in Business: Spirit and Leadership in the 21st Century*, edited by John Renesch. San Francisco: Berrett-Koehler, 1992.

Moyle, Henry D. *Conference Report*, April 1952, p. 37.

Myers, Ken. "A Culture of Value-added Leadership." *Executive Excellence* 10, no. 2 (February 1993): 4.

Myers, Scott M. *Every Employee a Manager*. New York: McGraw-Hill, 1970.

Nair, Keshavan. *A Higher Standard of Leadership: Lessons from the Life of Gandhi*. San Francisco: Berrett-Koehler, 1994.

Naisbitt, John. *Megatrends: Ten New Directions Transforming our Lives*. New York: Warner Books, 1982.

Nanus, Bert. *Visionary Leadership: Creating a Compelling Sense of Direction for Your Organization*. San Francisco: Jossey-Bass, 1992.

Nibley, Hugh. *Collected Works of Hugh Nibley*. Salt Lake City: Deseret Book Company, 1989, Vol. 8.

———. "Leadership Versus Management." *BYU Today*, February 1984, pp. 16, 47.

Nirenberg, John. Quoted in *The New Leaders* (Sterling and Stone, San Francisco) November/December 1994.

Nixon, Richard. *Leaders*. New York: Warner Books, 1982.

Noda, Mitz. "The Japanese Way." *Executive* 6, no. 3 (summer 1980): 22–25.

Nourse, Bartley B., Jr. Quoted in *The New Leaders* (Sterling and Stone, San Francisco) March/April 1995.

Novak, Michael. "Macbeth Sans Tragedy." *Forbes* 15, no. 3 (August 2, 1993): 95.

Osborn, Susan. *The New Leaders* (Sterling and Stone, San Francisco) November/December 1994.

Ott, Stephen. *The Organizational Culture Perspective*. Belmont, CA: The Dorsey Press, 1989.

Ouchi, William G. *Theory Z: How American Business Can Meet the Japanese Challenge*. New York: Avon Books, 1981.

Pascale, R. T., and Anthony G. Athos. *The Art of Japanese Management: Applications for American Executives*. New York: Simon and Schuster, 1981.

Pascerella, Perry. *The New Achievers*. New York: The Free Press, 1984.

Payne, Bruce. "A New and Right Spirit." Proceedings of the Leadership Education conference, University of Richmond, July 7, 1994.

Peck, M. Scott. *A World Waiting to Be Born: Civility Discovered*. New York: Bantam, 1993.

Peters, Tom. "Questions and Comments to Tom." *On Achieving Excellence*, 9, no. 7 (July 1994): 9–11.

Peters, Tom, and Watterman, Robert. *In Search of Excellence*. New York: Harper and Row, 1982.

Pinchot, Gifford, and Elizabeth Pinchot. *The End of Bureaucracy and the Rise of the Intelligent Organization*. San Francisco: Berrett-Koehler, 1994.

———. Quoted in *The New Leaders* (Sterling and Stone, San Francisco) July/August 1994a.

Pope, Alexander. *An Essay on Man*, Epistle III, line 248.

Rabbin, Robert. "Leading from Within," in *The New Leaders* (Sterling and Stone, San Francisco) spring 1994.

Ram, Dass. Quoted in *The New Leaders*, Bonus Issue (Sterling and Stone, San Francisco) spring 1994.

Range, Peter Ross. "Interview with William J. Bennett." *Modern Maturity*, March/April 1995.

Raspberry, William. "Churches Shouldn't Neglect Their Strong Inside Game." *The Richmond Times-Dispatch*, Thursday, February 16, 1995, p. A15.

Rasmussen, Tina. Quoted in *Leadership in a New Era*, edited by John Renesch. San Francisco: New Leaders Press, 1993.

Ray, Michael L. Quoted in *New Traditions in Business: Spirit and Leadership in the 21st Century*, edited by John Renesch. San Francisco: Berrett-Koehler, 1992.

Renesch, John. *The New Leaders* (Sterling and Stone, San Francisco) January/February 1995.

———. "Organizational Transformation and Healing: A Natural Alliance." *The New Leaders* (Sterling and Stone, San Francisco) January/February 1994, p. 9.

———. "Lessons from the Mystics." *The New Leaders*, Bonus Issue (Sterling and Stone, San Francisco) spring 1994a.

———. "Global Workplace Values Identified." *The New Leaders* (Sterling and Stone, San Francisco) May/June 1994b.

———. *The New Leaders* (Sterling and Stone, San Francisco) July/August 1994c.

———. *The New Leaders* (Sterling and Stone, San Francisco) September/October 1994d.

———, ed. *New Traditions in Business: Spirit and Leadership in the 21st Century*. San Francisco: Berrett-Koehler, 1992.

Reynolds, Joe. "Boards of Directors as Corporate Stewards." *Directorship*, July/August 1994.

Robins, Tom. "Thoughts," quoted in *The New Leaders* (Sterling and Stone, San Francisco) spring 1994.

Roddick, Anita. Speech read at Business for Social Responsibility Conference, November 1993, San Francisco.

———. *Body and Soul*. New York: Crown Publishers, 1991.

Rondeau, Ed. "The Goal Is Not Survival." *Office* 107, no. 1 (January 1988): 96.

Rosen, Robert H. "Developing a Healthy Organization." *New Traditions in Business: Spirit and Leadership in the 21st Century*, edited by John Renesch. San Francisco: Berrett-Koehler, 1992.

Rowan, Roy. *The Intuitive Manager*. Boston: Little, Brown, 1986.

Rue, John. Quoted in *The New Leaders* (Sterling and Stone, San Francisco) November/December 1994.

Ruppert, Paul. "Compelling Strategies for a Competitive Workplace." *Equifax* (1991): 15.

Sashkin, Marshall. "True Vision in Leadership." *Training and Development Journal*, May 1986, p. 58.

Schein, Edgar H. *Organizational Culture and Leadership*. San Francisco: Jossey-Bass, 1985.

Schlack, Robert F. "Economic Change in the People's Republic of China." *Journal of Economic Issues* 23, no. 1 (March 1989): 155–188.

Selznick, Phillip. *Leadership in Administration.* New York: Harper and Row, 1957.

Senge, Peter. Quoted in *New Traditions in Business: Spirit and Leadership in the 21st Century,* edited by John Renesch. San Francisco: Berrett-Koehler, 1992.

——. "The Leaders' New Work: Building Learning Organizations." *Sloan Management Review,* fall 1990.

Senge, Peter, Charlotte Roberts, Richard Ross, Bryan Smith, and Art Kleiner. *The Fifth Discipline Fieldbook: Strategies and Tools for Building a Learning Organization.* New York: Currency/Doubleday, 1994.

Shortell, Stephen M. "High-Performing Healthcare Organizations: Guidelines for the Pursuit of Excellence." *Hospital & Health Services Administration* 30, no. 4 (July/August 1985): 7–35.

Sonnenberg, Frank. *Managing with a Conscience.* New York: McGraw-Hill, 1993.

Stata, Ray. "The Role of the Chief Executive Officer in Articulating the Vision." *Interfaces* 18, no. 3 (May/June 1988): 3–9.

Terry, Robert W. "Authentic Leadership: Courage in Action." *The New Leaders,* January/February 1994.

Thaker, Vimala. Quoted in *The New Leaders,* Bonus Issue (Sterling and Stone, San Francisco) spring 1994.

Tocqueville, Alexis de. *Democracy in America.* New York: The New American Library, 1956.

Vaill, Peter. *Managing as a Performing Art.* San Francisco: Jossey-Bass, 1989.

Vanfleet, David D., and Gary A. Yukl. "A Century of Leadership Research." In *Contemporary Issues in Leadership,* edited by W. E. Rosenbach and R. L. Taylor. Boulder, Colo.: Westview Press, 1989.

Walker, Robert G. "The Imperative of Leaders to Create Leaders." *Directors & Boards* 13, no. 2 (winter 1989): 21–25.

Waterman, Robert. Quoted in *The New Leaders* (Sterling and Stone, San Francisco) September/October 1994.

Weaver, Dennis. Quoted in *The New Leaders,* Bonus Issue (Sterling and Stone, San Francisco) spring 1994.

Wheatley, Margaret J. *Leadership and The New Science.* San Francisco: Berrett-Koehler, 1992.

Whyte, David. Quoted in *The New Leaders* (Sterling and Stone, San Francisco) September/October 1994.

Wildavsky, Aaron. *The Nursing Father: Moses as a Political Leader.* Birmingham: University of Alabama Press, 1984.

Wilson, Ian. Quoted in *The New Leaders* (Sterling and Stone, San Francisco) July/August 1994.

Windle, Ralph. *The Poetry of Business Life: An Anthology.* San Francisco: Berrett-Koehler, 1994.

Wolf, James F. "Besieged British Public Service." *Bureaucrat* 16, no. 2 (summer 1987): 45–48.

Woodword, Kenneth. "On the Road Again." *Newsweek,* November 28, 1994, pp. 61–62.

Wright, Wayne L. "Escape from Mediocrity." *Personnel Administrator* 32, no. 9 (September 1987): 109–119.

Index

About the Author

GILBERT W. FAIRHOLM has been a teacher of Public Administration, Leadership, and Organizational Behavior for over twenty years at the University of Pittsburgh, Virginia Commonwealth University, and the University of Richmond. He is now visiting Professor of Political Science at Hampden-Sydney College in Virginia. He is the author of *Values Leadership* (Praeger, 1991) and *Leadership and the Culture of Trust* (Praeger, 1994), both used by several institutions of higher education as part of executive development and academic programs, and *Organizational Power Politics* (Praeger, 1993). Both *Organizational Power Politics* and *Leadership and the Culture of Trust* are *Choice* Outstanding Academic Books.